Thinking Through The Test

A Study Guide for
The Florida College Basic Skills Exit Tests

Writing

with Answer Key

D1621683

Third Edition

D. J. Henry
Daytona Beach Community College

Mimi Markus
Broward Community College

PEARSON
Longman

New York   Boston   San Francisco
London   Toronto   Sydney   Tokyo   Singapore   Madrid
Mexico City   Munich   Paris   Cape Town   Hong Kong   Montreal

Thinking Through the Test: A Study Guide for The Florida College Basic Skills Exit Tests: Writing, with Answer Key, Third Edition

Copyright ©2006 Pearson Education, Inc.

ISBN: 0-321-38741-4

9 10–BRR–10 09

Contents

PART THREE: EXIT EXAM

PART FOUR: CORRESPONDENCE CHARTS FOR TEST QUESTIONS

PART FIVE: STUDENT ANSWER SHEETS

PART SIX: ANSWER KEYS

APPENDIX: THINKING THROUGH THE WRITING SAMPLE

Introduction

"Chance favors the prepared mind."
—Louis Pasteur

You've been polishing your writing skills and studying grammar and punctuation rules. You feel confident now, ready to enroll in college-level English classes. However, you have one more challenge: to pass the Florida College Basic Skills Test in English. At this moment, thinking about passing a test as important as this one has probably raised your anxiety level! You can take comfort in the fact that there are many students like you who are concerned about this test. However, you should also know that hundreds of students have successfully passed it, and you can too. *Thinking Through the Test* will help you get ready.

You'll find *Thinking Through the Test* divided into six main parts:

Part One	Pretest (a 40-question test to determine what skills you'll want to focus on)
Part Two	Writing Workbook (with diagnostics and exercises for further practice)
Part Three	Exit Exam (a 40-question test to reinforce the skills you'll have acquired)
Part Four	Correspondence Charts for Test Questions
Part Five	Student Answer Sheets
Part Six	Answer Keys (brief answer keys followed by answers with explanations)

You will also find a new **Appendix**, "Thinking Through the Writing Sample," which shows how to write a passing 50-minute essay.

We have also added several features and enhanced the instructional content for this new edition, including:

- **A brand-new Pretest and Exit Exam** in the same format and question sequence as the State Exam, so you can test and re-test all the writing skills you will need to be successful
- **Subject-specific Diagnostics** following the introduction of each chapter, which test your proficiency in specific skills (the answers directly follow each diagnostic, so you can mark your own progress)
- **Easy to Understand Examples and Explanations** to illustrate the skills presented each chapter
- **Study Hints:** These features offer test-taking and study tips
- **A List of Correspondences** for each test question in the back of the book that shows the *type* of skill being tested
- **Answer Sheets** to help you track your progress and record your own thinking about your reasons for the choices you make in each activity and test

While these features are designed to help you make the most of your learning experience, remember: The more practice you have in *thinking through* your choices, the more likely you are to be successful on the state test and in future college courses.

In the meantime, as you study and practice for the test ahead, remember what baseball legend Ted Williams said: "Just keep going. Everybody gets better if they keep at it."

THINKING THROUGH THE FLORIDA COLLEGE BASIC SKILLS EXIT TESTS

The Florida Legislature enacted a law requiring students to pass an exit test after successfully completing their college preparatory classes. The purpose of the test is to assess your knowledge of the competencies taught in those classes. A passing grade on this test makes you eligible for college-level English classes.

The English Exit Test consists of two parts: an objective test and an essay test.

The objective subtest consists of 40 multiple-choice questions. The writing sample is a 50-minute timed essay on one of two topics provided.

The objective part tests your knowledge of twenty-three skills distributed among 40 questions. The skills tested include the following:

- Paragraph and essay skills: topic sentence/thesis statement, general and specific supporting details, arrangement of ideas and supporting details in logical patterns, relevant or irrelevant details, and effective transitional words and phrases.
- Language skills: proper expressions and misused words
- Sentence skills: modifiers, coordination and subordination, parallel structure, and fragments, comma splices, and run-ons (fused sentences)
- Grammar skills: verbs, pronouns, adjectives and adverbs, spelling, punctuation, and capitalization

The writing sample measures your ability to write an essay in 50 minutes. You will need to show that you can organize your essay, support your ideas with specific details, and use correct grammar and punctuation. (Some colleges request a well-developed paragraph instead of an essay. Be sure you know which will be expected of you.)

TIPS FOR STUDYING AND TEST TAKING

"It's not that I'm so smart; it's just that I stay with problems longer."
—Albert Einstein

The best way to overcome the fear and anxiety you may have about passing this test is to become test-wise, that is, to learn the format of the questions that are on the test, to work through practice questions that are similar to those on the test, and to review the competencies that you will be tested on. *Thinking Through the Test* has everything you need to get ready for the exam.

In addition to working through the chapters in this book, apply the study tips in this section. By using the **Get Ready, Get Set, Go** approach, you will get through the test like a champ.

Get Ready shows you what to do to prepare for the test
Get Set provides strategies to apply on the day of the test
Go gives pointers to help you during the test

Get Ready: What to Do to Prepare for the Test

- Start preparing early. Don't wait until a day or two before the test to cram.
- Plan a study schedule. Set aside some time, even if you can only devote ten minutes a day to study.
- Take the Pretest at the beginning of the book to find out which skills you need to spend more time reviewing. At the end of this book, you'll find a chart that shows you the skill tested in each of the questions.
- Take the subject diagnostic in each of the chapters; it will help you zero in on the skills taught in the chapter.
- Work in short periods rather than one long one. Each of the chapters of the book has three parts: a pre-test, an explanation of a specific skill, and a practice test. Therefore, you can work through each chapter in three short study sessions.
- Find extra help if you need it. Some people are uncomfortable about asking for help and want to tough it out alone. You don't have to! Go to your campus writing center. Talk to your instructor. Find out where you can get assistance.
- Form a study group. You'll find that each person in the group has a particular strength to share. Studying with others not only helps academically, but also emotionally. You become a team in which the members support each other.
- Practice relaxation techniques so that when the day of the test comes, you will be able to overcome your anxiety. Square breathing is one easy relaxation technique to master. Here's how you do it:

    1. Close your eyes.
    2. Take a slow, deep breath through your nose while you count to three.
    3. Hold your breath while you count to three slowly.
    4. Breathe out through your mouth, again counting to three slowly.
    5. Hold your breath for three slow counts.

    Repeat this several times. You will be surprised to see how well this works to get rid of stress. Use it any time you feel anxiety—and remember to use this method on the day of the test.

- The night before the test, get a good night's sleep. Don't try to stay up all night studying. Pulling an "all-nighter" will disrupt your ability to think clearly. Overdosing on caffeinated products will make you shaky and hyper, and you won't be able to concentrate.

Get Set: Strategies to Apply on the Day of the Test

Food   Don't take your test on an empty stomach. You may not be hungry before the exam, but sooner or later your hunger is going to kick in and cloud your thinking. Eat something light but avoid foods that can increase stress, like caffeine and sugar-laden products. Another thing you can do is bring a snack with you, like a health bar.

Time   Arrive early. You don't want to get stuck in a traffic jam and risk being late. Bring something interesting with you to read, so the wait won't be so nerve-wracking. Try the square breathing technique while you wait.

Seating   If you can, choose a seat away from distractions like doors or windows. Turn off your cell phone and put it out of sight so you won't be tempted to check for calls or messages. Also, avoid others in the room who show negative behavior, are not prepared, or are anxious.

Materials   Be sure to bring the materials required, such as a number 2 pencil and a scantron sheet.

Anxiety   Most people feel some anxiety at test time. Use that energy to motivate you to do your best. Don't turn that anxiety into negative self-talk. Turn negative thoughts, such as "I never do well on tests" or "Everyone else will do better than I will," into positive thoughts. When you find yourself thinking a negative thought, stop and replace it with a positive one. "I can pass this test with ease."

Go: Pointers to Help You During the Test

- Preview the test. Can you tell that some questions look more difficult than others? Work on the easiest parts first. Decide how to budget your time while you are taking the test.
- Read the directions for each question. Be sure you understand what the question is asking for.
- Read each question from beginning to end, including all the answers. Use the options in the answers to give you hints.
- Don't panic if you go blank. You can always come back to the question later.
- Answer every question. There's no penalty for guessing. Your first answer may be the correct one, so don't change your answers unless you are positive about the correction.
- "No change is necessary" options are sometimes correct.
- If others finish before you, don't try to hurry to finish too. When you think you are done, and you still have time left, use that time to make sure that you have answered every question and to go over your answers.

Finally, remember to congratulate yourself!

"Difficulties mastered are opportunities won."
—Winston Churchill

Part One: Pretest

Read the entire passage carefully, then answer the questions. (Note: Intentional errors may have been included in the passage.)

(1) _____.

(2) In early autumn of 1991, two hikers working their way along the edge of a melting glacier in the high Alps of northern Italy found what seemed to be the weathered remains of an unlucky mountain climber. (3) Next to him were a bow and several arrows, a wooden backpack, and a metal ax. (4) It was a man clothed in hand-sewn leather, frozen in glacial ice. (5) A closer look turned up a leather pouch and other tools. (6) The "Ice Man" turned out to be a leftover from the Stone Age, a young hunter who may have died from exhaustion and exposure some 5,000 years ago. (7) Although scientists knew that the Ice Man was ancient, they did not know where he was from. (8) In 1994, researchers reported that mitochondrial DNA from the Ice Man closely matched that of central and northern Europeans, not Native Americans. (9) DNA is unlikely to remain intact. (10) _____ the Ice Man remains frozen in the anatomy department of the University of Innsbruck. (11) Continuing analysis of DNA may provide more clues about his place in human evolution. (12) Scientists have reported fossils of a 65-million-year old dinosaur fossil. (Adapted from Neil A. Campbell, Lawrence G. Mitchell, and Jane B. Reece, *Biology*, 3rd ed., San Francisco: Benjamin Cummings, 2000.)

1. Which of the following sentences, if inserted into the blank labeled number 1, would provide the best thesis statement for the entire passage?
   A. Because it is difficult to obtain uncontaminated samples from fossils, DNA is very challenging.
   B. Science advances by the ebb and flow of ideas.
   C. The analysis of DNA from fossils provides an opportunity to learn about extinct life.
   D. The discovery of the "Ice Man" was highly publicized.

2. Which of the numbered sentences is NOT supported by sufficient details?
   A. 9
   B. 2
   C. 7
   D. 3

3. Select the order of sentences 3, 4, and 5 that presents the details in the most logical sequence of ideas. If no change is necessary, select option A.
   A. Next to him were a bow and several arrows, a wooden backpack, and a metal ax. It was a man clothed in hand-sewn leather, frozen in glacial ice. A closer look turned up a leather pouch and other tools.
   B. It was a man clothed in hand-sewn leather, frozen in glacial ice. Next to him were a bow and several arrows, a wooden backpack, and a metal ax. A closer look turned up a leather pouch and other tools.
   C. Next to him were a bow and several arrows, a wooden backpack, and a metal ax. A closer look turned up a leather pouch and other tools. It was a man clothed in hand-sewn leather, frozen in glacial ice.
   D. A closer look turned up a leather pouch and other tools. It was a man clothed in hand-sewn leather, frozen in glacial ice. Next to him were a bow and several arrows, a wooden backpack, and a metal ax.

4. Which numbered sentence is the LEAST relevant to the passage?
   A. 12
   B. 2
   C. 6
   D. 8

5. Which word or phrase, if inserted into the blank in the sentence labeled number 10, would make the relationship between sentences 8, 9, and 11 clear?
   A. In contrast,
   B. However,
   C. Although,
   D. Currently,

Read the entire passage carefully, then answer the questions. (Note: Intentional errors may have been included in the passage.)

(1) _____.

(2) Even when your use of a source may be perfectly legal, you may still be violating ethical standards if you do not give credit to the information source. (3) _____ assume that you are writ-

ing a research report on genetically modified foods. (4) In your research, you discover a very good paper on the Web. (5) Under copyright and fair use guidelines, you can reproduce portions of this paper without permission. (6) However, does this legal standard mean that you can use someone else's material freely, without giving that person credit? (7) Even though it might be legal under fair use guidelines to reprint the material without notifying the copyright holder, using someone else's material or ideas without giving them credit is plagiarism. (8) There are several systems for citing others' ideas. (9) Plagiarism is serious because it violates several of the reasonable criteria for ethical decision making. (10) It also violates your obligation to society to produce fair and accurate information. (11) Plagiarism violates your obligation to yourself to be truthful. (12) Finally, it violates your obligation to other students and researchers. (13) Students can be expelled from school. (Adapted from Laura J. Gurak, and John M. Lannon, *A Concise Guide to Technical Communication*, New York: Longman, 2001.)

6. Which of the following sentences, if inserted into the blank labeled number 1, would provide the best thesis statement for the entire passage?
   A. Plagiarism is using someone else's words and ideas without giving that person proper credit.
   B. People can lose their jobs if they plagiarize.
   C. Plagiarism violates ethical standards.
   D. Plagiarism is rampant in colleges and universities.

7. Which of the numbered sentences is NOT supported by sufficient details?
   A. 2
   B. 4
   C. 8
   D. 9

8. Select the order of sentences 10, 11, and 12 that presents the details in the most logical sequence of ideas. If no change is necessary, select option A.
   A. It also violates your obligation to society to produce fair and accurate information. Plagiarism violates your obligation to yourself to be truthful. Finally, it violates your obligation to other students and researchers.
   B. It also violates your obligation to society to produce fair and accurate information. Finally, it violates your obligation to other students and researchers. Plagiarism violates your obligation to yourself to be truthful.
   C. Plagiarism violates your obligation to yourself to be truthful. Finally, it violates your obligation to other students and researchers. It also violates your obligation to society to produce fair and accurate information.
   D. Plagiarism violates your obligation to yourself to be truthful. It also violates your obligation to society to produce fair and accurate information. Finally, it violates your obligation to other students and researchers.

9. Which numbered sentence is the LEAST relevant to the passage?
   A. 5
   B. 7
   C. 9
   D. 13

10. Which word or phrase, if inserted into the blank in the sentence labeled number 3, would make the relationship between sentences 2 and 4 clear?
    A. For example,
    B. Therefore,
    C. In addition,
    D. Being that,

11. DIRECTIONS: Choose the most effective word or phrase within the context suggested by the sentence.

    Martin's English skills are strong, but his math skills are _____, for he hasn't passed more than one math exam this semester.

    A. impaired
    B. deficient
    C. sufficient

12. DIRECTIONS: Choose the most effective word or phrase within the context suggested by the sentence.

    We have lived near the airport for so long that we are _____ of the noise of planes flying over our house, yet it annoys anyone who visits us.

    A. oblivious
    B. conscious
    C. negligent

13. DIRECTIONS: Choose the option that corrects an error in the underlined portion(s). If no error exists, choose "No change is necessary."

    Diana sat <u>beside</u> a person on the bus <u>who's</u> <u>clothes</u> were soaked with perspiration.
    　　　　　　 A　　　　　　　　　　　　　 B　　 C
    A. besides
    B. whose
    C. cloths
    D. No change is necessary.

14. DIRECTIONS: Choose the option that corrects an error in the underlined portion(s). If no error exists, choose "No change is necessary."

    Now that Steven is working on improving his health, he is drinking <u>fewer</u> cups of coffee,
    　　　　　　　　　　　　　　　　　　　　　　　　　　　　　　　 A

    cutting down on the <u>amount</u> of calories, and <u>losing</u> weight as a result.
    　　　　　　　　　　 B　　　　　　　　　　 C

A. less
B. number
C. loosing
D. No change is necessary.

15. DIRECTIONS: Choose the sentence in which the modifiers are correctly placed.
    A. They had a perfect view of the fireworks display sitting on the beach.
    B. Sitting on the beach was a perfect view of the fireworks display.
    C. Sitting on the beach, they had a perfect view of the fireworks display.

16. DIRECTIONS: Choose the sentence in which the modifiers are correctly placed.
    A. Natalie returned the garlic and herb cheese spread to the supermarket that was moldy.
    B. Natalie returned the garlic and herb cheese spread that was moldy to the supermarket.
    C. The garlic and cheese spread was returned by Natalie that was moldy to the supermarket.

17. DIRECTIONS: Choose the sentence that expresses the thought most clearly and effectively and has no error in structure.
    A. Because I have a job now, I can start saving money for a car.
    B. Although I have a job now, I can start saving money for a car.
    C. Unless I have a job now, I can start saving money for a car.

18. DIRECTIONS: Choose the most effective word or phrase within the context suggested by the sentence.

    Jeff's dog is very aggressive; _____, he has to keep Killer in his cage when Jeff has visitors.

    A. however
    B. otherwise
    C. finally
    D. therefore

19. DIRECTIONS: Choose the most effective word or phrase within the context suggested by the sentence.

    Drinking and driving a car can have several risks, such as harming innocent people, getting arrested, and _____.

    A. it can interfere with your brain functions.
    B. interferes with your brain functions.
    C. interfering with your brain functions.
    D. interference with your brain functions.

20. DIRECTONS: Choose the sentence that has no errors in structure.
    A. Since my car broke down, I have to figure out how to get to school every day; my choices are to ride the bus, taking a cab, or borrow my aunt's car.
    B. Since my car broke down, I have to figure out how to get to school every day; my choices are riding the bus, taking a cab, or borrow my aunt's car.
    C. Since my car broke down, I have to figure out how to get to school every day; my choices are to ride the bus, take a cab, or borrow my aunt's car.

21. DIRECTIONS: Choose the option that corrects an error in the underlined portion(s). If no error exists, choose "No change is necessary."

Even though I am not a high school cheerleader anymore, I still help out at my old
<u>school sometimes</u> I even cheer along with the cheerleaders just for fun.

A. school. Sometimes
B. school, sometimes
C. school, sometimes,
D. No change is necessary.

22. DIRECTIONS: Choose the option that corrects an error in the underlined portion(s). If no error exists, choose "No change is necessary."

In order to retrieve our anchor, I had to perform a perfect <u>dive. If</u> I dove too <u>fast, my</u>
                 A   B

body would not be able to adjust to the quick increase in <u>pressure, if</u> I dove too slowly,
                       C

I would run out of oxygen.

A. dive, if
B. fast. My
C. pressure; if
D. No change is necessary.

23. DIRECTIONS: Choose the option that corrects an error in the underlined portion(s). If no error exists, choose "No change is necessary."

In my house, there is always a task to be <u>accomplished. Such as</u> walking the dog, mowing the lawn, or planning a fishing trip.

A. accomplished; such as,
B. accomplished, such as
C. accomplished such as;
D. No change is necessary.

24. DIRECTIONS: Choose the option that corrects an error in the underlined portion(s). If no error exists, choose "No change is necessary."

When my mother first came to the United <u>States. She</u> could not speak a word of <u>English; she</u>
                   A   B

struggled with the language for a long <u>time, but</u> today she communicates in English very well.
                   C

A. States, she
B. English, she
C. time but,
D. No change is necessary.

25. DIRECTIONS: Choose the option that corrects an error in the underlined portion(s). If no error exists, choose "No change is necessary."

Jarred <u>had spoke</u> with his parents about going away to school, but they wanted him to go to the local community college.

A. had spoken
B. has spoke
C. speaking
D. No change is necessary.

26. DIRECTIONS: Choose the option that corrects an error in the underlined portion(s). If no error exists, choose "No change is necessary."

    Bonnie <u>worked</u> on hiring the caterer and the photographer, Jennifer <u>is looking</u> for a wedding
         A   B

    dress, and Dad <u>worried</u> about paying for everything.
                C

    A. works
    B. looked
    C. worrying
    D. No change is necessary.

27. DIRECTIONS: Choose the option that corrects an error in the underlined portion(s). If no error exists, choose "No change is necessary."

    I used every last bit of energy I had to catch up with the ball; then, I <u>dive</u> in the air to make the catch in the end zone.

    A. am diving
    B. dove
    C. had dove
    D. No change is necessary.

28. DIRECTIONS: Choose the option that corrects an error in the underlined portion(s). If no error exists, choose "No change is necessary."

    Some high schools <u>install</u> video cameras in the halls to see if there <u>are</u> any fights or if
                        A   B

    there <u>is</u> any drug sales.
         C

    A. installs
    B. is
    C. are
    D. No change is necessary.

29. DIRECTIONS: Choose the option that corrects an error in the underlined portion(s). If no error exists, choose "No change is necessary."

    Because of the heavy rains from the tropical storm that <u>is</u> moving through the area, neither
                                               A

    the grass nor the flowers <u>needs</u> any more water, but the weather service <u>predicts</u> five
                                B   C

    more inches of rain within the next three hours.

A. are
B. need
C. predict
D. No change is necessary.

30. DIRECTIONS: Choose the option that corrects an error in the underlined portion(s). If no error exists, choose "No change is necessary."

Even though each of the children forgot a few of <u>their</u> lines, the audience clapped <u>its</u>
                                                      A   B

hands eagerly to show <u>its</u> appreciation for the performance.
                            C

A. his or her
B. their
C. their
D. No change is necessary.

31. DIRECTIONS: Choose the option that corrects an error in the underlined portion(s). If no error exists, choose "No change is necessary."

One reason <u>we</u> like living in Florida is that <u>we</u> can play sports outdoors all year round,
                A   B

and <u>you</u> don't have to wear heavy coats.
         C

A. you
B. you
C. we
D. No change is necessary.

32. DIRECTIONS: Choose the option that corrects an error in the underlined portion(s). If no error exists, choose "No change is necessary."

<u>They</u> are always looking for good places to surf, but to find the most challenging waves,
 A

<u>we</u> have to travel to the northern coast, or <u>they</u> can wait for a big storm and surf at the
 B   C

local beach.

A. We
B. they
C. we
D. No change is necessary.

33. DIRECTIONS: Choose the option that corrects an error in the underlined portion(s). If no error exists, choose "No change is necessary."

Chris has always enjoyed antique car exhibits, so he decided to buy <u>it</u>.

A. them
B. an antique car exhibit
C. an antique car
D. No change is necessary.

34. DIRECTIONS: Choose the option that corrects an error in the underlined portion(s). If no error exists, choose "No change is necessary."

She and I had an argument, so our friends have to relay messages between her and I.
  A   B   C

A. Her
B. me
C. me
D. No change is necessary.

35. DIRECTIONS: Choose the option that corrects an error in the underlined portion(s). If no error exists, choose "No change is necessary."

Flea cocoons can live safe in your home for over a year without eating, surviving
                                  A

easily most pesticides as they hibernate in their secure shell.
  B   C

A. safely
B. easy
C. securely
D. No change is necessary.

36. DIRECTIONS: Choose the word or phrase that best completes the sentence.

The weather is getting _____, so we had better go inside.

A. worst
B. worse
C. the worst
D. worser

37. DIRECTIONS: Choose the option that corrects an error in the underlined portion(s). If no error exists, choose "No change is necessary."

Broccoli contains many cancer-fighting properties including fiber, beta-carotene, and
vitamin C.

A. Brocoli
B. Brocolli
C. Broccolli
D. No change is necessary.

38. DIRECTIONS: Choose the option that corrects an error in the underlined portion(s). If no error exists, choose "No change is necessary."

As part of my <u>job as</u> an after-school care <u>worker, I</u> am responsible for organizing the
              A   B

children's arts and crafts <u>activities, and</u> helping them with their homework.
                                 C

A. job, as
B. worker I
C. activities and
D. No change is necessary.

39. DIRECTIONS: Choose the sentence that is correctly punctuated.
A. Eric wanted to know where were the team members jerseys.
B. Eric wanted to know where the team members' jerseys were.
C. Eric wanted to know where were the team members' jerseys?

40. DIRECTIONS: Choose the option that corrects an error in the underlined portion(s). If no error exists, choose "No change is necessary."

Many people do not think that the <u>southern</u> part of Florida represents the <u>south</u> in terms
                                    A   B

of <u>culture</u> because most of the people living there come from other states or countries.
     C

A. Southern
B. South
C. Culture
D. No change is necessary.

Part Two: Writing Workbook

Chapter 1: Concept Skills

Competency 1.1	Conceptual and Organizational Skills
Skill Tested	Identifies a thesis statement or a topic sentence

The Skill

This item tests your ability to identify the best thesis statement or topic sentence in a passage. The thesis statement and the topic sentence both express a main idea, but they serve different purposes. The thesis statement is the main idea sentence of a piece of writing that consists of more than one paragraph. On the other hand, the topic sentence is the main idea sentence of a single paragraph.

Thesis Statement

The thesis statement is a sentence that usually appears in the introductory paragraph of a piece of writing. If you have studied essay writing, then you know how important the thesis statement is to the essay. The thesis will often appear at the end of the introductory paragraph, though this is not always the case. The thesis statement does two things:

1. Tells the readers what the limited subject will be
2. Gives the writer's point, opinion, idea, or attitude about the limited subject

In addition to revealing the limited subject and the writer's point about the subject, the thesis can also list the supporting points in the same sentence. Here's an example:

> Attending community college was the best decision I have ever made because of the excellent teachers, the convenient location, and the affordable cost.

The limited subject: Attending community college
The writer's point: was the best decision I have ever made
Supporting points: because of the excellent teachers, the convenient location, and the affordable cost.

The body paragraphs of the essay support the thesis statement. Each body paragraph has a topic sentence supported by details arranged in a specific pattern. As you read the following passage, notice how the thesis statement (in bold) expresses the main idea and lists the points that will be covered in the body. Also, look at how each body paragraph has a topic sentence (in bold), which is supported by proof details.

If you have ever stayed up late, say, studying or partying, and then awakened early the next morning, you have probably experienced sleep deprivation. In fact, you may be sleep deprived right now. If so, you have company. Many adults do not get enough sleep (defined as 8 hours). **Sleep deprivation affects us in at least three important psychological areas: attention, mood, and performance.**

One psychological area affected by sleep deprivation is the ability to perform tasks requiring sustained attention. Young adults who volunteered for a sleep deprivation study were allowed to sleep for only 5 hours each night, for a total of 7 nights. After 3 nights of restricted sleep, volunteers complained of cognitive, emotional, and physical difficulties. Moreover, their performance on a visual motor task declined after only 2 nights of restricted sleep. Visual motor tasks usually require participants to concentrate on detecting a change in a particular stimulus, and then to respond as quickly as they can after they perceive the change by pressing a button. Although you may be able to perform short mental tasks normally when sleep deprived, if a task requires sustained attention and a motor response, your performance will suffer. Driving a car is an example of such a task. In fact, in a survey by the National Sleep Foundation, 25% of the respondents reported that they had at some time fallen asleep at the wheel; sleepy drivers account for at least 100,000 car crashes each year.

Moods are also affected by sleep deprivation. Those who sleep less than 6 hours each weekday night are more likely to report being impatient or aggravated when faced with common minor frustrations such as being stuck in traffic or having to wait in line, and they were more dissatisfied with life in general, according to the National Sleep Foundation. The loss of even one night's sleep can lead to increases in the next day's level of cortisol. Cortisol helps the body meet the demands of stress. However, sleep deprivation can lead to a change in cortisol levels that, in turn, alters other biological functions. Regularly increased cortisol levels affect memory and cause a decrease in the immune system.

In addition to attention and mood, sleep deprivation affects performance. Many students take a series of all-nighters, when you get no sleep at all, as might occur during finals period. Results from volunteers who have gone without sleep for long stretches (finally sleeping after staying awake anywhere from 4 to 11 days) show profound psychological changes, such as hallucinations, feelings of losing control or going crazy, anxiety, and paranoia. Morevoer, going without sleep alters the normal circadian rhythms of changes in temperature, metabolism, and hormone secretion. Results of a study on sleep-deprived humans found a different pattern of brain activation when learning verbal material, compared to the pattern of activation when not sleep deprived, suggesting an attempt to compensate for the brain changes induced by sleep deprivation. (Adapted from Stephen M. Kosslyn and Robin S. Rosenberg, *Psychology*, Boston: Allyn and Bacon, 2004.)

Topic Sentence

The topic sentence states the main idea of a paragraph. The topic sentence is often the first sentence of a paragraph, but this is not always the case. Following the topic sentence are the specific details that develop the point that the topic sentence makes. The following paragraph shows how the topic sentence works in a paragraph.

Deborah Tannen, sociologist and author, explains that men and women have different listening behavior. Women seek to build rapport and establish a closer relationship and so use listening to achieve these ends. For example, women use more listening cues that let the other person know they are paying attention and are interested. On the other hand, men not only use fewer listening cues but interrupt more and will often change the topic to one they know more about or one that is less relational or people-oriented to one that is more factual, for example, sports, statistics, economic developments, or political problems. Research shows that men play up their expertise, emphasize it, and use it to dominate the conversation. Women play down their expertise. (Adapted from Joseph A. DeVito, *Essentials of Human Communication*, 3rd ed., New York: Longman, 1999.)

The Test Question

You will be tested on your ability to identify the best thesis statement or topic sentence in a passage of approximately 200 words. Incorrect answers may include supporting details and/or partial thesis statements rather than complete thesis statements.

SECTION 1 ◆ DIAGNOSTIC: THE TOPIC SENTENCE

Read the passages and apply the strategies described above for finding the topic sentence. When you are done, check your work with the answers immediately following the diagnostic. Even if you get a perfect score here, go ahead and complete the exercises in this section; they are designed to help build confidence and to give you practice for future test success.

PASSAGE #1

Read the passage and answer the question that follows.

> (1) _____. (2) Some instructors, for example, have a teaching style that promotes social interaction among students. (3) An instructor may organize small group activities, encourage class participation, or require students to work in pairs or teams to complete a specific task. (4) A lecture class is an example. (5) Other instructors offer little or no opportunity for social interaction. (6) Some instructors are very applied; they teach by example. (7) Others are more conceptual; they focus on presenting ideas, rules, theories, and so forth. (8) To an extent, of course, the subject matter also dictates how the instructor teaches. (9) _____ a biology instructor has a large body of factual information to present and may feel he or she has little time to schedule group interaction. (10) Some instructors' teaching styles are boring. (11) Once you are aware of your learning style and then consider the instructor's teaching style, you can begin to understand why you can learn better from one instructor than another and why you feel more comfortable in certain instructors' classes than others. (Adapted from Kathleen McWhorter, *Study and Critical Thinking Skills in College*, 5th ed., New York: Longman, 2003.)

1. Which sentence, if inserted in the blank labeled number 1, is the **best** main idea or topic sentence?
   A. Learning from both textbooks and lectures is the biggest challenge you face as a college student.
   B. The reasons instructors don't tell their students how to learn is simple.
   C. Just as each student has his or her own learning style, so does each instructor have his or her own teaching style.
   D. Variations in how people learn are known as learning styles.

PASSAGE #2

Read the passage and answer the question that follows.

> (1) _____. (2) As early as the 1920s, psychologists attempted to teach language to chimpanzees to find out whether

they could communicate. (3) Chimps don't have the appropriate vocal apparatus to produce spoken language, so researchers had to devise other methods of communication. (4) For instance, a chimp named Washoe was taught a highly simplified version of American Sign Language. (5) In addition, a chimp named Sarah was taught to manipulate symbols on a magnetic board. (6) Skeptics wondered if the chimps' combination of gestures and symbols constituted any kind of meaningful language. (7) Recent research has provided more solid insights into the language capabilities of chimps. (8) Bonobos and chimps can be raised together. (9) Sue Savage-Rumbaugh and her team work primarily with *bonobos*, a species of great ape that is evolutionarily nearer to humans than even the common chimpanzees. (10) Remarkably, two of the bonobos in her studies, Kanzi and Mulika, learned the meanings of plastic symbols at the same time. (11) They did not receive direct training; rather, they acquired the symbols by watching humans and other bonobos. (12) _____ Kanzi and Mulika can understand some spoken English. (13) For example, when Kanzi hears a spoken word, he is able to locate either the symbol for the word or a picture of the object. (Adapted from Richard J. Gerrig and Philip G. Zimbardo, *Psychology and Life*, 16th ed., Boston: Allyn and Bacon, 2002.)

2. Which sentence, if inserted in the blank labeled number 1, is the **best** main idea or topic sentence?
   A. Bonobos are more intelligent than chimpanzees because bonobos are closer to humans in their evolution.
   B. Research over the years has demonstrated that bonobos and chimpanzees can understand some spoken English words.
   C. Researchers derive much satisfaction from teaching language to apes.
   D. Some chimps can communicate with sign language and plastic symbols.

PASSAGE #3

Read the passage and answer the question that follows.

(1) _____. (2) The relationship between temperature and assault is actually strongest in the late evening and early morning hours, from 9 p.m. to 3 a.m. (3) One explanation is that people are more likely to commit assault when they are out and about. (4) That is, in warmer weather, people are usually outdoors more and, therefore, are also more "available" as assault victims. (5) In the 9 p.m. to 3 a.m. hours, people are typically not working or bound by other responsibilities. (6) The time of day is another factor. (7) Furthermore, by the late evening hours, people may have been drinking alcohol or using other substances that lower their inhibition to aggression. (8) Substance abuse is a big problem in our society. (9) Another part of the explanation is the way in which people cope with and interpret the discomfort associated with high temperatures. (10) As the day goes on, it may be harder to remember, "I'm feeling this way because it's hot" and just conclude, "I'm feeling this way because this person is making me crazy." (11)_____, assaults decline when temperatures become very hot. (12) Researchers have speculated that at very high temperatures, people might experience sufficient discomfort to withdraw from abrasive situations rather than stay and fight. (Adapted from Richard J. Gerrig and Philip G. Zimbardo, *Psychology and Life*, 16th ed., Boston: Allyn and Bacon, 2002.)

3. Which sentence, if inserted in the blank labeled number 1, is the **best** main idea or topic sentence?
   A. Inappropriate levels of serotonin may impair the brain's ability to regulate aggressive behavior.
   B. Aggression is behavior that causes psychological or physical harm to another individual.

C. Many individuals use aggression to solve their problems.
D. Psychologists have learned that there is a strong relationship between how cold or hot it is and how likely it is that people will commit assaults.

PASSAGE #4

Read the passage and answer the question that follows.

(1) _____. (2) The Hare Indians of Colville Lake are a small group of Canadian Inuit. (3) Savishinsky lived with the Hare Indians to study them. (4) They survive by hunting, trapping, and fishing in one of the harshest environments in the world. (5)_____, dogs are economically useful. (6) Dog teams give the Inuit a means for travel during the harshest seasons of the year. (7) The temperatures are extremely cold, and the winters are long and severe. (8) Finding food can be difficult. (9) The Inuit estimate that six dogs are required for travel, and some households have as many as four dog teams, with an average of 6.2 dogs per team. (10) The dogs are a frequent topic of conversation. (11) More than being only economically useful, dogs play a significant role in people's emotional lives. (12) Members of the community constantly compare and comment on the care, condition, and growth of one another's animals. (13) They note special qualities of size, strength, color, speed, and alertness. (14) Emotional displays, uncommon among the Hare, are significant between people and their dogs. (15) All people participate in the affectionate and concerned treatment of young dogs. (Adapted from Barbara D. Miller, *Cultural Anthropology*, 2nd ed., Boston: Allyn and Bacon, 2002.)

4. Which sentence, if inserted in the blank labeled number 1, is the **best** main idea or topic sentence?
   A. Inuit refers to the people formerly called Eskimos.
   B. Dogs play a significant role in the lives of the Hare Indians.
   C. The roots of the Inuit dog, or Qimmiq, date back 4,000 years, possibly more.
   D. The Inuit sled dog is bred for its overwhelming desire to work.

PASSAGE #5

Read the passage and answer the question that follows.

(1) _____. (2) The robin searches for food by selecting only those items that provide the greatest energy return for the energy expended. (3) This can be illustrated by the robin's behavior, which has four parts. (4) First, the robin has to decide where to hunt for food. (5) Once on the lawn, it has to search for food items. (6) Because the robin forages on lawns, it is vulnerable to pesticide poisoning. (7) Having located some potential food, the robin has to decide whether to pursue it. (8) If it begins pursuit by pecking, the robin has to attempt a capture, in which it might or might not be successful. (9) If a food item is too large, it requires too much time to handle; if it is too small, it does not deliver enough energy to cover the costs of capture. (10) The robin should reject or ignore less valuable items, such as small beetles and caterpillars, and give preference to small and medium-sized earthworms. (11) _____ by capturing an earthworm, the robin earns some units of energy. (12) These more valuable food items would be classified as preferred food. (13) If the robin fails to find suitable and sufficient food in the area of the lawn it is searching, it leaves to search elsewhere. (14) If successful, the bird probably will return until the spot is no longer an economical place to feed. (Adapted from Robert Leo Smith and Thomas M. Smith, *Elements of Ecology*, 5th ed., San Francisco: Benjamin Cummings, 2003.)

5. Which sentence, if inserted in the blank labeled number 1, is the **best** main idea or topic sentence?
   A. To the robin, time is energy.
   B. The robin is noted for feeding in lawns where it finds earthworms.
   C. Robins eat different types of food depending on the time of day; in the morning they eat earthworms, and in the afternoon they eat fruits and berries.
   D. The American robin is a common occupant of residential areas during the breeding season.

PASSAGE #6

Read the passage and answer the question that follows.

(1) _____. (2) Beach-nesting birds such as the piping plover and the least tern are so disturbed by bathers and dune buggies that both species are in danger of extinction. (3) Other terns and shore birds are subjected to competition for nest sites and to egg predators by rapidly growing populations of large gulls. (4) These gulls are highly tolerant of humans and thrive on human garbage. (5) Sea turtles and the horseshoe crab, dependent on sandy beaches for nesting sites, find themselves evicted. (6) _____, they are declining rapidly. (7) Furthermore, each incoming tide brings onto the beaches feces-contaminated water that makes them unhealthy for humans and wildlife alike. (8) This contaminated water comes from a number of different sources, such as sewer overflows, failing private and commercial septic systems, animal and wildlife waste, and swimmers' illnesses. (9) The oceans have become dumping grounds. (10) Major chronic pollutants are oil that is released from tanker accidents, seepage from offshore drilling and other sources, toxic materials such as pesticides and heavy metals from industrial, urban, and agricultural sources. (11) The most devastating human activity in reefs is overfishing, especially in the Philippines and the Caribbean. (12) Tides also carry in old fishing lines, plastic debris, and other wastes hazardous to wildlife. (Adapted from Robert Leo Smith, and Thomas M. Smith, *Elements of Ecology*, 5th ed., San Francisco: Benjamin Cummings, 2003.)

6. Which sentence, if inserted in the blank labeled number 1, is the **best** main idea or topic sentence?
   A. Oil has become a major pollutant of the seas.
   B. Where the land meets the sea, we find the complex world of the seashore.
   C. Human intrusion onto the seashore has had serious effects on wildlife of the sandy shores.
   D. Ocean bathers face the risk of respiratory infections and gastroenteritis due to water pollution.

PASSAGE #7

Read the passage and answer the question that follows.

(1) _____. (2) About 21 million people trace their origin to Mexico, 3 million to Puerto Rico, 1 million to Cuba, and almost 5 million to Central or South America, primarily Venezuela or Colombia. (3) Officially tallied at 35 million in the year 2000 census, the actual number of Latinos is higher because, not surprisingly, many who are in the country illegally avoid contact with both public officials and census forms. (4) Each year, more than 1 million people are apprehended at the border or at points inland and are deported to Mexico. (5) Perhaps another million or so manage to enter the United States. (6) _____ many migrate for temporary work and then return to their homes and families. (7) To gain an understanding of how vast these numbers are, we can note that there are millions more Latinos in the United States than there

are Canadians in Canada (31 million). (8) To Midwesterners, such a comparison often comes as a surprise, for Latinos are absent from vast stretches of mid-America. (9) Sixty-nine percent are concentrated in just four states: California, Texas, New York, and Florida. (10) In the next twenty-five years, changes in the U.S. racial-ethnic mix will be dramatic. (Adapted from James M. Henslin, *Sociology*, 6th ed., Boston: Allyn and Bacon, 2003.)

7. Which sentence, if inserted in the blank labeled number 1, is the **best** main idea or topic sentence?
   A. In the United States, 20 million people speak Spanish at home.
   B. Today Latinos are a growing minority group in the United States.
   C. People from different Latin nations feel little in common with one another.
   D. *Latino* refers to ethnic groups, not race.

Answers and Explanations to Diagnostic: The Topic Sentence

1. Answer   C
This passage gives examples of different teaching styles.

False choices
>   Choice A leads the reader to think that the paragraph will be about learning from both textbooks and lectures.
>   Choice B indicates that the paragraph will discuss reasons instructors don't tell students how to learn.
>   Choice D defines learning style. A fact can not be a topic sentence.

2. Answer   B
The passage describes research done over the years that has taught researchers that bonobos and chimpanzees can understand some English.

False choices
>   Choice A leads the reader to believe that the entire paragraph will contrast the intelligence of bonobos and chimpanzees. While the author mentions that bonobos are evolutionarily closer to humans and indicates that bonobos are better at recognizing English, this is not the focus of the paragraph.
>   Choice C refers to the satisfaction researchers derive from this work; however, the topic is not covered in the paragraph.
>   Choice D is a fact from the paragraph, not the main idea.

3. Answer   D
This passage explains the relationship between temperature and assaults.

False choices
>   Choice A refers to serotonin levels in the brain as a factor that contributes to aggressive behavior, but this is not covered in the passage.
>   Choice B defines the term "aggression." Definitions are not main idea sentences.
>   Choice C is too general in its statement that many people use aggression to solve problems. This paragraph clearly explains that there is a correlation between temperature and assaults.

4. Answer   B
The passage tells the reader how dogs are economically and emotionally helpful to the Hare Indians.

False choices
>   Choice A provides a definition of Inuit. Since it is a fact, the definition can not be a topic sentence.
>   Choice C speaks of the root of the Inuit dog. While the paragraph is about these dogs, it does not discuss the history and evolution of the species.

Choice D gives the reason that the sled dog is bred; however, the paragraph does not describe sled dog breeding.

5. Answer   A

The passage explains that the robin should find food without expending too much energy.

False choices

Choice B gives a fact about robins—that they look for earthworms on lawns. A topic sentence may not be a fact.

Choice C also gives a fact about what robins eat at different times of the day.

Choice D leads the reader to believe that the paragraph will talk about the kinds of residential areas the robin occupies, not the way it feeds.

6. Answer   C

The passage explains the effects of human intrusion on the seashore.

False choices

Choice A leads the reader to believe that the passage will focus on the effects of oil pollution on the oceans.

Choice B indicates that the discussion will be about the "complex world of the seashore." This might include the various plants and animals that live at the water's edge or in the sand.

Choice D tells the reader that the passage will talk about the risks ocean bathers face as a result of ocean pollution. Risks to bathers is mentioned in the passage, but it is not the main idea.

7. Answer   B

This passage gives specific information on how the Latino population is increasing in the United States.

False choices

Choice A presents a fact, which cannot be a topic sentence.

Choice C leads the reader to think that the paragraph will discuss the fact that people from different Latin countries do not have much in common; however, the passage focuses on population, not commonalities.

Choice D tells the reader the meaning of *Latino*. This is a definition, not a topic sentence.

SECTION 1 ◆ EXERCISES: THE TOPIC SENTENCE

PASSAGE #1

Read the passage and answer the question that follows.

1 _____
_____.
2First of all, because e-mail messages are informal and quick, writers may be sloppy in transferring their thoughts to the screen. 3Misspellings and ungrammatical sentences can project a negative image if users do not take time to edit what they write on e-mail. 4Second, the messages are sent and read online, often leaving no paper trail at all. 5As a result, some important messages are forgotten or lost. 6It is easy to read your electronic mail and delete it instead of printing out a copy of the message to keep in a file or filing the message electronically in your e-mail file folder. 7Although generally thought of as a quick method of communication, e-mail's efficiency is only as good as the recipient's care in routinely checking e-mail messages. 8Electronic communication can be slow if people don't check their messages. 9Moreover, you have no privacy. 10Another disadvantage is the increasing use of e-mail as a replacement for the personal contact of a phone call or face-to-face meeting. 11The

1986 Electronic Communications Privacy Act considers e-mail to be the property of the company paying for the mail system. [12]_____, writing on a computer screen often encourages people to drop inhibitions and write things in e-mail that they would never write in a paper letter or say over the telephone. (Adapted from Kristin R. Woolever, *Writing for the Technical Professions*, 2nd ed., New York: Longman, 2002.)

1. Which sentence, if inserted in the blank labeled number 1, is the **best** main idea or topic sentence?
   A. Electronic mail is a beneficial form of communication.
   B. When using e-mail to communicate in the workplace, always maintain a level of professionalism and courtesy.
   C. Although electronic mail has become a medium of choice for business communication, e-mail has disadvantages for users.
   D. At work, people are using e-mail as a primary form of communication.

PASSAGE #2

Read the passage and answer the question that follows.

[1]_____.

[2]Although women have served in every branch of the armed services since World War II, two differences between the treatment of men and women in the military persist. [3]First, only men must register for the draft when they turn eighteen. [4]In 1981, the Supreme Court ruled that male-only registration for the military did not violate the Fifth Amendment. [5]Second, statutes and regulations also prohibit women from serving in combat. [6]A breach exists between policy and practice, however, as the Persian Gulf war showed. [7]Women piloted helicopters at the front and helped to operate antimissile systems; some were taken as prisoners of war. [8]_____, women are not permitted to serve as combat pilots in the navy and air force and to serve on navy warships. [9]They are still not permitted to serve in ground combat units in the army or marines. [10]These actions have reopened the debate over whether women should serve in combat. [11]Others argue that men will not be able to fight effectively beside wounded or dying women. [12]Critics of these views point out that some women surpass men in body strength and that we do not know how well men and women will fight together. [13]Some experts insist that because women, on the average, have less body strength than men, they are less suited for combat. [14]This debate is not only a controversy about ability, but it also touches on the question of whether engaging in combat is a burden or a privilege. (Adapted from George C. Edwards, Martin P. Wattenberg, and Robert L. Lineberry, *Government in America*, 9th ed., New York: Longman, 2000.)

2. Which sentence, if inserted in the blank labeled number 1, is the **best** main idea or topic sentence?
   A. Women have overcome many obstacles to serving in the military.
   B. The U.S. has had a volunteer military force since 1973.
   C. Women are less suited for combat than men.
   D. Military service is still a controversial issue of gender equality.

PASSAGE #3

Read the passage and answer the question that follows.

[1]_____.

[2]Jaime Escalante taught calculus in an East Los Angeles inner-city school that was plagued with poverty, crime, drugs, and gangs. [3]As a result of his methods, his students earned the

highest Advanced Placement scores in the city. 4_____, Escalante had to open his students' minds to the possibility of success in learning. 5Most Latino students were tracked into craft classes where they made jewelry and birdhouses. 6Escalante felt that his students were talented and needed an opportunity to show it. 7Also, the students needed to see learning as a way out of the barrio, as a path to good jobs. 8By arranging for foundations to provide money for students to attend colleges of their choice, Escalante showed students that if they did well, their poverty would not stop them. 9When Escalante first came to the United States, he worked as a busboy and attended Pasadena Community College. 10Escalante also changed the system of instruction. 11Before class, his students did "warm-ups," hand clapping and foot stomping to a rock song. 12To foster team identity, students wore team jackets, caps, and T-shirts with logos that identified them as part of the math team. 13He had his students think of themselves as a team, of him as the coach, and the national math exams as a sort of Olympics for which they were preparing. 14Escalante thought it was important to teach his classes in English, not Spanish. 15Escalante demonstrated that a teacher can motivate students to believe in their ability to achieve at high levels, no matter how great their problems. (Adapted from James M. Henslin, *Sociology*, 6th ed., Boston: Allyn and Bacon, 2003.)

3. Which sentence, if inserted in the blank labeled number 1, is the **best** main idea or topic sentence?
   A. Jaime Escalante, the Bolivian who did not know how to speak English when he came to the U.S., graduated from California State University in 1974 with a bachelor's degree in mathematics and electronics.
   B. Jaime Escalante's dramatic success in teaching calculus to students in an East Los Angeles inner-city school plagued with poverty, crime, drugs, and gangs, was a result of changes he made to classroom instruction.
   C. The story of Jaime Escalante's success in teaching calculus to low-income Latino high school students in Los Angeles was the subject of the movie *Stand and Deliver*.
   D. Jaime Escalante believed that all a person needs to succeed is desire that comes from within.

PASSAGE #4

Read the passage and answer the question that follows.

1
_____.
2Anorexia nervosa literally means loss of appetite, but this is a misnomer. 3The anorexic individual approaches weight loss with a fervor, convinced that her body is too large. 4A person with anorexia nervosa is hungry, but he or she denies the hunger because of an irrational fear of becoming fat. 5Therefore, the first characteristic is a significant weight loss due to a relentless drive for thinness. 6She is unable to recognize that her appearance is abnormal. 7She will insist that her emaciated figure is just right or is too fat. 8There is a strong argument that eating disorders are a form of addiction. 9This condition is more than a simple eating disorder. 10_____, Anorexia is a distinct psychological disorder with a wide range of psychological disturbances. 11Anorexics are typically compulsive, perfectionistic, and very competitive. 12Food preoccupation and rituals and compulsive exercising are other characteristics. 13The anorexic sometimes suffers from low self-image due to a feeling of incompetence, so she becomes consumed with losing weight to demonstrate to herself and others that she is in total control. 14Additional features of the disease develop from the effects of starvation over time. 15Untreated anorexia can be fatal. 16Causes of death include starvation, infections due to poor nutrition, irregular heartbeat due to potassium deficiency, and suicide due to depression.

(Adapted from David J. Anspaugh and Gene Ezell, *Teaching Today's Health*, 7th ed., San Francisco: Pearson, 2004.)

4. Which sentence, if inserted in the blank labeled number 1, is the **best** main idea or topic sentence?
   A. Eating disorders are one of the most common psychological problems facing young women around the world.
   B. Some of the physical symptoms of anorexia nervosa are directly related to the effects of starvation.
   C. Anorexia nervosa has the poorest prognosis of all the eating disorders; however, the prognosis is moderately improved if the disorder is detected and treated in its early stages.
   D. The central features of anorexia nervosa are a complex mixture of symptoms.

PASSAGE #5

Read the passage and answer the question that follows.

1 _____.

[2]Bare-knuckle boxing, the forerunner of modern boxing, was a brutal, bloody sport. [3]Two men fought bare-fisted until one could not continue. [4]A round lasted until one of the men knocked or threw down his opponent. [5]At that point, both men rested for thirty seconds and then started to fight again. [6]Fights often lasted over one hundred rounds and as long as seven or eight hours. [7]After such a fight, it took months for the fighters to recover. [8]During the 1800s, boxing underwent a series of reforms. [9]There have been periodic efforts to outlaw the sport. [10]The challenge system was replaced by modern promotional techniques. [11]Fighters deserted bare-fisted combat and started wearing gloves. [12]Most importantly, professional boxers adopted the Marquis of Queensberry Rules, which standardized a round at three minutes, allowing a one-minute rest period between rounds, and outlawed all wrestling throws and holds. [13]_____, the fight to the finish was replaced with a fight to a decision over a specified number of rounds. [14]A bell and a referee told fighters when to fight and when to rest. [15]Currently there are eight major professional divisions. [16]Although the new rules did not reduce the violence, they did provide for more orderly bouts. (Adapted from James Kirby Martin et al., *America and Its Peoples*, 5th ed., New York: Longman, 2003.)

5. Which sentence, if inserted in the blank labeled number 1, is the **best** main idea or topic sentence?
   A. Boxing originated when a person first lifted a fist against another in competition.
   B. Boxing began as a largely unstructured sport, but by 1900 new rules had standardized the sport.
   C. The sport of boxing did not catch on in the United States until the late 1800s.
   D. Boxing is one of the most popular sports in the history of modern sport.

PASSAGE #6

Read the passage and answer the question that follows.

1 _____.

[2]For example, with eye movements you can seek feedback. [3]In talking with someone, you look at her or him intently, as if to say, "Well, what do you think?" [4]Your pupils enlarge when you are interested or emotionally aroused. [5]You can also inform the other person that the channel of communication is open and that he or she should now speak. [6]You see this in the college classroom, when the instructor asks a question and then locks eyes with a student.

[7]Without saying anything, the instructor expects that student to answer the question and the student knows it.[8]Eye movements may also signal the nature of a relationship, whether positive (an attentive glance) or negative (eye avoidance). [9]_____, you can signal your power through visual dominance behavior. [10]The average speaker, for example, maintains a high level of eye contact while listening and a lower level while speaking. [11]When people want to signal dominance, they may reverse this pattern: maintaining a high level of eye contact while talking but a lower level while listening. [12]Eye contact can also change the psychological distance between yourself and another person. [13]When you catch someone's eye at a party, for example, you become psychologically close even though far apart. [14]By avoiding eye contact—even when physically close as in a crowded elevator—you increase the psychological distance between you. (Adapted from Joseph A. DeVito, *Essentials of Human Communication*, 3rd ed., New York: Longman, 1999.)

6. Which sentence, if inserted in the blank labeled number 1, is the **best** main idea or topic sentence?
   A. Eye movements have been widely researched.
   B. Eye movements communicate a variety of messages.
   C. Eye messages vary from one culture to another.
   D. The eyes are regarded as the most important nonverbal message system.

PASSAGE #7

Read the passage and answer the question that follows.

1 _____.
[2]It even drinks seawater, which is much saltier than its body fluids. [3]Few animals can tolerate such salty liquid because the salt draws water out of their tissues, and they become severely dehydrated. [4]An albatross can thrive on salt water because it has special salt-excreting glands in its nostrils. [5]The glands dispose of excess salts, allowing the bird to eat salty fish and squid and drink all it needs without ever visiting land. [6]Their scientific name, *Diomedea exulans*, means exiled warrior in Greek. [7]_____ its remarkable salt tolerance, the wandering albatross has extraordinary flight abilities specially suited to its seafaring life. [8]Its wingspan is greater than that of any other bird—about 3.6 meters (nearly twelve feet). [9]Most birds have to flap their wings to stay up in the air very long, but the albatross's long wings provide so much lift that the bird can stay aloft for hours by gliding up and down on wind currents. [10]The wandering albatross spends most of its time in an area of high winds and rough seas, far from land, often alone on the open ocean. [11]The winds carry it from west to east, and in a year's time, an albatross may circle the globe, seeing little land except New Zealand and the tip of South America. (Adapted from Neil A. Campbell, Lawrence G. Mitchell, and Jane B. Reece, *Biology*, 3rd ed., San Francisco: Benjamin Cummings, 2000.)

7. Which sentence, if inserted in the blank labeled number 1, is the **best** main idea or topic sentence?
   A. Only a few birds can live at sea, but the albatross is a model of fitness for its environment.
   B. Albatrosses frequent areas where steady winds blow over the ocean.
   C. The albatross's body has special structural adaptations.
   D. An albatross takes full advantage of the energy of ocean winds to stay aloft.

PASSAGE #8

Read the passage and answer the question that follows.

1 _____.

[2]Testosterone is a male hormone that causes a general buildup in muscle and bone mass during puberty in males and maintains masculine traits throughout life. [3]Anabolic steroids are synthetic variants of the male hormone testosterone. [4]Pharmaceutical companies first produced and marketed anabolic steroids in the early 1950s as a treatment for certain diseases that destroy body muscle. [5]About a decade later, some athletes began using anabolic steroids to build up their muscles quickly and enhance their performance with less hard work. [6]It is not surprising that some of the heaviest users are weight lifters, football players, and body builders. [7]Today, anabolic steroids, along with other drugs, are banned by most athletic organizations. [8]Black market sales bring in up to $400 million a year. [9]Medical research indicates that these substances can cause serious physical and mental problems. [10]Overdosing in males can cause acne, baldness, and breast development. [11]Mental effects can range from mood swings to deep depression. [12]Internally, there may be liver damage leading to cancer. [13]_____, anabolic steroids can make blood cholesterol levels rise, perhaps increasing a user's chances of developing serious cardiovascular problems. [14]Heavy users may also experience a reduced sex drive and become infertile because anabolic steroids often make the body reduce its normal output of sex hormones. (Adapted from Neil A. Campbell, Lawrence G. Mitchell, and Jane B. Reece, *Biology*, 3rd ed., San Francisco: Benjamin Cummings, 2000.)

8. Which sentence, if inserted in the blank labeled number 1, is the **best** main idea or topic sentence?
   A. Athletes who use anabolic steroids to increase body mass should not be allowed to compete.
   B. The only way to promote fair athletic competition is to test the athletes for anabolic steroids.
   C. While using anabolic steroids is a fast way to increase general body size, their health hazards support the argument for banning their use in athletics.
   D. There are many ways to increase your strength or improve your appearance.

PASSAGE #9

Read the passage and answer the question that follows.

1 _____.

[2]In most cases, the child continually learns from the parent. [3]In the area of computer and Internet-mediated communication, however, the child may be able to teach the parent. [4]_____, one five-year-old learned a graphics program before she could read. [5]The child taught herself how to operate the rather intuitive program. [6]Not only did the computer provide the child with a valuable learning process, but the parents totally depended on the child when they wanted to use the program she knew. [7]In another case, a young boy taught his parents how to use PowerPoint. [8]The examples are endless. [9]Children are more apt to interact with the computer as if it were alive. [10]A child may be able to understand a concept differently from the parent, and the role reversal of the child-as-teacher can be an important way the computer and the Internet can enhance a child's self-esteem. [11]The child and parent alike may feel positive toward themselves when they are able to learn new things, master a program, or win an Internet game. [12]Their self-confidence may increase when others seek their advice, for example, because they are the family computer experts. (Adapted from Leonard J. Shedletsky and Joan E. Aitken, *Human Communication on the Internet*, Boston: Allyn and Bacon, 2004.)

9. Which sentence, if inserted in the blank labeled number 1, is the **best** main idea or topic sentence?
   A. Young children often relate to the computer in creative and fun ways.
   B. Sharing information and teaching each other about their computer and the Internet can strengthen the parent-child relationship.

C. The lure of computers can come between family members.

D. The computer can have positive and negative effects on the family.

PASSAGE #10

Read the passage and answer the question that follows.

[1]_____.
[2]Highlighting is a strategy for condensing textbook material and emphasizing what is important. [3]_____, the process of highlighting forces you to sift through what you have read to identify important information. [4]This sifting or sorting is an active thought process; you are forced to weigh and evaluate what you read. [5]One mistake to avoid is highlighting almost every idea on a page. [6]Another benefit of highlighting is that it keeps you physically active while you are reading. [7]In addition, highlighting can help you discover the organization of facts and ideas as well as their connections and relationships. [8]Highlighting demonstrates to you whether you have understood a passage you have just read. [9]When combined with annotation, highlighting is a quick and easy way to review so that you do not have to reread everything when studying for an exam. [10]If you highlight 20 percent of a chapter, you will be able to avoid rereading 80 percent of the material. [11]If it normally takes two hours to read a chapter, you should be able to review a highlighted chapter in less than a half hour. [12]Highlighting has many benefits, but it is not by itself a sufficient study method; you must process the information by organizing it, expressing it in your own words, and testing yourself periodically. (Adapted from Kathleen T. McWhorter, *Study and Critical Thinking Skills in College*, 5th ed., New York: Longman, 2003.)

10. Which sentence, if inserted in the blank labeled number 1, is the **best** main idea or topic sentence?

A. If you have understood a paragraph or section, then your highlighting should be fast and efficient.

B. To highlight textbook material most efficiently, apply these guidelines.

C. College students should know how to highlight their textbooks properly.

D. Highlighting is an extremely effective way of making a textbook review manageable.

SECTION 2 ◆ SUPPORTING DETAILS

Competency 1.2   Conceptual and Organizational Skills
Skill Tested   **Recognizes adequate support provided by generalized and specific details**

The Skill

This item tests your ability to recognize whether or not an idea is supported adequately. A supporting detail is not an opinion, a restatement of the main idea, or a generality. Instead, a supporting detail is a statement providing evidence for the claim of the topic sentence. Supporting details can be:

facts	brief stories
reasons	steps in a process
statistics	definitions
examples	quotations from experts
descriptions	comparisons
effects	contrasts

You may find it helpful to remember the mnemonic **RECAPS** to identify statements of specific, concrete detail:

- Reasons
- Examples
- Characteristics
- Analysis and explanations
- People and places
- Senses (sight, sound, smell, taste, touch)

Read the following two paragraphs. Which one is adequately supported?

Sample 1

> Caffeine, a common stimulant found in coffee, tea, cola drinks, and even chocolate, is a drug and should be recognized as one that can lead to health problems. Because it is not viewed as a dangerous drug, caffeine use for its own sake is overlooked.

Sample 2

> Caffeine, a common stimulant found in coffee, tea, cola drinks, and even chocolate, is a drug and should be recognized as one that can lead to health problems. Caffeine increases mental alertness and provides a feeling of energy. However, high doses of caffeine can over stimulate and cause nervousness and increased heart rate. Caffeine can also cause sleeplessness, excitement, and irritability. In some cases, high doses of caffeine can induce convulsions. Because it is not viewed as a dangerous drug, caffeine use for its own sake is overlooked. (Adapted from David J. Anspaugh and Gene Ezell, *Teaching Today's Health*, 7th ed., San Francisco: Benjamin Cummings, 2004.)

Sample 1 does not provide any supporting details explaining the possible health problems from caffeine use; however, Sample 2 does. Three statements give examples of the kinds of problems a person who uses caffeine might have:

> However, high doses of caffeine can over stimulate and cause nervousness and increased heart rate. Caffeine can also cause sleeplessness, excitement, and irritability. In some cases, high doses of caffeine can induce convulsions.

The Test Question
You will be tested on your ability to recognize adequate supporting details in one of two ways:

1. You may be asked to identify which sentence in a passage is NOT supported by sufficient details. You must decide if a statement is a general statement that needs additional support.
2. You may be given several sentences and asked to choose which sentence provides support for a specified sentence in the passage. You must choose the best statement of detail for a general idea.

SECTION 2 ◆ DIAGNOSTIC: SUPPORTING DETAILS

Read the passages and apply the strategies described above for finding supporting details. When you are done, check your work with the answers immediately following the diagnostic. Even if you get a perfect score here, go ahead and complete the exercises in this section; they are designed to help build confidence and to give you practice for future test success.

PASSAGE #1

Read the passage and answer the question that follows.

(1) _____.
(2) Some instructors, for example, have a teaching style that promotes social interaction among students. (3) An instructor may organize small group activities, encourage class participation, or require students to work in pairs or teams to complete a specific task. (4) A lecture class is an example. (5) Other instructors offer little or no opportunity for social interaction. (6) Some instructors are very applied; they teach by example. (7) Others are more conceptual; they focus on presenting ideas, rules, theories, and so forth. (8) To an extent, of course, the subject matter also dictates how the instructor teaches. (9) _____ a biology instructor has a large body of factual information to present and may feel he or she has little time to schedule group interaction. (10) Some instructors' teaching styles are boring. (11) Once you are aware of your learning style and then consider the instructor's teaching style, you can begin to understand why you can learn better from one instructor than another and why you feel more comfortable in certain instructors' classes than others. (Adapted from Kathleen McWhorter, *Study and Critical Thinking Skills in College*, 5th ed., New York: Longman, 2003.)

1. Which sentence provides specific support for sentence 8 in the passage?
   A. Some instructors' teaching styles are boring. (sentence 10)
   B. _____, a biology instructor has a large body of factual information to present and may feel he or she has little time to schedule group interaction. (sentence 9)
   C. Once you are aware of your learning style and then consider the instructor's teaching style, you can begin to understand why you can learn better from one instructor than another and why you feel more comfortable in certain instructors' classes than others. (sentence 11)
   D. A lecture class is an example. (sentence 4)

PASSAGE #2

Read the passage and answer the question that follows.

(1) _____.
(2) As early as the 1920s, psychologists attempted to teach language to chimpanzees to find out whether they could communicate. (3) Chimps don't have the appropriate vocal apparatus to produce spoken language, so researchers had to devise other methods of communication. (4) For instance, a chimp named Washoe was taught a highly simplified version of American Sign Language. (5) In addition, a chimp named Sarah was taught to manipulate symbols on a magnetic board. (6) Skeptics wondered if the chimps' combination of gestures and symbols constituted any kind of meaningful language. (7) Recent research has provided more solid insights into the language capabilities of chimps. (8) Bonobos and chimps can be raised together. (9) Sue Savage-Rumbaugh and her team work primarily with *bonobos*, a species of great ape that is evolutionarily nearer to humans than even the common chimpanzees. (10) Remarkably, two of the bonobos in her studies, Kanzi and Mulika, learned the meanings of plastic symbols at the same time. (11) They did not receive direct training; rather, they acquired the symbols by watching humans and other bonobos. (12) _____ Kanzi and Mulika can understand some spoken English. (13) For example, when Kanzi hears a spoken word, he is able to locate either the symbol for the word or a picture of the object.

(Adapted from Richard J. Gerrig and Philip G. Zimbardo, *Psychology and Life*, 16th ed., Boston: Allyn and Bacon, 2002.)

2. Which sentence provides specific support for sentence 3 in the passage?
   A. In addition, a chimp named Sarah was taught to manipulate symbols on a magnetic board. (sentence 5)
   B. Skeptics wondered if the chimps' combination of gestures and symbols constituted any kind of meaningful language. (sentence 6)
   C. Recent research has provided more solid insights into the language capabilities of chimps. (sentence 7)
   D. Bonobos and chimps can be raised together. (sentence 8)

PASSAGE #3

Read the passage and answer the question that follows.

(1) _____.
(2) The relationship between temperature and assault is actually strongest in the late evening and early morning hours, from 9 p.m. to 3 a.m. (3) One explanation is that people are more likely to commit assault when they are out and about. (4) That is, in warmer weather, people are usually outdoors more and, therefore, are also more "available" as assault victims. (5) In the 9 p.m. to 3 a.m. hours, people are typically not working or bound by other responsibilities. (6) The time of day is another factor. (7) Furthermore, by the late evening hours, people may have been drinking alcohol or using other substances that lower their inhibition to aggression. (8) Substance abuse is a big problem in our society. (9) Another part of the explanation is the way in which people cope with and interpret the discomfort associated with high temperatures. (10) As the day goes on, it may be harder to remember, "I'm feeling this way because it's hot" and just conclude, "I'm feeling this way because this person is making me crazy." (11)_____, assaults decline when temperatures become very hot. (12) Researchers have speculated that at very high temperatures, people might experience sufficient discomfort to withdraw from abrasive situations rather than stay and fight. (Adapted from Richard J. Gerrig and Philip G. Zimbardo, *Psychology and Life*, 16th ed., Boston: Allyn and Bacon, 2002.)

3. Which of the numbered sentences is not supported by sufficient specific details?
   A. 2
   B. 6
   C. 9
   D. 12

PASSAGE #4

Read the passage and answer the question that follows.

(1) _____.
(2) The Hare Indians of Colville Lake are a small group of Canadian Inuit. (3) Savishinsky lived with the Hare Indians to study them. (4) They survive by hunting, trapping, and fishing in one of the harshest environments in the world. (5)_____, dogs are economically useful. (6) Dog teams give the Inuit a means for travel during the harshest seasons of the year. (7) The temperatures are extremely cold, and the winters are long and severe. (8) Finding food can be difficult. (9) The Inuit estimate that six dogs are required for travel, and some

households have as many as four dog teams, with an average of 6.2 dogs per team. (10) The dogs are a frequent topic of conversation. (11) More than being only economically useful, dogs play a significant role in people's emotional lives. (12) Members of the community constantly compare and comment on the care, condition, and growth of one another's animals. (13) They note special qualities of size, strength, color, speed, and alertness. (14) Emotional displays, uncommon among the Hare, are significant between people and their dogs. (15) All people participate in the affectionate and concerned treatment of young dogs. (Adapted from Barbara D. Miller, *Cultural Anthropology*, 2nd ed., Boston: Allyn and Bacon, 2002.)

4. Which of the numbered sentences is not supported by sufficient specific details?
   A. 3
   B. 5
   C. 10
   D. 12

PASSAGE #5

Read the passage and answer the question that follows.

(1) _____.
(2) The robin searches for food by selecting only those items that provide the greatest energy return for the energy expended. (3) This can be illustrated by the robin's behavior, which has four parts. (4) First, the robin has to decide where to hunt for food. (5) Once on the lawn, it has to search for food items. (6) Because the robin forages on lawns, it is vulnerable to pesticide poisoning. (7) Having located some potential food, the robin has to decide whether to pursue it. (8) If it begins pursuit by pecking, the robin has to attempt a capture, in which it might or might not be successful. (9) If a food item is too large, it requires too much time to handle; if it is too small, it does not deliver enough energy to cover the costs of capture. (10) The robin should reject or ignore less valuable items, such as small beetles and caterpillars, and give preference to small and medium-sized earthworms. (11) _____ by capturing an earthworm, the robin earns some units of energy. (12) These more valuable food items would be classified as preferred food. (13) If the robin fails to find suitable and sufficient food in the area of the lawn it is searching, it leaves to search elsewhere. (14) If successful, the bird probably will return until the spot is no longer an economical place to feed. (Adapted from Robert Leo Smith and Thomas M. Smith, *Elements of Ecology*, 5th ed., San Francisco: Benjamin Cummings, 2003.)

5. Which sentence provides specific support for sentence 3 in the passage?
   A. The robin searches for food by selecting only those items that provide the greatest energy return for the energy expended. (sentence 2)
   B. Once on the lawn, it has to search for food items. (sentence 5)
   C. Because the robin forages on lawns, it is vulnerable to pesticide poisoning. (sentence 6)
   D. These more valuable food items would be classified as preferred food. (sentence 12)

PASSAGE #6

Read the passage and answer the question that follows.

(1) _____.
(2) Beach-nesting birds such as the piping plover and the least tern are so disturbed by bathers and dune buggies that both species are in danger of extinction. (3) Other terns and shore birds are subjected to competition for nest sites and to egg predators by rapidly growing populations

of large gulls. (4) These gulls are highly tolerant of humans and thrive on human garbage. (5) Sea turtles and the horseshoe crab, dependent on sandy beaches for nesting sites, find themselves evicted. (6) _____, they are declining rapidly. (7) Furthermore, each incoming tide brings onto the beaches feces-contaminated water that makes them unhealthy for humans and wildlife alike. (8) This contaminated water comes from a number of different sources, such as sewer overflows, failing private and commercial septic systems, animal and wildlife waste, and swimmers' illnesses. (9) The oceans have become dumping grounds. (10) Major chronic pollutants are oil that is released from tanker accidents, seepage from offshore drilling and other sources, toxic materials such as pesticides and heavy metals from industrial, urban, and agricultural sources. (11) The most devastating human activity in reefs is overfishing, especially in the Philippines and the Caribbean. (12) Tides also carry in old fishing lines, plastic debris, and other wastes hazardous to wildlife. (Adapted from Robert Leo Smith and Thomas M. Smith, *Elements of Ecology*, 5th ed., San Francisco: Benjamin Cummings, 2003.)

6. Which sentence provides specific support for sentence 7 in the passage?
   A. The oceans have become dumping grounds. (sentence 9)
   B. Major chronic pollutants are oil that is released from tanker accidents, seepage from offshore drilling and other sources, toxic materials such as pesticides and heavy metals from industrial, urban, and agricultural sources. (sentence 10)
   C. This contaminated water comes from a number of different sources, such as sewer overflows, failing private and commercial septic systems, animal and wildlife waste, and swimmers' illnesses. (sentence 8)
   D. Tides also carry in old fishing lines, plastic debris, and other wastes hazardous to wildlife. (sentence 12)

PASSAGE #7

Read the passage and answer the question that follows.

(1) _____.
(2) About 21 million people trace their origin to Mexico, 3 million to Puerto Rico, 1 million to Cuba, and almost 5 million to Central or South America, primarily Venezuela or Colombia. (3) Officially tallied at 35 million in the year 2000 census, the actual number of Latinos is higher because, not surprisingly, many who are in the country illegally avoid contact with both public officials and census forms. (4) Each year, more than 1 million people are apprehended at the border or at points inland and are deported to Mexico. (5) Perhaps another million or so manage to enter the United States. (6) _____ many migrate for temporary work and then return to their homes and families. (7) To gain an understanding of how vast these numbers are, we can note that there are millions more Latinos in the United States than there are Canadians in Canada (31 million). (8) To Midwesterners, such a comparison often comes as a surprise, for Latinos are absent from vast stretches of mid-America. (9) Sixty-nine percent are concentrated in just four states: California, Texas, New York, and Florida. (10) In the next twenty-five years, changes in the U.S. racial-ethnic mix will be dramatic. (Adapted from James M. Henslin, *Sociology*, 6th ed., Boston: Allyn and Bacon, 2003.)

7. Which sentence provides specific support for sentence 3 in the passage?
   A. 5
   B. 7
   C. 8
   D. 9

Answers and Explanations to Diagnostic: Supporting Details

1. Answer   B

Sentence 9 gives an example for sentence 8. Sentence 9 explains that a biology teacher may teach a certain way because he or she has so much factual material to cover.

False choices

Choice A is a statement of opinion and does not support sentence 8.

Choice C is the concluding statement of the paragraph, not a supporting statement.

Choice D supports sentence 5, a class where there is no opportunity for social interaction.

2. Answer   A

Sentence 3 introduces the idea that researchers had to devise ways to communicate with chimps and bonobos because they can't talk. Sentence 5 gives a supporting example; a chimp was taught to manipulate symbols on a magnetic board.

False choices

Choice B introduces a new point about the researchers' skepticism about whether chimps were learning meaningful language.

Choice C supports the sentence before it. Recent research is showing that chimps do have language capabilities.

Choice D does not support any sentence in the paragraph.

3. Answer   D

Sentence 12 introduces an opinion of researchers for the reasons that keep people from assaulting others when the temperature is higher. This is not supported by specific details.

False choices

Choice A is supported by sentence 3.

Choice B is supported by sentence 5.

Choice C is supported by sentence 10.

4. Answer   A

Sentence 3 mentions that the researcher Savishinsky lived with the Hare Indians to study them. No further explanation is given on this point.

False choices

Choice B is supported by sentence 6.

Choice C is supported by sentence 12.

Choice D is supported by sentence 13.

5. Answer   B

Sentence 5 is one of the steps in the process introduced by sentence 3.

False choices

Choice A provides specific support for the topic sentence.

Choice C does not support any sentence in the paragraph.

Choice D provides specific support for sentence 11.

6. Answer   C

Sentence 8 describes where the contaminated water comes from, supporting sentence 7, which explains that incoming tide brings feces-contaminated water to the beaches.

False choices

Choice A makes a general statement, not a specific supporting statement for sentence 7.

Choice B talks about oil pollution and does not support sentence 7.

Choice D describes debris carried in by tides, such as plastic and fishing lines. It does not talk about human or animal waste products.

7. Answer   A

Sentence 3 explains that the number of Latinos is higher than the number tallied by the census taken in 2000 because of those who come to the U.S. illegally and avoid census forms. Sentence 5 supports sentence 3 by stating that about a million people enter illegally.

False choices

Choice B does not support sentence 3. Sentence 7 provides an example of comparison to show how large the Latino population is.

Choice C supports sentence 7.

Choice D supports sentence 8.

SECTION 2 ◆ EXERCISES: SUPPORTING DETAILS

PASSAGE #1

Read the passage and answer the question that follows.

1 _____.

[2]First of all, because e-mail messages are informal and quick, writers may be sloppy in transferring their thoughts to the screen. [3]Misspellings and ungrammatical sentences can project a negative image if users do not take time to edit what they write on e-mail. [4]Second, the messages are sent and read online, often leaving no paper trail at all. [5]As a result, some important messages are forgotten or lost. [6]It is easy to read your electronic mail and delete it instead of printing out a copy of the message to keep in a file or filing the message electronically in your e-mail file folder. [7]Although generally thought of as a quick method of communication, e-mail's efficiency is only as good as the recipient's care in routinely checking e-mail messages. [8]Electronic communication can be slow if people don't check their messages. [9]Moreover, you have no privacy. [10]Another disadvantage is the increasing use of e-mail as a replacement for the personal contact of a phone call or face-to-face meeting. [11]The 1986 Electronic Communications Privacy Act considers e-mail to be the property of the company paying for the mail system. [12]_____, writing on a computer screen often encourages people to drop inhibitions and write things in e-mail that they would never write in a paper letter or say over the telephone. (Adapted from Kristin R. Woolever, *Writing for the Technical Professions*, 2nd ed., New York: Longman, 2002.)

1. Which of the numbered sentences is not supported by sufficient specific details?
   A. 9
   B. 4
   C. 2
   D. 7

PASSAGE #2

Read the passage and answer the question that follows.

1 _____.

[2]Although women have served in every branch of the armed services since World War II, two differences between the treatment of men and women in the military persist. [3]First, only men

must register for the draft when they turn eighteen. [4]In 1981, the Supreme Court ruled that male-only registration for the military did not violate the Fifth Amendment. [5]Second, statutes and regulations also prohibit women from serving in combat. [6]A breach exists between policy and practice, however, as the Persian Gulf War showed. [7]Women piloted helicopters at the front and helped to operate antimissile systems; some were taken as prisoners of war. [8]_____, women are not permitted to serve as combat pilots in the navy and air force and to serve on navy warships. [9]They are still not permitted to serve in ground combat units in the army or marines. [10]These actions have reopened the debate over whether women should serve in combat. [11]Others argue that men will not be able to fight effectively beside wounded or dying women. [12]Critics of these views point out that some women surpass men in body strength and that we do not know how well men and women will fight together. [13]Some experts insist that because women, on the average, have less body strength than men, they are less suited for combat. [14]This debate is not only a controversy about ability, but it also touches on the question of whether engaging in combat is a burden or a privilege. (Adapted from George C. Edwards, Martin P. Wattenberg, and Robert L. Lineberry, *Government in America*, 9th ed., New York: Longman, 2000.)

2. Which of the numbered sentences is not supported by sufficient specific details?
   A. 10
   B. 14
   C. 6
   D. 2

PASSAGE #3

Read the passage and answer the question that follows.

[1]_____

[2]_____.

[2]Jaime Escalante taught calculus in an East Los Angeles inner-city school that was plagued with poverty, crime, drugs, and gangs. [3]As a result of his methods, his students earned the highest Advanced Placement scores in the city. [4]_____, Escalante had to open his students' minds to the possibility of success in learning. [5]Most Latino students were tracked into craft classes where they made jewelry and birdhouses. [6]Escalante felt that his students were talented and needed an opportunity to show it. [7]Also, the students needed to see learning as a way out of the barrio, as a path to good jobs. [8]By arranging for foundations to provide money for students to attend colleges of their choice, Escalante showed students that if they did well, their poverty would not stop them. [9]When Escalante first came to the United States, he worked as a busboy and attended Pasadena Community College. [10]Escalante also changed the system of instruction. [11]Before class, his students did "warm-ups," hand clapping and foot stomping to a rock song. [12]To foster team identity, students wore team jackets, caps, and T-shirts with logos that identified them as part of the math team. [13]He had his students think of themselves as a team, of him as the coach, and the national math exams as a sort of Olympics for which they were preparing. [14]Escalante thought it was important to teach his classes in English, not Spanish. [15]Escalante demonstrated that a teacher can motivate students to believe in their ability to achieve at high levels, no matter how great their problems. (Adapted from James M. Henslin, *Sociology*, 6th ed., Boston: Allyn and Bacon, 2003.)

3. Which sentence provides specific support for sentence 10 in the passage?
   A. As a result of his methods, his students earned the highest Advanced Placement scores in the city. (sentence 3)

B. Escalante felt that his students were talented and needed an opportunity to show it. (sentence 6)

C. Most Latino students were tracked into craft classes where they made jewelry and birdhouses. (sentence 5)

D. Before class, his students did "warm-ups," hand clapping and foot stomping to a rock song. (sentence 11)

PASSAGE #4

Read the passage and answer the question that follows.

1 _____.
[2]Anorexia nervosa literally means loss of appetite, but this is a misnomer. [3]The anorexic individual approaches weight loss with a fervor, convinced that her body is too large. [4]A person with anorexia nervosa is hungry, but he or she denies the hunger because of an irrational fear of becoming fat. [5]Therefore, the first characteristic is a significant weight loss due to a relentless drive for thinness. [6]She is unable to recognize that her appearance is abnormal. [7]She will insist that her emaciated figure is just right or is too fat. [8]There is a strong argument that eating disorders are a form of addiction. [9]This condition is more than a simple eating disorder. [10]_____, anorexia is a distinct psychological disorder with a wide range of psychological disturbances. [11]Anorexics are typically compulsive, perfectionistic, and very competitive. [12]Food preoccupation and rituals and compulsive exercising are other characteristics. [13]The anorexic sometimes suffers from low self-image due to a feeling of incompetence, so she becomes consumed with losing weight to demonstrate to herself and others that she is in total control. [14]Additional features of the disease develop from the effects of starvation over time. [15]Untreated anorexia can be fatal. [16]Causes of death include starvation, infections due to poor nutrition, irregular heartbeat due to potassium deficiency, and suicide due to depression. (Adapted from David J. Anspaugh and Gene Ezell, *Teaching Today's Health*, 7th ed., San Francisco: Pearson, 2004.)

4. Which sentence provides specific support for sentence 9 in the passage?
   A. A person with anorexia nervosa is hungry, but he or she denies the hunger because of an irrational fear of becoming fat. (sentence 4)
   B. Anorexia nervosa literally means loss of appetite, but this is a misnomer. (sentence 2)
   C. _____, anorexia is a distinct psychological disorder with a wide range of psychological disturbances. (sentence 10)
   D. Therefore, the first characteristic is a significant weight loss due to a relentless drive for thinness. (sentence 5)

PASSAGE #5

Read the passage and answer the question that follows.

1 _____.
[2]Bare-knuckle boxing, the forerunner of modern boxing, was a brutal, bloody sport. [3]Two men fought bare-fisted until one could not continue. [4]A round lasted until one of the men knocked or threw down his opponent. [5]At that point, both men rested for thirty seconds and then started to fight again. [6]Fights often lasted over one hundred rounds and as long as seven or eight hours. [7]After such a fight, it took months for the fighters to recover. [8]During the 1800s, boxing underwent a series of reforms. [9]There have been periodic efforts to outlaw the sport. [10]The challenge system was replaced by modern promotional techniques. [11]Fighters

deserted bare-fisted combat and started wearing gloves. [12]Most importantly, professional boxers adopted the Marquis of Queensberry Rules, which standardized a round at three minutes, allowing a one-minute rest period between rounds, and outlawed all wrestling throws and holds. [13]_____, the fight to the finish was replaced with a fight to a decision over a specified number of rounds. [14]A bell and a referee told fighters when to fight and when to rest. [15]Currently there are eight major professional divisions. [16]Although the new rules did not reduce the violence, they did provide for more orderly bouts. (Adapted from James Kirby Martin et al., *America and Its Peoples*, 5th ed., New York: Longman, 2003.)

5. Which of the numbered sentences is not supported by sufficient specific details?
   A. 8
   B. 2
   C. 9
   D. 12

PASSAGE #6

Read the passage and answer the question that follows.

[1]_____.
[2]For example, with eye movements you can seek feedback. [3]In talking with someone, you look at her or him intently, as if to say, "Well, what do you think?" [4]Your pupils enlarge when you are interested or emotionally aroused. [5]You can also inform the other person that the channel of communication is open and that he or she should now speak. [6]You see this in the college classroom, when the instructor asks a question and then locks eyes with a student. [7]Without saying anything, the instructor expects that student to answer the question and the student knows it. [8]Eye movements may also signal the nature of a relationship, whether positive (an attentive glance) or negative (eye avoidance). [9]_____, you can signal your power through visual dominance behavior. [10]The average speaker, for example, maintains a high level of eye contact while listening and a lower level while speaking. [11]When people want to signal dominance, they may reverse this pattern: maintaining a high level of eye contact while talking but a lower level while listening. [12]Eye contact can also change the psychological distance between yourself and another person. [13]When you catch someone's eye at a party, for example, you become psychologically close even though far apart. [14]By avoiding eye contact—even when physically close as in a crowded elevator—you increase the psychological distance between you. (Adapted from Joseph A. DeVito, *Essentials of Human Communication*, 3rd ed., New York: Longman, 1999.)

6. Which of the numbered sentences is not supported by sufficient specific details?
   A. 12
   B. 6
   C. 8
   D. 2

PASSAGE #7

Read the passage and answer the question that follows.

[1]_____.
[2]It even drinks seawater, which is much saltier than its body fluids. [3]Few animals can tolerate such salty liquid because the salt draws water out of their tissues, and they become severe-

ly dehydrated. [4]An albatross can thrive on salt water because it has special salt-excreting glands in its nostrils. [5]The glands dispose of excess salts, allowing the bird to eat salty fish and squid and drink all it needs without ever visiting land. [6]Their scientific name, *Diomedea exulans*, means exiled warrior in Greek. [7]_____ its remarkable salt tolerance, the wandering albatross has extraordinary flight abilities specially suited to its seafaring life. [8]Its wingspan is greater than that of any other bird—about 3.6 meters (nearly twelve feet). [9]Most birds have to flap their wings to stay up in the air very long, but the albatross's long wings provide so much lift that the bird can stay aloft for hours by gliding up and down on wind currents. [10]The wandering albatross spends most of its time in an area of high winds and rough seas, far from land, often alone on the open ocean. [11]The winds carry it from west to east, and in a year's time, an albatross may circle the globe, seeing little land except New Zealand and the tip of South America. (Adapted from Neil A. Campbell, Lawrence G. Mitchell, and Jane B. Reece, *Biology*, 3rd ed., San Francisco: Benjamin Cummings, 2000.)

7. Which sentence provides specific support for sentence 4 in the passage?
   A. It even drinks seawater, which is much saltier than its body fluids. (sentence 2)
   B. The glands dispose of excess salts, allowing the bird to eat salty fish and squid and drink all it needs without ever visiting land. (sentence 5)
   C. Few animals can tolerate such salty liquid because the salt draws water out of their tissues, and they become severely dehydrated. (sentence 3)
   D. The wandering albatross spends most of its time in an area of high winds and rough seas, far from land, often alone on the open ocean. (sentence 10)

PASSAGE #8

Read the passage and answer the question that follows.

[1]_____.
[2]Testosterone is a male hormone that causes a general buildup in muscle and bone mass during puberty in males and maintains masculine traits throughout life. [3]Anabolic steroids are synthetic variants of the male hormone testosterone. [4]Pharmaceutical companies first produced and marketed anabolic steroids in the early 1950s as a treatment for certain diseases that destroy body muscle. [5]About a decade later, some athletes began using anabolic steroids to build up their muscles quickly and enhance their performance with less hard work. [6]It is not surprising that some of the heaviest users are weight lifters, football players, and body builders. [7]Today, anabolic steroids, along with other drugs, are banned by most athletic organizations. [8]Black market sales bring in up to $400 million a year. [9]Medical research indicates that these substances can cause serious physical and mental problems. [10]Overdosing in males can cause acne, baldness, and breast development. [11]Mental effects can range from mood swings to deep depression. [12]Internally, there may be liver damage leading to cancer. [13]_____, anabolic steroids can make blood cholesterol levels rise, perhaps increasing a user's chances of developing serious cardiovascular problems. [14]Heavy users may also experience a reduced sex drive and become infertile because anabolic steroids often make the body reduce its normal output of sex hormones. (Adapted from Neil A. Campbell, Lawrence G. Mitchell, and Jane B. Reece, *Biology*, 3rd ed., San Francisco: Benjamin Cummings, 2000.)

8. Which sentence provides specific support for sentence 9 in the passage?
   A. _____, anabolic steroids can make blood cholesterol levels rise, perhaps increasing a user's chances of developing serious cardiovascular problems. (sentence 13)

B. Today, anabolic steroids, along with other drugs, are banned by most athletic organizations. (sentence 7)
C. It is not surprising that some of the heaviest users are weight lifters, football players, and body builders. (sentence 6)
D. Anabolic steroids are synthetic variants of the male hormone testosterone. (sentence 3)

PASSAGE #9

Read the passage and answer the question that follows.

1 _____.
²In most cases, the child continually learns from the parent. ³In the area of computer and Internet-mediated communication, however, the child may be able to teach the parent. ⁴_____, one five-year-old learned a graphics program before she could read. ⁵The child taught herself how to operate the rather intuitive program. ⁶Not only did the computer provide the child with a valuable learning process, but the parents totally depended on the child when they wanted to use the program she knew. ⁷In another case, a young boy taught his parents how to use PowerPoint. ⁸The examples are endless. ⁹Children are more apt to interact with the computer as if it were alive. ¹⁰A child may be able to understand a concept differently from the parent, and the role reversal of the child-as-teacher can be an important way the computer and the Internet can enhance a child's self-esteem. ¹¹The child and parent alike may feel positive toward themselves when they are able to learn new things, master a program, or win an Internet game. ¹²Their self-confidence may increase when others seek their advice, for example, because they are the family computer experts. (Adapted from Leonard J. Shedletsky and Joan E. Aitken, *Human Communication on the Internet*, Boston: Allyn and Bacon, 2004.)

9. Which of the numbered sentences is not supported by specific details?
   A. 3
   B. 4
   C. 5
   D. 9

PASSAGE #10

Read the passage and answer the question that follows.

1 _____.
²Highlighting is a strategy for condensing textbook material and emphasizing what is important. ³_____, the process of highlighting forces you to sift through what you have read to identify important information. ⁴This sifting or sorting is an active thought process; you are forced to weigh and evaluate what you read. ⁵One mistake to avoid is highlighting almost every idea on a page. ⁶Another benefit of highlighting is that it keeps you physically active while you are reading. ⁷In addition, highlighting can help you discover the organization of facts and ideas as well as their connections and relationships. ⁸Highlighting demonstrates to you whether you have understood a passage you have just read. ⁹When combined with annotation, highlighting is a quick and easy way to review so that you do not have to reread everything when studying for an exam. ¹⁰If you highlight 20 percent of a chapter, you will be able to avoid rereading 80 percent of the material. ¹¹If it normally takes two hours to read a chapter, you should be able to review a highlighted chapter in less than a half hour. ¹²Highlighting has many benefits, but it is not by itself a sufficient study method; you must process the infor-

mation by organizing it, expressing it in your own words, and testing yourself periodically. (Adapted from Kathleen T. McWhorter, *Study and Critical Thinking Skills in College*, 5th ed., New York: Longman, 2003.)

10. Which sentence provides specific support for sentence 3 in the passage?
    A. If you highlight 20 percent of a chapter, you will be able to avoid rereading 80 percent of the material. (sentence 10)
    B. This sifting or sorting is an active thought process; you are forced to weigh and evaluate what you read. (sentence 4)
    C. Highlighting is a strategy for condensing textbook material and emphasizing what is important. (sentence 2)
    D. One mistake to avoid is highlighting almost every idea on a page. (sentence 5)

SECTION 3 ◆ LOGICAL PATTERNS

Competency 1.3	Conceptual and Organizational Skills
Skill Tested	**Arranges ideas and supporting details in a logical pattern**

The Skill

This item tests your ability to arrange ideas and supporting details in a logical pattern. A well-organized piece of writing is easy to read and understand because it follows a plan or pattern of organization. When writing does not follow a pattern of organization, the ideas do not seem to fit together, so the piece is difficult to read and understand. Your ability to recognize plans of organization will help you discover the correct answer to the test questions on this skill.

You may have learned patterns of organization for writing paragraphs or essays in your English class. Two characteristics of good organization are the order in which the details are presented and the use of patterns of development. Sometimes order and method overlap or are combined in a piece of writing.

Order

Order refers to the method used to organize the supporting material. Three commonly used methods are time order, spatial order, and order of importance.

Time Order	Details are listed as they happen in time
Spatial Order	Details are organized according to their physical positions
Order of Importance	Details are written from least important to most important, simplest to most difficult, or most familiar to least familiar

Patterns

Patterns are plans of development. Some essays follow one pattern throughout while others use several patterns to develop individual paragraphs within the essay.

Pattern	Supporting Details
Description	Creates a word picture of a person, place, thing, or emotion through the use of sensory words (sight, touch, taste, smell, sound)
Narration	Tells a story

Pattern	Supporting Details
Illustration	Uses specific examples to support or present a main idea.
Process	Tells how to do something or how something is done by breaking the process into steps or stages
Cause and Effect	Explains reasons (cause) or results (effect) of a particular situation or event
Comparison/Contrast	Shows how people, places, things, events, or ideas are similar (comparison) or how they are different (contrast)
Classification	Analyzes a subject according to a single organizing principle, breaking the subject into categories or types
Definition	Gives the meaning of a word in a variety of ways, including its formal definition and extending the meaning by using other patterns of development
Argumentation/Persuasion	Makes a clear statement of the author's position and supports that position with details that convince or persuade the reader that the position is correct and possibly to take action

The Test Question

You will be tested on your ability to recognize adequate supporting details in one of two ways:

1. You will be given a passage to read and asked to select the most logical arrangement or sequence of several sentences. Each choice will contain the same sentences, but they will be arranged in a different order. You need to decide which set expresses the idea most logically.
2. You will be given a short passage of three sentences and asked to figure out the most logical placement of the fourth sentence.

SECTION 3 ◆ DIAGNOSTIC: LOGICAL PATTERNS

Read the passages and apply the strategies described above for finding logical patterns. When you are done, check your work with the answers immediately following the diagnostic. Even if you get a perfect score here, go ahead and complete the exercises in this section; they are designed to help build confidence and to give you practice for future test success.

PASSAGE #1

Read the passage and answer the question that follows.

(1) _____.
(2) Some instructors, for example, have a teaching style that promotes social interaction among students. (3) An instructor may organize small group activities, encourage class participation, or require students to work in pairs or teams to complete a specific task. (4) A lecture class is an example. (5) Other instructors offer little or no opportunity for social interaction. (6) Some instructors are very applied; they teach by example. (7) Others are more conceptual; they focus on presenting ideas, rules, theories, and so forth. (8) To an extent, of course, the subject matter also dictates how the instructor teaches. (9) _____ a biology instructor has a large body of factual information to present and may feel he or she has little time to schedule group interaction. (10) Some instructors' teaching styles are boring. (11) Once you are

aware of your learning style and then consider the instructor's teaching style, you can begin to understand why you can learn better from one instructor than another and why you feel more comfortable in certain instructors' classes than others. (Adapted from Kathleen McWhorter, *Study and Critical Thinking Skills in College*, 5th ed., New York: Longman, 2003.)

1. Select the arrangement of sentences 3, 4, and 5 that provides the most logical sequence of ideas and supporting details in the paragraph. If no change is needed, select option A.
   A. An instructor may organize small group activities, encourage class participation, or require students to work in pairs or teams to complete a specific task. A lecture class is an example. Other instructors offer little or no opportunity for social interaction.
   B. An instructor may organize small group activities, encourage class participation, or require students to work in pairs or teams to complete a specific task. Other instructors offer little or no opportunity for social interaction. A lecture class is an example.
   C. Other instructors offer little or no opportunity for social interaction. An instructor may organize small group activities, encourage class participation, or require students to work in pairs or teams to complete a specific task. A lecture class is an example.
   D. A lecture class is an example. An instructor may organize small groups, encourage class participation, or require students to work in pairs or teams to complete a specific task. Other instructors offer little or no opportunity for social interaction.

PASSAGE #2

Read the passage and answer the question that follows.

(1) _____.
(2) As early as the 1920s, psychologists attempted to teach language to chimpanzees to find out whether they could communicate. (3) Chimps don't have the appropriate vocal apparatus to produce spoken language, so researchers had to devise other methods of communication. (4) For instance, a chimp named Washoe was taught a highly simplified version of American Sign Language. (5) In addition, a chimp named Sarah was taught to manipulate symbols on a magnetic board. (6) Skeptics wondered if the chimps' combination of gestures and symbols constituted any kind of meaningful language. (7) Recent research has provided more solid insights into the language capabilities of chimps. (8) Bonobos and chimps can be raised together. (9) Sue Savage-Rumbaugh and her team work primarily with *bonobos*, a species of great ape that is evolutionarily nearer to humans than even the common chimpanzees. (10) Remarkably, two of the bonobos in her studies, Kanzi and Mulika, learned the meanings of plastic symbols at the same time. (11) They did not receive direct training; rather, they acquired the symbols by watching humans and other bonobos. (12) _____ Kanzi and Mulika can understand some spoken English. (13) For example, when Kanzi hears a spoken word, he is able to locate either the symbol for the word or a picture of the object. (Adapted from Richard J. Gerrig and Philip G. Zimbardo, *Psychology and Life*, 16th ed., Boston: Allyn and Bacon, 2002.)

2. Select the arrangement of sentences 9, 10, and 11 that provides the most logical sequence of ideas and supporting details in the paragraph. If no change is needed, select option A.
   A. Sue Savage-Rumbaugh and her team work primarily with *bonobos*, a species of great ape that is evolutionarily nearer to humans than even the common chimpanzees. Remarkably, two of the bonobos in her studies, Kanzi and Mulika, learned the meanings of plastic symbols at the same time. They did not receive direct training; rather, they acquired the symbols by watching humans and other bonobos.

B. Remarkably, two of the bonobos in her studies, Kanzi and Mulika, learned the meanings of plastic symbols at the same time. They did not receive direct training; rather they acquired the symbols by watching humans and other bonobos. Sue Savage-Rumbaugh and her team work primarily with *bonobos*, a species of great ape that is evolutionarily nearer to humans than even the common chimpanzees.

C. They did not receive direct training; rather they acquired the symbols by watching humans and other bonobos. Remarkably, two of the bonobos in her studies, Kanzi and Mulika, learned the meanings of the plastic symbols at the same time. Sue Savage-Rumbaugh and her team work primarily with *bonobos*, a species of great ape that is evolutionarily nearer to humans than even common chimpanzees.

D. Sue Savage-Rumbaugh and her team work primarily with *bonobos*, a species of great ape that is evolutionarily nearer to humans than even common chimpanzees. They did not receive direct training; rather they acquired the symbols by watching humans and other bonobos. Remarkably, two of the bonobos in her studies, Kanzi and Mulika, learned the meanings of the plastic symbols at the same time.

PASSAGE #3

Read the passage and answer the question that follows.

(1) _____.
(2) The relationship between temperature and assault is actually strongest in the late evening and early morning hours, from 9 p.m. to 3 a.m. (3) One explanation is that people are more likely to commit assault when they are out and about. (4) That is, in warmer weather, people are usually outdoors more and, therefore, are also more "available" as assault victims. (5) In the 9 p.m. to 3 a.m. hours, people are typically not working or bound by other responsibilities. (6) The time of day is another factor. (7) Furthermore, by the late evening hours, people may have been drinking alcohol or using other substances that lower their inhibition to aggression. (8) Substance abuse is a big problem in our society. (9) Another part of the explanation is the way in which people cope with and interpret the discomfort associated with high temperatures. (10) As the day goes on, it may be harder to remember, "I'm feeling this way because it's hot" and just conclude, "I'm feeling this way because this person is making me crazy." (11)_____, assaults decline when temperatures become very hot. (12) Researchers have speculated that at very high temperatures, people might experience sufficient discomfort to withdraw from abrasive situations rather than stay and fight. (Adapted from Richard J. Gerrig and Philip G. Zimbardo, *Psychology and Life*, 16th ed., Boston: Allyn and Bacon, 2002.)

3. Select the arrangement of sentences 5, 6, and 7 that provides the most logical sequence of ideas and supporting details in the paragraph. If no change is needed, select option A.
A. In the 9 p.m. to 3 a.m. hours, people are typically not working or bound by other responsibilities. The time of day is another factor. Furthermore, by the late evening hours, people may have been drinking alcohol or using other substances that lower their inhibition to aggression.
B. Furthermore, by the late evening hours, people may have been drinking alcohol or using other substances that lower their inhibition to aggression. The time of day is another factor. In the 9 p.m. to 3 a.m. hours, people are typically not working or bound by other responsibilities.
C. In the 9 p.m. to 3 a.m. hours, people are typically not working or bound by other responsibilities. Furthermore, by the late evening hours, people may have been drinking alcohol

or using other substances that lower their inhibition to aggression. The time of day is another factor.

  D. The time of day is another factor. In the 9 p.m. to 3 a.m. hours, people are typically not working or bound by other responsibilities. Furthermore, by the late evening hours, people may have been drinking alcohol or using other substances that lower their inhibition to aggression.

PASSAGE #4

Read the passage and answer the question that follows.

(1) _____.
(2) The Hare Indians of Colville Lake are a small group of Canadian Inuit. (3) Savishinsky lived with the Hare Indians to study them. (4) They survive by hunting, trapping, and fishing in one of the harshest environments in the world. (5)_____, dogs are economically useful. (6) Dog teams give the Inuit a means for travel during the harshest seasons of the year. (7) The temperatures are extremely cold, and the winters are long and severe. (8) Finding food can be difficult. (9) The Inuit estimate that six dogs are required for travel, and some households have as many as four dog teams, with an average of 6.2 dogs per team. (10) The dogs are a frequent topic of conversation. (11) More than being only economically useful, dogs play a significant role in people's emotional lives. (12) Members of the community constantly compare and comment on the care, condition, and growth of one another's animals. (13) They note special qualities of size, strength, color, speed, and alertness. (14) Emotional displays, uncommon among the Hare, are significant between people and their dogs. (15) All people participate in the affectionate and concerned treatment of young dogs. (Adapted from Barbara D. Miller, *Cultural Anthropology*, 2nd ed., Boston: Allyn and Bacon, 2002.)

  4. Select the arrangement of sentences 10, 11, and 12 that provides the most logical sequence of ideas and supporting details in the paragraph. If no change is needed, select option A.
  A. The dogs are a frequent topic of conversation. More than being only economically useful, dogs play a significant role in people's emotional lives. Members of the community constantly compare and comment on the care, condition, and growth of one another's animals.
  B. Members of the community constantly compare and comment on the care, condition, and growth of one another's animals. More than being only economically useful, dogs play a significant role in people's emotional lives. The dogs are a frequent topic of conversation.
  C. More than being only economically useful, dogs play a significant role in people's emotional lives. The dogs are a frequent topic of conversation. Members of the community constantly compare and comment on the care, condition, and growth of one another's animals.
  D. Members of the community constantly compare and comment on the care, condition, and growth of one another's animals. The dogs are a frequent topic of conversation. More than being only economically useful, dogs play a significant role in people's emotional lives.

PASSAGE #5

Read the passage and answer the question that follows.

(1) _____.
(2) The robin searches for food by selecting only those items that provide the greatest energy return for the energy expended. (3) This can be illustrated by the robin's behavior, which

has four parts. (4) First, the robin has to decide where to hunt for food. (5) Once on the lawn, it has to search for food items. (6) Because the robin forages on lawns, it is vulnerable to pesticide poisoning. (7) Having located some potential food, the robin has to decide whether to pursue it. (8) If it begins pursuit by pecking, the robin has to attempt a capture, in which it might or might not be successful. (9) If a food item is too large, it requires too much time to handle; if it is too small, it does not deliver enough energy to cover the costs of capture. (10) The robin should reject or ignore less valuable items, such as small beetles and caterpillars, and give preference to small and medium-sized earthworms. (11) _____ by capturing an earthworm, the robin earns some units of energy. (12) These more valuable food items would be classified as preferred food. (13) If the robin fails to find suitable and sufficient food in the area of the lawn it is searching, it leaves to search elsewhere. (14) If successful, the bird probably will return until the spot is no longer an economical place to feed. (Adapted from Robert Leo Smith and Thomas M. Smith, *Elements of Ecology*, 5th ed., San Francisco: Benjamin Cummings, 2003.)

5. Which is the best placement for the sentence below to make the sequence of ideas in the paragraph clear?

   It stands stock-still with its head cocked to one side as though listening for its prey but actually discovering it by sight.

   A. immediately after sentence 5
   B. immediately after sentence 9
   C. immediately before sentence 12
   D. immediately after sentence 12

PASSAGE #6

Read the passage and answer the question that follows.

(1) _____.
(2) Beach-nesting birds such as the piping plover and the least tern are so disturbed by bathers and dune buggies that both species are in danger of extinction. (3) Other terns and shore birds are subjected to competition for nest sites and to egg predators by rapidly growing populations of large gulls. (4) These gulls are highly tolerant of humans and thrive on human garbage. (5) Sea turtles and the horseshoe crab, dependent on sandy beaches for nesting sites, find themselves evicted. (6) _____, they are declining rapidly. (7) Furthermore, each incoming tide brings onto the beaches feces-contaminated water that makes them unhealthy for humans and wildlife alike. (8) This contaminated water comes from a number of different sources, such as sewer overflows, failing private and commercial septic systems, animal and wildlife waste, and swimmers' illnesses. (9) The oceans have become dumping grounds. (10) Major chronic pollutants are oil that is released from tanker accidents, seepage from offshore drilling and other sources, toxic materials such as pesticides and heavy metals from industrial, urban, and agricultural sources. (11) The most devastating human activity in reefs is overfishing, especially in the Philippines and the Caribbean. (12) Tides also carry in old fishing lines, plastic debris, and other wastes hazardous to wildlife. (Adapted from Robert Leo Smith and Thomas M. Smith, *Elements of Ecology*, 5th ed., San Francisco: Benjamin Cummings, 2003.)

6. Which is the best placement for the sentence below to make the sequence of ideas in the paragraph clear?

Increase in the development of coastal housing such as condominiums destroy the sea turtles' nesting habitat, and the lights from these homes disorient the turtle hatchlings so that many do not make it safely to the ocean.

A. immediately after sentence 3
B. immediately before sentence 6
C. immediately before sentence 9
D. immediately after sentence 12

PASSAGE #7

Read the passage and answer the question that follows.

(1) _____.
(2) About 21 million people trace their origin to Mexico, 3 million to Puerto Rico, 1 million to Cuba, and almost 5 million to Central or South America, primarily Venezuela or Colombia. (3) Officially tallied at 35 million in the year 2000 census, the actual number of Latinos is higher because, not surprisingly, many who are in the country illegally avoid contact with both public officials and census forms. (4) Each year, more than 1 million people are apprehended at the border or at points inland and are deported to Mexico. (5) Perhaps another million or so manage to enter the United States. (6) _____ many migrate for temporary work and then return to their homes and families. (7) To gain an understanding of how vast these numbers are, we can note that there are millions more Latinos in the United States than there are Canadians in Canada (31 million). (8) To Midwesterners, such a comparison often comes as a surprise, for Latinos are absent from vast stretches of mid-America. (9) Sixty-nine percent are concentrated in just four states: California, Texas, New York, and Florida. (10) In the next twenty-five years, changes in the U.S. racial-ethnic mix will be dramatic. (Adapted from James M. Henslin, *Sociology*, 6th ed., Boston: Allyn and Bacon, 2003.)

7. Which is the best placement for the sentence below to make the sequence of ideas in the paragraph clear?

Latinos are the largest minority group in several major cities, including Los Angeles, San Antonio, Miami, and Houston.

A. immediately after sentence 2
B. immediately before sentence 6
C. immediately before sentence 8
D. immediately after sentence 9

Answers and Explanations to Diagnostic: Logical Patterns

Some of the questions in this section ask you to select the arrangement of sentences that provides the most logical sequence of ideas and supporting details in the passage. For those questions, only the correct answer is explained. All other options do not provide a logical sequence of ideas.

1. Answer   B
The first sentence in the sequence supports sentence 2. This first sentence provides an example of ways in which an instructor may promote social interaction among students. The next sentence explains another teaching style, which offers little opportunity for social interaction. The last sentence gives the lecture class as an example of the teaching style that does not offer social interaction.

2. Answer   A

This series of sentences gives an example of how recent research has provided insights into language capabilities of chimps. The first sentence explains that Savage-Rumbaugh and her team worked with bonobos; this species is closer to humans than common chimpanzees. The next sentence gives the example of two bonobos who learned meanings of plastic symbols at the same time. The last sentence emphasizes that these two bonobos learned the meanings of the plastic symbols without direct instruction, further supporting the fact that these animals do have language capabilities as proved by the research.

3. Answer   D

These three sentences provide support and explanation for the time of day as a factor contributing to assault. The first sentence makes the point that the time of day is another factor. The next sentence explains that people are usually not bound by work or other responsibilities between 9 p.m. and 3 a.m. Finally, the last sentence supports the one before it by suggesting that some people are more likely to be drinking or using other substances during those hours.

4. Answer   C

This group of sentences begins by making the point that dogs play an important part in the emotional lives of the Hare Indians. The next sentence provides support by explaining that people talk about their dogs. This is elaborated on in the sentence that follows; people in the community compare their dogs and comment on the dogs' condition and growth.

5. Answer   A

This sentence, which describes the way the robin looks for prey, should follow sentence 5. Sentence 5 tells the reader that the second step in the robin's quest for food is that it must search for food once on the lawn.

False choices

Choice B would place the sentence at a later point in the process, after the robin has captured its prey.

Choice C would place the sentence after the robin had caught an earthworm. Since the sentence refers to the robin's actions before catching prey, choice C would not be in the appropriate sequence.

Choice D also places the sentence out of sequence. Sentence 12 talks about the earthworm as preferred food, not the hunting process.

6. Answer   B

Sentence 5 tells the reader that the sea turtles find themselves evicted from their nesting sites on the beach. The suggested sentence further develops this idea by explaining that coastal housing has destroyed the turtles' habitat and that the lights from these homes confuse the baby turtles who, as a result, may not make it to the ocean.

False choices

Choice A would place the sentence about sea turtles after the statement about sea birds, which compete for nest sites and are subjected to egg predators.

Choice C would place the sentence about sea turtles before the sentence that describes the ocean as a dumping ground, which does not correspond.

Choice D would place the sentence at the end of the passage after sentence 12, which gives examples of materials washed in by the tide. This does not make the sequence of ideas clear.

7. Answer   D

This sentence logically follows sentence 9, which offers the statistic that 69 percent of Latinos in the United States live in four states: California, Texas, New York, and Florida. The suggested sentence then lists the major cities in which Latinos are the largest minority groups.

False choices

Choice A places the sentence after sentence 2. Sentence 2 gives the numbers of Latinos who trace their origins to various countries. This has nothing to do with the suggested sentence.

Choice B places the suggested sentence before sentence 6. Sentence 6 suggests one way in which Latinos come to the U.S.—to work and then to return home. The two sentences do not support each other.

Choice C places the suggested sentence before sentence 8. Sentence 7 compares the number of Latinos in the U. S. to the number of Canadians in Canada. The suggested sentence does add information to make the sequence of ideas clearer.

SECTION 3 ◆ EXERCISES: LOGICAL PATTERNS

PASSAGE #1

Read the passage and answer the question that follows.

1 _____.
^{2}First of all, because e-mail messages are informal and quick, writers may be sloppy in transferring their thoughts to the screen. ^{3}Misspellings and ungrammatical sentences can project a negative image if users do not take time to edit what they write on e-mail. ^{4}Second, the messages are sent and read online, often leaving no paper trail at all. ^{5}As a result, some important messages are forgotten or lost. ^{6}It is easy to read your electronic mail and delete it instead of printing out a copy of the message to keep in a file or filing the message electronically in your e-mail file folder. ^{7}Although generally thought of as a quick method of communication, e-mail's efficiency is only as good as the recipient's care in routinely checking e-mail messages. ^{8}Electronic communication can be slow if people don't check their messages. ^{9}Moreover, you have no privacy. ^{10}Another disadvantage is the increasing use of e-mail as a replacement for the personal contact of a phone call or face-to-face meeting. ^{11}The 1986 Electronic Communications Privacy Act considers e-mail to be the property of the company paying for the mail system. ^{12}_____, writing on a computer screen often encourages people to drop inhibitions and write things in e-mail that they would never write in a paper letter or say over the telephone. (Adapted from Kristin R. Woolever, *Writing for the Technical Professions*, 2nd ed., New York: Longman, 2002.)

1. Select the arrangement of sentences 4, 5, and 6 that provides the most logical sequence of ideas and supporting details in the paragraph. If no change is needed, select option A.
   A. Second, the messages are sent and read online, often leaving no paper trail at all. As a result, some important messages are forgotten or lost. It is easy to read your electronic mail and delete it instead of printing out a copy of the message to keep in a file or filing the message electronically in your e-mail file folder.
   B. Second, the messages are sent and read online, often leaving no paper trail at all. It is easy to read your electronic mail and delete it instead of printing out a copy of the message to keep in a file or filing the message electronically in your e-mail file folder. As a result, some important messages are forgotten or lost.
   C. It is easy to read your electronic mail and delete it instead of printing out a copy of the message to keep in a file or filing the message electronically in your e-mail file folder. As a result, some important messages are forgotten or lost. Second, the messages are sent and read online, often leaving no paper trail at all.

D. As a result, some important messages are forgotten or lost. Second, the messages are sent and read online, often leaving no paper trail at all. It is easy to read your electronic mail and delete it instead of printing out a copy of the message to keep in a file or filing the message electronically in your e-mail file folder.

PASSAGE #2

Read the passage and answer the question that follows.

1 _____.

[2]Although women have served in every branch of the armed services since World War II, two differences between the treatment of men and women in the military persist. [3]First, only men must register for the draft when they turn eighteen. [4]In 1981, the Supreme Court ruled that male-only registration for the military did not violate the Fifth Amendment. [5]Second, statutes and regulations also prohibit women from serving in combat. [6]A breach exists between policy and practice, however, as the Persian Gulf War showed. [7]Women piloted helicopters at the front and helped to operate antimissile systems; some were taken as prisoners of war. [8]_____, women are not permitted to serve as combat pilots in the navy and air force and to serve on navy warships. [9]They are still not permitted to serve in ground combat units in the army or marines. [10]These actions have reopened the debate over whether women should serve in combat. [11]Others argue that men will not be able to fight effectively beside wounded or dying women. [12]Critics of these views point out that some women surpass men in body strength and that we do not know how well men and women will fight together. [13]Some experts insist that because women, on the average, have less body strength than men, they are less suited for combat. [14]This debate is not only a controversy about ability, but it also touches on the question of whether engaging in combat is a burden or a privilege. (Adapted from George C. Edwards, Martin P. Wattenberg, and Robert L. Lineberry, *Government in America*, 9th ed., New York: Longman, 2000.)

2. Select the arrangement of sentences 11, 12, and 13 that provides the most logical sequence of ideas and supporting details in the paragraph. If no change is needed, select option A.
   A. Others argue that men will not be able to fight effectively beside wounded or dying women. Critics of these views point out that some women surpass men in body strength and that we do not know how well men and women will fight together. Some experts insist that because women, on the average, have less body strength than men, they are less suited for combat.
   B. Critics of these views point out that some women surpass men in body strength and that we do not know how well men and women will fight together. Some experts insist that because women, on the average, have less body strength than men, they are less suited for combat. Others argue that men will not be able to fight effectively beside wounded or dying women.
   C. Some experts insist that because women, on the average, have less body strength than men, they are less suited for combat. Others argue that men will not be able to fight effectively beside wounded or dying women. Critics of these views point out that some women surpass men in body strength and that we do not know how well men and women will fight together.
   D. Some experts insist that because women, on the average, have less body strength than men, they are less suited for combat. Critics of these views point out that some women surpass men in body strength and that we do not know how well men and women will

fight together. Others argue that men will not be able to fight effectively beside wounded or dying women.

PASSAGE #3

Read the passage and answer the question that follows.

1 _____.

[2]Jaime Escalante taught calculus in an East Los Angeles inner-city school that was plagued with poverty, crime, drugs, and gangs. [3]As a result of his methods, his students earned the highest Advanced Placement scores in the city. [4]_____, Escalante had to open his students' minds to the possibility of success in learning. [5]Most Latino students were tracked into craft classes where they made jewelry and birdhouses. [6]Escalante felt that his students were talented and needed an opportunity to show it. [7]Also, the students needed to see learning as a way out of the barrio, as a path to good jobs. [8]By arranging for foundations to provide money for students to attend colleges of their choice, Escalante showed students that if they did well, their poverty would not stop them. [9]When Escalante first came to the United States, he worked as a busboy and attended Pasadena Community College. [10]Escalante also changed the system of instruction. [11]Before class, his students did "warm-ups," hand clapping and foot stomping to a rock song. [12]To foster team identity, students wore team jackets, caps, and T-shirts with logos that identified them as part of the math team. [13]He had his students think of themselves as a team, of him as the coach, and the national math exams as a sort of Olympics for which they were preparing. [14]Escalante thought it was important to teach his classes in English, not Spanish. [15]Escalante demonstrated that a teacher can motivate students to believe in their ability to achieve at high levels, no matter how great their problems. (Adapted from James M. Henslin, *Sociology*, 6th ed., Boston: Allyn and Bacon, 2003.)

3. Select the arrangement of sentences 11, 12, and 13 that provides the most logical sequence of ideas and supporting details in the paragraph. If no change is needed, select option A.
   A. Before class, his students did "warm-ups," hand clapping and foot stomping to a rock song. To foster team identity, students wore team jackets, caps, and T-shirts with logos that identified them as part of the math team. He had his students think of themselves as a team, of him as the coach, and the national math exams as a sort of Olympics for which they were preparing.
   B. He had his students think of themselves as a team, of him as the coach, and the national math exams as a sort of Olympics for which they were preparing. To foster team identity, students wore team jackets, caps, and T-shirts with logos that identified them as part of the math team. Before class, his students did "warm-ups," hand clapping and foot stomping to a rock song.
   C. To foster team identity, students wore team jackets, caps, and T-shirts with logos that identified them as part of the math team. Before class, his students did "warm-ups," hand clapping and foot stomping to a rock song. He had his students think of themselves as a team, of him as the coach, and the national math exams as a sort of Olympics for which they were preparing.
   D. He had his students think of themselves as a team, of him as the coach, and the national math exams as a sort of Olympics for which they were preparing. Before class, his students did "warm-ups," hand clapping and foot stomping to a rock song. To foster team identity, students wore team jackets, caps, and T-shirts with logos that identified them as part of the math team.

Read the passage and answer the question that follows.

1 _____.

²Anorexia nervosa literally means loss of appetite, but this is a misnomer. ³The anorexic individual approaches weight loss with a fervor, convinced that her body is too large. ⁴A person with anorexia nervosa is hungry, but he or she denies the hunger because of an irrational fear of becoming fat. ⁵Therefore, the first characteristic is a significant weight loss due to a relentless drive for thinness. ⁶She is unable to recognize that her appearance is abnormal. ⁷She will insist that her emaciated figure is just right or is too fat. ⁸There is a strong argument that eating disorders are a form of addiction. ⁹This condition is more than a simple eating disorder. ¹⁰_____, anorexia is a distinct psychological disorder with a wide range of psychological disturbances. ¹¹Anorexics are typically compulsive, perfectionistic, and very competitive. ¹²Food preoccupation and rituals and compulsive exercising are other characteristics. ¹³The anorexic sometimes suffers from low self-image due to a feeling of incompetence, so she becomes consumed with losing weight to demonstrate to herself and others that she is in total control. ¹⁴Additional features of the disease develop from the effects of starvation over time. ¹⁵Untreated anorexia can be fatal. ¹⁶Causes of death include starvation, infections due to poor nutrition, irregular heartbeat due to potassium deficiency, and suicide due to depression. (Adapted from David J. Anspaugh and Gene Ezell, *Teaching Today's Health*, 7th ed., San Francisco: Pearson, 2004.)

4. Select the arrangement of sentences 3, 4, and 5 that provides the most logical sequence of ideas and supporting details in the paragraph. If no change is needed, select option A.
   A. The anorexic individual approaches weight loss with a fervor, convinced that her body is too large. A person with anorexia nervosa is hungry, but he or she denies the hunger because of an irrational fear of becoming fat. Therefore, the first characteristic is a significant weight loss due to a relentless drive for thinness.
   B. Therefore, the first characteristic is a significant weight loss due to a relentless drive for thinness. The anorexic individual approaches weight loss with a fervor, convinced that her body is too large. A person with anorexia nervosa is hungry, but he or she denies the hunger because of an irrational fear of becoming fat.
   C. A person with anorexia nervosa is hungry, but he or she denies the hunger because of an irrational fear of becoming fat. Therefore, the first characteristic is a significant weight loss due to a relentless drive for thinness. The anorexic individual approaches weight loss with a fervor, convinced that her body is too large.
   D. The anorexic individual approaches weight loss with a fervor, convinced that her body is too large. Therefore, the first characteristic is a significant weight loss due to a relentless drive for thinness. A person with anorexia nervosa is hungry, but he or she denies the hunger because of an irrational fear of becoming fat.

PASSAGE #5

Read the passage and answer the question that follows.

1 _____.

²Bare-knuckle boxing, the forerunner of modern boxing, was a brutal, bloody sport. ³Two men fought bare-fisted until one could not continue. ⁴A round lasted until one of the men knocked or threw down his opponent. ⁵At that point, both men rested for thirty seconds and then started to fight again. ⁶Fights often lasted over one hundred rounds and as long as seven

or eight hours. [7]After such a fight, it took months for the fighters to recover. [8]During the 1800s, boxing underwent a series of reforms. [9]There have been periodic efforts to outlaw the sport. [10]The challenge system was replaced by modern promotional techniques. [11]Fighters deserted bare-fisted combat and started wearing gloves. [12]Most importantly, professional boxers adopted the Marquis of Queensberry Rules, which standardized a round at three minutes, allowing a one-minute rest period between rounds, and outlawed all wrestling throws and holds. [13]_____, the fight to the finish was replaced with a fight to a decision over a specified number of rounds. [14]A bell and a referee told fighters when to fight and when to rest. [15]Currently there are eight major professional divisions. [16]Although the new rules did not reduce the violence, they did provide for more orderly bouts. (Adapted from James Kirby Martin et al., *America and Its Peoples*, 5th ed., New York: Longman, 2003.)

5. Select the arrangement of sentences 3, 4, and 5 that provides the most logical sequence of ideas and supporting details in the paragraph. If no change is needed, select option A.
   A. Two men fought bare-fisted until one could not continue. A round lasted until one of the men knocked or threw down his opponent. At that point, both men rested for thirty seconds and then started to fight again.
   B. At that point, both men rested for thirty seconds and then started to fight again. Two men fought bare-fisted until one could not continue. A round lasted until one of the men knocked or threw down his opponent.
   C. A round lasted until one of the men knocked or threw down his opponent. At that point, both men rested for thirty seconds and then started to fight again. Two men fought bare-fisted until one could not continue.
   D. A round lasted until one of the men knocked or threw down his opponent. Two men fought bare-fisted until one could not continue. At that point, both men rested for thirty seconds and then started to fight again.

PASSAGE #6

Read the passage and answer the question that follows.

[1] _____.
[2]For example, with eye movements you can seek feedback. [3]In talking with someone, you look at her or him intently, as if to say, "Well, what do you think?" [4]Your pupils enlarge when you are interested or emotionally aroused. [5]You can also inform the other person that the channel of communication is open and that he or she should now speak. [6]You see this in the college classroom, when the instructor asks a question and then locks eyes with a student. [7]Without saying anything, the instructor expects that student to answer the question and the student knows it. [8]Eye movements may also signal the nature of a relationship, whether positive (an attentive glance) or negative (eye avoidance). [9]_____, you can signal your power through visual dominance behavior. [10]The average speaker, for example, maintains a high level of eye contact while listening and a lower level while speaking. [11]When people want to signal dominance, they may reverse this pattern: maintaining a high level of eye contact while talking but a lower level while listening. [12]Eye contact can also change the psychological distance between yourself and another person. [13]When you catch someone's eye at a party, for example, you become psychologically close even though far apart. [14]By avoiding eye contact—even when physically close as in a crowded elevator—you increase the psychological distance between you. (Adapted from Joseph A. DeVito, *Essentials of Human Communication*, 3rd ed., New York: Longman, 1999.)

6. Which is the best placement for the sentence below to make the sequence of ideas in the paragraph clear?

   When you avoid eye contact, such as looking away from a couple fighting, you help others maintain their privacy.

   A. immediately after sentence 11
   B. immediately after sentence 12
   C. immediately after sentence 13
   D. immediately after sentence 14

PASSAGE # 7

Read the passage and answer the question that follows.

1_____.
2It even drinks seawater, which is much saltier than its body fluids. 3Few animals can tolerate such salty liquid because the salt draws water out of their tissues, and they become severely dehydrated. 4An albatross can thrive on salt water because it has special salt-excreting glands in its nostrils. 5The glands dispose of excess salts, allowing the bird to eat salty fish and squid and drink all it needs without ever visiting land. 6Their scientific name, *Diomedea exulans*, means exiled warrior in Greek. 7_____ its remarkable salt tolerance, the wandering albatross has extraordinary flight abilities specially suited to its seafaring life. 8Its wingspan is greater than that of any other bird—about 3.6 meters (nearly twelve feet). 9Most birds have to flap their wings to stay up in the air very long, but the albatross's long wings provide so much lift that the bird can stay aloft for hours by gliding up and down on wind currents. 10The wandering albatross spends most of its time in an area of high winds and rough seas, far from land, often alone on the open ocean. 11The winds carry it from west to east, and in a year's time, an albatross may circle the globe, seeing little land except New Zealand and the tip of South America. (Adapted from Neil A. Campbell, Lawrence G. Mitchell, and Jane B. Reece, *Biology*, 3rd ed., San Francisco: Benjamin Cummings, 2000.)

7. Which is the best placement for the sentence below to make the sequence of ideas in the paragraph clear?

   The albatross's feathers insulate it against the chill of the strong sea wind, and its wings remain dry because they are lightly coated with oil.

   A. immediately after sentence 8
   B. immediately after sentence 9
   C. immediately after sentence 10
   D. immediately after sentence 11

PASSAGE #8

Read the passage and answer the question that follows.

1_____.
2Testosterone is a male hormone that causes a general buildup in muscle and bone mass during puberty in males and maintains masculine traits throughout life. 3Anabolic steroids are synthetic variants of the male hormone testosterone. 4Pharmaceutical companies first produced and marketed anabolic steroids in the early 1950s as a treatment for certain diseases that destroy body muscle. 5About a decade later, some athletes began using anabolic steroids to build up their muscles quickly and enhance their performance with less hard work. 6It is

not surprising that some of the heaviest users are weight lifters, football players, and body builders. [7]Today, anabolic steroids, along with other drugs, are banned by most athletic organizations. [8]Black market sales bring in up to $400 million a year. [9]Medical research indicates that these substances can cause serious physical and mental problems. [10]Overdosing in males can cause acne, baldness, and breast development. [11]Mental effects can range from mood swings to deep depression. [12]Internally, there may be liver damage leading to cancer. [13]_____, anabolic steroids can make blood cholesterol levels rise, perhaps increasing a user's chances of developing serious cardiovascular problems. [14]Heavy users may also experience a reduced sex drive and become infertile because anabolic steroids often make the body reduce its normal output of sex hormones. (Adapted from Neil A. Campbell, Lawrence G. Mitchell, and Jane B. Reece, *Biology*, 3rd ed., San Francisco: Benjamin Cummings, 2000.)

8. Which is the best placement for the sentence below to make the sequence of ideas in the paragraph clear?

   Another effect of steroids on mind and behavior is known as "roid rage," which is severe, aggressive behavior that may result in violence, such as fighting or destroying property.

   A. immediately after sentence 11
   B. immediately after sentence 12
   C. immediately after sentence 13
   D. immediately after sentence 14

PASSAGE #9

Read the passage and answer the question that follows.

[1]_____.
[2]In most cases, the child continually learns from the parent. [3]In the area of computer and Internet-mediated communication, however, the child may be able to teach the parent. [4]_____, one five-year-old learned a graphics program before she could read. [5]The child taught herself how to operate the rather intuitive program. [6]Not only did the computer provide the child with a valuable learning process, but the parents totally depended on the child when they wanted to use the program she knew. [7]In another case, a young boy taught his parents how to use PowerPoint. [8]The examples are endless. [9]Children are more apt to interact with the computer as if it were alive. [10]A child may be able to understand a concept differently from the parent, and the role reversal of the child-as-teacher can be an important way the computer and the Internet can enhance a child's self-esteem. [11]The child and parent alike may feel positive toward themselves when they are able to learn new things, master a program, or win an Internet game. [12]Their self-confidence may increase when others seek their advice, for example, because they are the family computer experts. (Adapted from Leonard J. Shedletsky and Joan E. Aitken, *Human Communication on the Internet*, Boston: Allyn and Bacon, 2004.)

9. Which is the best placement for the sentence below to make the sequence of ideas in the paragraph clear?

   A preteen taught his parents how to download music to their computer, set up a music library, and upload songs to their iPod.

   A. immediately after sentence 1
   B. immediately after sentence 4

C. immediately after sentence 5
D. immediately after sentence 7

PASSAGE #10

Read the passage and answer the question that follows.

^{1}_____.
^{2}Highlighting is a strategy for condensing textbook material and emphasizing what is important. ^{3}_____, the process of highlighting forces you to sift through what you have read to identify important information. ^{4}This sifting or sorting is an active thought process; you are forced to weigh and evaluate what you read. ^{5}One mistake to avoid is highlighting almost every idea on a page. ^{6}Another benefit of highlighting is that it keeps you physically active while you are reading. ^{7}In addition, highlighting can help you discover the organization of facts and ideas as well as their connections and relationships. ^{8}Highlighting demonstrates to you whether you have understood a passage you have just read. ^{9}When combined with annotation, highlighting is a quick and easy way to review so that you do not have to reread everything when studying for an exam. ^{10}If you highlight 20 percent of a chapter, you will be able to avoid rereading 80 percent of the material. ^{11}If it normally takes two hours to read a chapter, you should be able to review a highlighted chapter in less than a half hour. ^{12}Highlighting has many benefits, but it is not by itself a sufficient study method; you must process the information by organizing it, expressing it in your own words, and testing yourself periodically. (Adapted from Kathleen T. McWhorter, *Study and Critical Thinking Skills in College*, 5th ed., New York: Longman, 2003.)

10. Which is the best placement for the sentence below to make the sequence of ideas in the paragraph clear?

    If you have difficulty highlighting, or your highlighting is not helpful or meaningful after you have finished reading, you will know that you did not understand the passage.

    A. immediately after sentence 9
    B. immediately after sentence 6
    C. immediately after sentence 8
    D. immediately after sentence 7

SECTION 4 ◆ RELEVANCE OF DETAILS

Competency 1.4	Conceptual and Organizational Skills
Skill Tested	**Identifies supporting material that is relevant or irrelevant to the thesis statement or topic sentence**

The Skill

This skill tests your ability to distinguish between elements that do and do not provide adequate and relevant support for the thesis statement or topic sentence. In addition, the skill tests your ability to understand how sentences work together to provide unity.

Details that are irrelevant do not relate to the main idea being expressed in the topic or thesis statement. For example, if the topic sentence is about the differences in spoken communication styles between men and women, then all the details must relate to

---

- men and women
- spoken communication styles
- differences

There should be no discussion about other species (like chimpanzees or pets); there should be no details about non-spoken communication (like hugging or frowning); and there should be no information about similarities.

The following questions can help you determine if a detail is relevant or not.

- What is the writing trying to say, explain, or prove?
- How does this sentence help explain or prove the writer's point?
- What is the logical pattern used by the writer?
- How does this sentence explain or complete that pattern?
- Does this sentence talk about a different topic or pattern?

The Test Question
You will be asked to read a passage of approximately 200 words and then choose the sentence that is the **least** relevant to the thesis statement or topic sentence.

When making your choice, keep in mind that the sentence that is least relevant will not seem to support the sentence(s) before it. The point may be an interesting detail, but as you read the passage, you will wonder why the sentence is there.

SECTION 4 ◆ DIAGNOSTIC: RELEVANCE OF DETAILS

Read the passages and apply the strategies described above for finding relevant details. When you are done, check your work with the answers immediately following the diagnostic. Even if you get a perfect score here, go ahead and complete the exercises in this section; they are designed to help build confidence and to give you practice for future test success.

PASSAGE #1
Read the passage and answer the question that follows.

(1) _____.
(2) Some instructors, for example, have a teaching style that promotes social interaction among students. (3) An instructor may organize small group activities, encourage class participation, or require students to work in pairs or teams to complete a specific task. (4) A lecture class is an example. (5) Other instructors offer little or no opportunity for social interaction. (6) Some instructors are very applied; they teach by example. (7) Others are more conceptual; they focus on presenting ideas, rules, theories, and so forth. (8) To an extent, of course, the subject matter also dictates how the instructor teaches. (9) _____ a biology instructor has a large body of factual information to present and may feel he or she has little time to schedule group interaction. (10) Some instructors' teaching styles are boring. (11) Once you are aware of your learning style and then consider the instructor's teaching style, you can begin to understand why you can learn better from one instructor than another and why you feel more comfortable in certain instructors' classes than others. (Adapted from Kathleen McWhorter, *Study and Critical Thinking Skills in College*, 5th ed., New York: Longman, 2003.)

1. Which numbered sentence is **least** relevant to the passage?
   A. 2
   B. 4
   C. 8
   D. 10

PASSAGE #2

Read the passage and answer the question that follows.

(1) _____.
(2) As early as the 1920s, psychologists attempted to teach language to chimpanzees to find out whether they could communicate. (3) Chimps don't have the appropriate vocal apparatus to produce spoken language, so researchers had to devise other methods of communication. (4) For instance, a chimp named Washoe was taught a highly simplified version of American Sign Language. (5) In addition, a chimp named Sarah was taught to manipulate symbols on a magnetic board. (6) Skeptics wondered if the chimps' combination of gestures and symbols constituted any kind of meaningful language. (7) Recent research has provided more solid insights into the language capabilities of chimps. (8) Bonobos and chimps can be raised together. (9) Sue Savage-Rumbaugh and her team work primarily with *bonobos*, a species of great ape that is evolutionarily nearer to humans than even the common chimpanzees. (10) Remarkably, two of the bonobos in her studies, Kanzi and Mulika, learned the meanings of plastic symbols at the same time. (11) They did not receive direct training; rather, they acquired the symbols by watching humans and other bonobos. (12) _____ Kanzi and Mulika can understand some spoken English. (13) For example, when Kanzi hears a spoken word, he is able to locate either the symbol for the word or a picture of the object. (Adapted from Richard J. Gerrig and Philip G. Zimbardo, *Psychology and Life*, 16th ed., Boston: Allyn and Bacon, 2002.)

2. Which numbered sentence is **least** relevant to the passage?
   A. 2
   B. 3
   C. 8
   D. 12

PASSAGE #3

Read the passage and answer the question that follows.

(1) _____.
(2) The relationship between temperature and assault is actually strongest in the late evening and early morning hours, from 9 p.m. to 3 a.m. (3) One explanation is that people are more likely to commit assault when they are out and about. (4) That is, in warmer weather, people are usually outdoors more and, therefore, are also more "available" as assault victims. (5) In the 9 p.m. to 3 a.m. hours, people are typically not working or bound by other responsibilities. (6) The time of day is another factor. (7) Furthermore, by the late evening hours, people may have been drinking alcohol or using other substances that lower their inhibition to aggression. (8) Substance abuse is a big problem in our society. (9) Another part of the explanation is the way in which people cope with and interpret the discomfort associated with high temperatures. (10) As the day goes on, it may be harder to remember, "I'm feeling this way because it's hot" and just conclude, "I'm feeling this way because this person is mak-

ing me crazy." (11)_____, assaults decline when temperatures become very hot. (12) Researchers have speculated that at very high temperatures, people might experience sufficient discomfort to withdraw from abrasive situations rather than stay and fight. (Adapted from Richard J. Gerrig and Philip G. Zimbardo, *Psychology and Life*, 16th ed., Boston: Allyn and Bacon, 2002.)

3. Which numbered sentence is **least** relevant to the passage?
   A. 8
   B. 10
   C. 11
   D. 12

PASSAGE #4

Read the passage and answer the question that follows.

(1) _____.
(2) The Hare Indians of Colville Lake are a small group of Canadian Inuit. (3) Savishinsky lived with the Hare Indians to study them. (4) They survive by hunting, trapping, and fishing in one of the harshest environments in the world. (5)_____, dogs are economically useful. (6) Dog teams give the Inuit a means for travel during the harshest seasons of the year. (7) The temperatures are extremely cold, and the winters are long and severe. (8) Finding food can be difficult. (9) The Inuit estimate that six dogs are required for travel, and some households have as many as four dog teams, with an average of 6.2 dogs per team. (10) The dogs are a frequent topic of conversation. (11) More than being only economically useful, dogs play a significant role in people's emotional lives. (12) Members of the community constantly compare and comment on the care, condition, and growth of one another's animals. (13) They note special qualities of size, strength, color, speed, and alertness. (14) Emotional displays, uncommon among the Hare, are significant between people and their dogs. (15) All people participate in the affectionate and concerned treatment of young dogs. (Adapted from Barbara D. Miller, *Cultural Anthropology*, 2nd ed., Boston: Allyn and Bacon, 2002.)

4. Which numbered sentence is **least** relevant to the passage?
   A. 3
   B. 4
   C. 7
   D. 8

PASSAGE #5

Read the passage and answer the question that follows.

(1) _____.
(2) The robin searches for food by selecting only those items that provide the greatest energy return for the energy expended. (3) This can be illustrated by the robin's behavior, which has four parts. (4) First, the robin has to decide where to hunt for food. (5) Once on the lawn, it has to search for food items. (6) Because the robin forages on lawns, it is vulnerable to pesticide poisoning. (7) Having located some potential food, the robin has to decide whether to pursue it. (8) If it begins pursuit by pecking, the robin has to attempt a capture, in which it might or might not be successful. (9) If a food item is too large, it requires too much time to handle; if it is too small, it does not deliver enough energy to cover the costs of capture.

(10) The robin should reject or ignore less valuable items, such as small beetles and caterpillars, and give preference to small and medium-sized earthworms. (11) _____ by capturing an earthworm, the robin earns some units of energy. (12) These more valuable food items would be classified as preferred food. (13) If the robin fails to find suitable and sufficient food in the area of the lawn it is searching, it leaves to search elsewhere. (14) If successful, the bird probably will return until the spot is no longer an economical place to feed. (Adapted from Robert Leo Smith and Thomas M. Smith, *Elements of Ecology*, 5th ed., San Francisco: Benjamin Cummings, 2003.)

5. Which numbered sentence is **least** relevant to the passage?
   A. 2
   B. 6
   C. 11
   D. 13

PASSAGE #6

Read the passage and answer the question that follows.

(1) _____.
(2) Beach-nesting birds such as the piping plover and the least tern are so disturbed by bathers and dune buggies that both species are in danger of extinction. (3) Other terns and shore birds are subjected to competition for nest sites and to egg predators by rapidly growing populations of large gulls. (4) These gulls are highly tolerant of humans and thrive on human garbage. (5) Sea turtles and the horseshoe crab, dependent on sandy beaches for nesting sites, find themselves evicted. (6) _____, they are declining rapidly. (7) Furthermore, each incoming tide brings onto the beaches feces-contaminated water that makes them unhealthy for humans and wildlife alike. (8) This contaminated water comes from a number of different sources, such as sewer overflows, failing private and commercial septic systems, animal and wildlife waste, and swimmers' illnesses. (9) The oceans have become dumping grounds. (10) Major chronic pollutants are oil that is released from tanker accidents, seepage from offshore drilling and other sources, toxic materials such as pesticides and heavy metals from industrial, urban, and agricultural sources. (11) The most devastating human activity in reefs is overfishing, especially in the Philippines and the Caribbean. (12) Tides also carry in old fishing lines, plastic debris, and other wastes hazardous to wildlife. (Adapted from Robert Leo Smith and Thomas M. Smith, *Elements of Ecology*, 5th ed., San Francisco: Benjamin Cummings, 2003.)

6. Which numbered sentence is **least** relevant to the passage?
   A. 4
   B. 6
   C. 10
   D. 11

PASSAGE #7

Read the passage and answer the question that follows.

(1) _____.
(2) About 21 million people trace their origin to Mexico, 3 million to Puerto Rico, 1 million to Cuba, and almost 5 million to Central or South America, primarily Venezuela or

Colombia. (3) Officially tallied at 35 million in the year 2000 census, the actual number of Latinos is higher because, not surprisingly, many who are in the country illegally avoid contact with both public officials and census forms. (4) Each year, more than 1 million people are apprehended at the border or at points inland and are deported to Mexico. (5) Perhaps another million or so manage to enter the United States. (6) _____ many migrate for temporary work and then return to their homes and families. (7) To gain an understanding of how vast these numbers are, we can note that there are millions more Latinos in the United States than there are Canadians in Canada (31 million). (8) To Midwesterners, such a comparison often comes as a surprise, for Latinos are absent from vast stretches of mid-America. (9) Sixty-nine percent are concentrated in just four states: California, Texas, New York, and Florida. (10) In the next twenty-five years, changes in the U.S. racial-ethnic mix will be dramatic. (Adapted from James M. Henslin, *Sociology*, 6th ed., Boston: Allyn and Bacon, 2003.)

7. Which numbered sentence is **least** relevant to the passage?
   A. 10
   B. 9
   C. 3
   D. 2

Answers and Explanations to Diagnostic: Relevance of Details

1. Answer   D
This statement is an opinion that is not supported. Whether or not an instructor's style of teaching is boring does not support the purpose of the passage, which is to explain that each instructor has a particular teaching style that is sometimes dependent on the kind of material he or she has to cover.

False choices
   Choice A provides the first example in support of instructors' different teaching styles.
   Choice B offers an example of a teaching style that offers no opportunity for social interaction.
   Choice C is a relevant detail that makes the point that it is the subject matter that affects the way an instructor teaches.

2. Answer   C
The passage offers no information about bonobos and chimpanzees being raised together and whether or not that fact influences their understanding of English.

False choices
   Choice A is a fact that is relevant to the passage. The statement tells the reader that the first research done to teach chimpanzees language was attempted in the 1920s.
   Choice B is another relevant point to the passage. It explains that researchers had to develop methods to communicate with chimps because they cannot speak.
   Choice D states that two bonobos, Kanzi and Mulika, can both understand some spoken English. This is a relevant statement that is a finding of current research.

3. Answer   A
The opinion that substance abuse is a big problem in our society has nothing to do with the main idea of the passage. The passage discusses the relationship between temperature and assault.

False choices
   Choice B is relevant because it supports sentence 9. The sentence gives an example of how people cope with the discomfort of high temperatures.

Choice C adds an important finding regarding temperature and assault. People are less likely to assault one another when the temperatures are very hot.

Choice D builds on the previous statement and is relevant to the passage. The sentence explains that researchers suggest that people are uncomfortable in very hot weather, and, therefore, they would rather withdraw than stay and fight.

4. Answer   A

Sentence 3 tells the reader that a person named Savishinsky lived with the Hare Indians to study them; however, no other information related to this fact is presented in the passage. Therefore, it is not relevant to the passage.

False choices

Choice B is relevant because it tells the reader how the Hare Indians survive in their harsh environment, thus giving background for the necessity of their dogs.

Choice C builds on the idea that winters are harsh and that dogs help the Hare travel during that time.

Choice D is also relevant by adding that finding food during the harsh winter is difficult. This adds to the description of the cold and isolation that the Hare experience.

5. Answer   B

The paragraph illustrates why it is important for the robin to conserve its energy while hunting for prey. The passage includes the steps the robin takes to hunt. However, the topic of pesticides is not relevant to the discussion.

False choices

Choice A sets up the premise of the passage.

Choice C is relevant because it explains that by catching an earthworm, the robin has expended the least amount of energy for the more valuable food.

Choice D is another step in the robin's process of searching for food, which is explained in the passage.

6. Answer   D

This sentence about overfishing in the Caribbean and the Philippines has nothing to do with the subject of the paragraph. The paragraph tells the reader about problems on the beaches for humans and animals.

False choices

Choice A is relevant because it further supports the sea gull encroachment on the territory needed by other sea birds.

Choice B gives the effect of the previous sentence. The sea turtles and horseshoe crabs are losing their nesting sites on the beaches; therefore, their populations are declining.

Choice C presents another support for problems on the beaches: oil as a major, chronic pollutant.

7. Answer   A

The passage explains that Latinos are the largest minority in the United States. It does not make projections for the next 25 years for Latinos or any other group. Therefore, the sentence is not relevant.

False choices

Choice B is relevant because it supplies data on the large number of Latinos who live in four states.

Choice C supports the main idea of the passage by providing data on the number of Latinos counted by the census; in addition, it explains that the number is larger due to illegal immigration.

Choice D presents data that is relevant to the main idea. It lists the numbers of Latinos who trace their origins to Mexico, Puerto Rico, Cuba, Central America, and South America.

PASSAGE #1

Read the passage and answer the question that follows.

1 _____.

[2]First of all, because e-mail messages are informal and quick, writers may be sloppy in transferring their thoughts to the screen. [3]Misspellings and ungrammatical sentences can project a negative image if users do not take time to edit what they write on e-mail. [4]Second, the messages are sent and read online, often leaving no paper trail at all. [5]As a result, some important messages are forgotten or lost. [6]It is easy to read your electronic mail and delete it instead of printing out a copy of the message to keep in a file or filing the message electronically in your e-mail file folder. [7]Although generally thought of as a quick method of communication, e-mail's efficiency is only as good as the recipient's care in routinely checking e-mail messages. [8]Electronic communication can be slow if people don't check their messages. [9]Moreover, you have no privacy. [10]Another disadvantage is the increasing use of e-mail as a replacement for personal contact of a phone call or face-to-face meeting. [11]The 1986 Electronic Communications Privacy Act considers e-mail to be the property of the company paying for the mail system. [12]_____, writing on a computer screen often encourages people to drop inhibitions and write things in e-mail that they would never write in a paper letter or say over the telephone. (Adapted from Kristin R. Woolever, *Writing for the Technical Professions*, 2nd ed., New York: Longman, 2002.)

1. Which numbered sentence is **least** relevant to the passage?
   A. 5
   B. 3
   C. 8
   D. 11

PASSAGE #2

Read the passage and answer the question that follows.

1 _____.

[2]Although women have served in every branch of the armed services since World War II, two differences between the treatment of men and women in the military persist. [3]First, only men must register for the draft when they turn eighteen. [4]In 1981, the Supreme Court ruled that male-only registration for the military did not violate the Fifth Amendment. [5]Second, statutes and regulations also prohibit women from serving in combat. [6]A breach exists between policy and practice, however, as the Persian Gulf war showed. [7]Women piloted helicopters at the front and helped to operate antimissile systems; some were taken as prisoners of war. [8]_____, women are not permitted to serve as combat pilots in the navy and air force and to serve on navy warships. [9]They are still not permitted to serve in ground combat units in the army or marines. [10]These actions have reopened the debate over whether women should serve in combat. [11]Others argue that men will not be able to fight effectively beside wounded or dying women. [12]Critics of these views point out that some women surpass men in body strength and that we do not know how well men and women will fight together. [13]Some experts insist that because women, on the average, have less body strength than men, they are less suited for combat. [14]This debate is not only a controversy about ability, but it

also touches on the question of whether engaging in combat is a burden or a privilege. (Adapted from George C. Edwards, Martin P. Wattenberg, and Robert L. Lineberry, *Government in America*, 9th ed., New York: Longman, 2000.)

2. Which numbered sentence is **least** relevant to the passage?
   A. 14
   B. 4
   C. 3
   D. 10

PASSAGE #3

Read the passage and answer the question that follows.

1
_____.
²Jaime Escalante taught calculus in an East Los Angeles inner-city school that was plagued with poverty, crime, drugs, and gangs. ³As a result of his methods, his students earned the highest Advanced Placement scores in the city. ⁴_____, Escalante had to open his students' minds to the possibility of success in learning. ⁵Most Latino students were tracked into craft classes where they made jewelry and birdhouses. ⁶Escalante felt that his students were talented and needed an opportunity to show it. ⁷Also, the students needed to see learning as a way out of the barrio, as a path to good jobs. ⁸By arranging for foundations to provide money for students to attend colleges of their choice, Escalante showed students that if they did well, their poverty would not stop them. ⁹When Escalante first came to the United States, he worked as a busboy and attended Pasadena Community College. ¹⁰Escalante also changed the system of instruction. ¹¹Before class, his students did "warm-ups," hand clapping and foot stomping to a rock song. ¹²To foster team identity, students wore team jackets, caps, and T-shirts with logos that identified them as part of the math team. ¹³He had his students think of themselves as a team, of him as the coach, and the national math exams as a sort of Olympics for which they were preparing. ¹⁴Escalante thought it was important to teach his classes in English, not Spanish. ¹⁵Escalante demonstrated that a teacher can motivate students to believe in their ability to achieve at high levels, no matter how great their problems. (Adapted from James M. Henslin, *Sociology*, 6th ed., Boston: Allyn and Bacon, 2003.)

3. Which numbered sentence is **least** relevant to the passage?
   A. 9
   B. 3
   C. 7
   D. 5

PASSAGE #4

Read the passage and answer the question that follows.

1
_____.
²Anorexia nervosa literally means loss of appetite, but this is a misnomer. ³The anorexic individual approaches weight loss with a fervor, convinced that her body is too large. ⁴A person with anorexia nervosa is hungry, but he or she denies the hunger because of an irrational fear of becoming fat. ⁵Therefore, the first characteristic is a significant weight loss due to a relentless drive for thinness. ⁶She is unable to recognize that her appearance is abnormal. ⁷She will insist that her emaciated figure is just right or is too fat. ⁸There is a strong argument that

eating disorders are a form of addiction. [9]This condition is more than a simple eating disorder. [10]_____, anorexia is a distinct psychological disorder with a wide range of psychological disturbances. [11]Anorexics are typically compulsive, perfectionistic, and very competitive. [12]Food preoccupation and rituals and compulsive exercising are other characteristics. [13]The anorexic sometimes suffers from low self-image due to a feeling of incompetence, so she becomes consumed with losing weight to demonstrate to herself and others that she is in total control. [14]Additional features of the disease develop from the effects of starvation over time. [15]Untreated anorexia can be fatal. [16]Causes of death include starvation, infections due to poor nutrition, irregular heartbeat due to potassium deficiency, and suicide due to depression. (Adapted from David J. Anspaugh and Gene Ezell, *Teaching Today's Health*, 7th ed., San Francisco: Pearson, 2004.)

4. Which numbered sentence is **least** relevant to the passage?
   A. 8
   B. 9
   C. 12
   D. 15

PASSAGE #5

Read the passage and answer the question that follows.

[1]_____.
[2]Bare-knuckle boxing, the forerunner of modern boxing, was a brutal, bloody sport. [3]Two men fought bare-fisted until one could not continue. [4]A round lasted until one of the men knocked or threw down his opponent. [5]At that point, both men rested for thirty seconds and then started to fight again. [6]Fights often lasted over one hundred rounds and as long as seven or eight hours. [7]After such a fight, it took months for the fighters to recover. [8]During the 1800s, boxing underwent a series of reforms. [9]There have been periodic efforts to outlaw the sport. [10]The challenge system was replaced by modern promotional techniques. [11]Fighters deserted bare-fisted combat and started wearing gloves. [12]Most importantly, professional boxers adopted the Marquis of Queensberry Rules, which standardized a round at three minutes, allowing a one-minute rest period between rounds, and outlawed all wrestling throws and holds. [13]_____, the fight to the finish was replaced with a fight to a decision over a specified number of rounds. [14]A bell and a referee told fighters when to fight and when to rest. [15]Currently there are eight major professional divisions. [16]Although the new rules did not reduce the violence, they did provide for more orderly bouts. (Adapted from James Kirby Martin et al., *America and Its Peoples*, 5th ed., New York: Longman, 2003.)

5. Which numbered sentence is **least** relevant to the passage?
   A. 11
   B. 3
   C. 15
   D. 6

PASSAGE #6

Read the passage and answer the question that follows.

[1]_____.
[2]For example, with eye movements you can seek feedback. [3]In talking with someone, you

look at her or him intently, as if to say, "Well, what do you think?" [4]Your pupils enlarge when you are interested or emotionally aroused. [5]You can also inform the other person that the channel of communication is open and that he or she should now speak. [6]You see this in the college classroom, when the instructor asks a question and then locks eyes with a student. [7]Without saying anything, the instructor expects that student to answer the question and the student knows it.[8]Eye movements may also signal the nature of a relationship, whether positive (an attentive glance) or negative (eye avoidance). [9]_____, you can signal your power through visual dominance behavior. [10]The average speaker, for example, maintains a high level of eye contact while listening and a lower level while speaking. [11]When people want to signal dominance, they may reverse this pattern: maintaining a high level of eye contact while talking but a lower level while listening. [12]Eye contact can also change the psychological distance between yourself and another person. [13]When you catch someone's eye at a party, for example, you become psychologically close even though far apart. [14]By avoiding eye contact—even when physically close as in a crowded elevator—you increase the psychological distance between you. (Adapted from Joseph A. DeVito, *Essentials of Human Communication*, 3rd ed., New York: Longman, 1999.)

6. Which numbered sentence is **least** relevant to the passage?
   A. 7
   B. 5
   C. 4
   D. 10

PASSAGE # 7

Read the passage and answer the question that follows.

[1]_____.
[2]It even drinks seawater, which is much saltier than its body fluids. [3]Few animals can tolerate such salty liquid, because the salt draws water out of their tissues, and they become severely dehydrated. [4]An albatross can thrive on salt water because it has special salt-excreting glands in its nostrils. [5]The glands dispose of excess salts, allowing the bird to eat salty fish and squid and drink all it needs without ever visiting land. [6]Their scientific name, *Diomedea exulans*, means exiled warrior in Greek. [7]_____ its remarkable salt tolerance, the wandering albatross has extraordinary flight abilities specially suited to its seafaring life. [8]Its wingspan is greater than that of any other bird—about 3.6 meters (nearly twelve feet). [9]Most birds have to flap their wings to stay up in the air very long, but the albatross's long wings provide so much lift that the bird can stay aloft for hours by gliding up and down on wind currents. [10]The wandering albatross spends most of its time in an area of high winds and rough seas, far from land, often alone on the open ocean. [11]The winds carry it from west to east, and in a year's time, an albatross may circle the globe, seeing little land except New Zealand and the tip of South America. (Adapted from Neil A. Campbell, Lawrence G. Mitchell, and Jane B. Reece, *Biology*, 3rd ed., San Francisco: Benjamin Cummings, 2000.)

7. Which numbered sentence is **least** relevant to the passage?
   A. 3
   B. 8
   C. 10
   D. 6

PASSAGE #8

Read the passage and answer the question that follows.

1 _____ .

[2]Testosterone is a male hormone that causes a general buildup in muscle and bone mass during puberty in males and maintains masculine traits throughout life. [3]Anabolic steroids are synthetic variants of the male hormone testosterone. [4]Pharmaceutical companies first produced and marketed anabolic steroids in the early 1950s as a treatment for certain diseases that destroy body muscle. [5]About a decade later, some athletes began using anabolic steroids to build up their muscles quickly and enhance their performance with less hard work. [6]It is not surprising that some of the heaviest users are weight lifters, football players, and body builders. [7]Today, anabolic steroids, along with other drugs, are banned by most athletic organizations. [8]Black market sales bring in up to $400 million a year. [9]Medical research indicates that these substances can cause serious physical and mental problems. [10]Overdosing in males can cause acne, baldness, and breast development. [11]Mental effects can range from mood swings to deep depression. [12]Internally, there may be liver damage leading to cancer. [13]_____, anabolic steroids can make blood cholesterol levels rise, perhaps increasing a user's chances of developing serious cardiovascular problems. [14]Heavy users may also experience a reduced sex drive and become infertile because anabolic steroids often make the body reduce its normal output of sex hormones. (Adapted from Neil A. Campbell, Lawrence G. Mitchell, and Jane B. Reece, *Biology*, 3rd ed., San Francisco: Benjamin Cummings, 2000.)

8. Which numbered sentence is **least** relevant to the passage?
   A. 2
   B. 8
   C. 4
   D. 3

PASSAGE #9

Read the passage and answer the question that follows.

1 _____ .

[2]In most cases, the child continually learns from the parent. [3]In the area of computer and Internet-mediated communication, however, the child may be able to teach the parent. [4]_____, one five-year-old learned a graphics program before she could read. [5]The child taught herself how to operate the rather intuitive program. [6]Not only did the computer provide the child with a valuable learning process, but the parents totally depended on the child when they wanted to use the program she knew. [7]In another case, a young boy taught his parents how to use PowerPoint. [8]The examples are endless. [9]Children are more apt to interact with the computer as if it were alive. [10]A child may be able to understand a concept differently from the parent, and the role reversal of the child-as-teacher can be an important way the computer and the Internet can enhance a child's self-esteem. [11]The child and parent alike may feel positive toward themselves when they are able to learn new things, master a program, or win an Internet game. [12]Their self-confidence may increase when others seek their advice, for example, because they are the family computer experts. (Adapted from Leonard J. Shedletsky and Joan E. Aitken, *Human Communication on the Internet*, Boston: Allyn and Bacon, 2004.)

9. Which numbered sentence is **least** relevant to the passage?
   A. 9
   B. 3
   C. 12
   D. 4

PASSAGE #10

Read the passage and answer the question that follows.

1 _____.
²Highlighting is a strategy for condensing textbook material and emphasizing what is impor-tant. ³_____, the process of highlighting forces you to sift through what you have read to identify important information. ⁴This sifting or sorting is an active thought process; you are forced to weigh and evaluate what you read. ⁵One mistake to avoid is highlighting almost every idea on a page. ⁶Another benefit of highlighting is that it keeps you physically active while you are reading. ⁷In addition, highlighting can help you discover the organization of facts and ideas as well as their connections and relationships. ⁸Highlighting demonstrates to you whether you have understood a passage you have just read. ⁹When combined with anno-tation, highlighting is a quick and easy way to review so that you do not have to reread every-thing when studying for an exam. ¹⁰If you highlight 20 percent of a chapter, you will be able to avoid rereading 80 percent of the material. ¹¹If it normally takes two hours to read a chap-ter, you should be able to review a highlighted chapter in less than a half hour. ¹²Highlighting has many benefits, but it is not by itself a sufficient study method; you must process the infor-mation by organizing it, expressing it in your own words, and testing yourself periodically.
(Adapted from Kathleen T. McWhorter, *Study and Critical Thinking Skills in College*, 5th ed., New York: Longman, 2003.)

10. Which numbered sentence is **least** relevant to the passage?
    A. 3
    B. 7
    C. 9
    D. 5

SECTION 5 ◆ TRANSITIONAL DEVICES

Competency 1.5	Conceptual and Organizational Skills
Skill Tested	**Recognizes effective transitional devices within the context of the passage**

The Skill

This item tests your ability to identify effective transitions that reflect the organization pattern used in a piece of writing. Transitions are words that connect one idea to another so that they flow smoothly and logically. They tell you the logical relationship of ideas **within** and **between** sentences. Transitional devices can appear at the beginning of a sentence or somewhere within a sentence.

Study the following chart of transition words and phrases so that you will recognize them in the test question.

Relationship Expressed	Transition Words and Phrases
Addition	also, in addition, too, moreover, and, besides, furthermore, equally important, then, finally, first, next, second
Example	for example, for instance, thus, as an illustration, namely, specifically, to illustrate
Contrast	yet, but, however, on the one hand/on the other hand, nevertheless, conversely, in contrast, still, although, despite that, on the contrary, otherwise, whereas
Comparison	similarly, likewise, in the same way
Concession	of course, certainly, granted, although it is true that, I admit that, it may appear that
Emphasis	indeed, in fact, of course
Place	here, there, above, below, beyond, closer to, far, near, nearby, to the left, to the right
Result	therefore, thus, consequently, as a result, so
Summary	in summary, in conclusion, finally, hence, on the whole, to summarize, as mentioned earlier, in other words, in short, therefore
Time	first, second, third, next, then, finally, after, afterwards, before, soon, later, meanwhile, subsequently, immediately, eventually, currently, after a while, earlier, presently, simultaneously, when, shortly

Here is an example of a passage that effectively uses transitions, which are underlined.

> The carefully planned wedding quickly turned into a disaster. <u>After</u> months of phone calls to the florists, photographer, minister, and caterer, the day seemed perfectly planned. <u>In fact</u>, the weather forecaster predicted a beautiful, picture perfect day. <u>However</u>, an unexpected summer rainstorm drove the wedding party off the beach after the bride, groom, minister, family, and guests had been thoroughly soaked. <u>Furthermore</u>, as if the rain and wind were not enough to ruin the day, the groom became violently ill with food poisoning and had to be hospitalized on his wedding night.

The Test Question

You will be given a passage of approximately 200 words containing numbered sentences, one of which contains a blank or underlined transitional word or phrase. You will be asked to choose the best word or phrase that, if inserted into the blank, would make the relationship of the ideas clear.

SECTION 5 ◆ DIAGNOSTIC: TRANSITIONAL DEVICES

Read the passages and apply the strategies described above for identifying transitional devices. When you are done, check your work with the answers immediately following the diagnostic. Even if you get a perfect score here, go ahead and complete the exercises in this section; they are designed to help build confidence and to give you practice for future test success.

PASSAGE #1

Read the passage and answer the question that follows.

(1) _____.
(2) Some instructors, for example, have a teaching style that promotes social interaction among students. (3) An instructor may organize small group activities, encourage class participation, or require students to work in pairs or teams to complete a specific task. (4) A lecture class is an example. (5) Other instructors offer little or no opportunity for social interaction. (6) Some instructors are very applied; they teach by example. (7) Others are more conceptual; they focus on presenting ideas, rules, theories, and so forth. (8) To an extent, of course, the subject matter also dictates how the instructor teaches. (9) _____ a biology instructor has a large body of factual information to present and may feel he or she has little time to schedule group interaction. (10) Some instructors' teaching styles are boring. (11) Once you are aware of your learning style and then consider the instructor's teaching style, you can begin to understand why you can learn better from one instructor than another and why you feel more comfortable in certain instructors' classes than others. (Adapted from Kathleen McWhorter, *Study and Critical Thinking Skills in College*, 5th ed., New York: Longman, 2003.)

1. Which word or phrase, if inserted in the blank in sentence 9, would make the relationship of the ideas clear?
   A. Therefore,
   B. However,
   C. In contrast,
   D. For example,

PASSAGE #2

Read the passage and answer the question that follows.

(1) _____.
(2) As early as the 1920s, psychologists attempted to teach language to chimpanzees to find out whether they could communicate. (3) Chimps don't have the appropriate vocal apparatus to produce spoken language, so researchers had to devise other methods of communication. (4) For instance, a chimp named Washoe was taught a highly simplified version of American Sign Language. (5) In addition, a chimp named Sarah was taught to manipulate symbols on a magnetic board. (6) Skeptics wondered if the chimps' combination of gestures and symbols constituted any kind of meaningful language. (7) Recent research has provided more solid insights into the language capabilities of chimps. (8) Bonobos and chimps can be raised together. (9) Sue Savage-Rumbaugh and her team work primarily with *bonobos*, a species of great ape that is evolutionarily nearer to humans than even the common chimpanzees. (10) Remarkably, two of the bonobos in her studies, Kanzi and Mulika, learned the meanings of plastic symbols at the same time. (11) They did not receive direct training; rather, they acquired the symbols by watching humans and other bonobos. (12) _____ Kanzi and Mulika can understand some spoken English. (13) For example, when Kanzi hears a spoken word, he is able to locate either the symbol for the word or a picture of the object. (Adapted from Richard J. Gerrig and Philip G. Zimbardo, *Psychology and Life*, 16th ed., Boston: Allyn and Bacon, 2002.)

2. Which word or phrase, if inserted in the blank in sentence 12, would make the relationship of the ideas clear?
   A. In contrast,
   B. Moreover,
   C. Next,
   D. In conclusion,

PASSAGE #3

Read the passage and answer the question that follows.

(1) _____.
(2) The relationship between temperature and assault is actually strongest in the late evening and early morning hours, from 9 p.m. to 3 a.m. (3) One explanation is that people are more likely to commit assault when they are out and about. (4) That is, in warmer weather, people are usually outdoors more and, therefore, are also more "available" as assault victims. (5) In the 9 p.m. to 3 a.m. hours, people are typically not working or bound by other responsibilities. (6) The time of day is another factor. (7) Furthermore, by the late evening hours, people may have been drinking alcohol or using other substances that lower their inhibition to aggression. (8) Substance abuse is a big problem in our society. (9) Another part of the explanation is the way in which people cope with and interpret the discomfort associated with high temperatures. (10) As the day goes on, it may be harder to remember, "I'm feeling this way because it's hot" and just conclude, "I'm feeling this way because this person is making me crazy." (11)_____, assaults decline when temperatures become very hot. (12) Researchers have speculated that at very high temperatures, people might experience sufficient discomfort to withdraw from abrasive situations rather than stay and fight. (Adapted from Richard J. Gerrig and Philip G. Zimbardo, *Psychology and Life*, 16th ed., Boston: Allyn and Bacon, 2002.)

3. Which word or phrase, if inserted in the blank in sentence 11, would make the relationship of the ideas clear?
   A. On the other hand,
   B. In fact,
   C. Now,
   D. In conclusion,

PASSAGE #4

Read the passage and answer the question that follows.

(1) _____.
(2) The Hare Indians of Colville Lake are a small group of Canadian Inuit. (3) Savishinsky lived with the Hare Indians to study them. (4) They survive by hunting, trapping, and fishing in one of the harshest environments in the world. (5)_____, dogs are economically useful. (6) Dog teams give the Inuit a means for travel during the harshest seasons of the year. (7) The temperatures are extremely cold, and the winters are long and severe. (8) Finding food can be difficult. (9) The Inuit estimate that six dogs are required for travel, and some households have as many as four dog teams, with an average of 6.2 dogs per team. (10) The dogs are a frequent topic of conversation. (11) More than being only economically useful,

dogs play a significant role in people's emotional lives. (12) Members of the community constantly compare and comment on the care, condition, and growth of one another's animals. (13) They note special qualities of size, strength, color, speed, and alertness. (14) Emotional displays, uncommon among the hare, are significant between people and their dogs. (15) All people participate in the affectionate and concerned treatment of young dogs. (Adapted from Barbara D. Miller, *Cultural Anthropology*, 2nd ed., Boston: Allyn and Bacon, 2002.)

4. Which word or phrase, if inserted in the blank in sentence 5, would make the relationship of the ideas clear?
   A. In contrast,
   B. Then,
   C. First of all,
   D. Nevertheless,

PASSAGE #5

Read the passage and answer the question that follows.

(1) _____.
(2) The robin searches for food by selecting only those items that provide the greatest energy return for the energy expended. (3) This can be illustrated by the robin's behavior, which has four parts. (4) First, the robin has to decide where to hunt for food. (5) Once on the lawn, it has to search for food items. (6) Because the robin forages on lawns, it is vulnerable to pesticide poisoning. (7) Having located some potential food, the robin has to decide whether to pursue it. (8) If it begins pursuit by pecking, the robin has to attempt a capture, in which it might or might not be successful. (9) If a food item is too large, it requires too much time to handle; if it is too small, it does not deliver enough energy to cover the costs of capture. (10) The robin should reject or ignore less valuable items, such as small beetles and caterpillars, and give preference to small and medium-sized earthworms. (11) _____ by capturing an earthworm, the robin earns some units of energy. (12) These more valuable food items would be classified as preferred food. (13) If the robin fails to find suitable and sufficient food in the area of the lawn it is searching, it leaves to search elsewhere. (14) If successful, the bird probably will return until the spot is no longer an economical place to feed. (Adapted from Robert Leo Smith and Thomas M. Smith, *Elements of Ecology*, 5th ed., San Francisco: Benjamin Cummings, 2003.)

5. Which word or phrase, if inserted in the blank in sentence 11, would make the relationship of the ideas clear?
   A. However,
   B. On the other hand,
   C. Therefore,
   D. In conclusion,

PASSAGE #6

Read the passage and answer the question that follows.

(1) _____.
(2) Beach-nesting birds such as the piping plover and the least tern are so disturbed by bathers and dune buggies that both species are in danger of extinction. (3) Other terns and shore birds are subjected to competition for nest sites and to egg predators by rapidly growing pop-

ulations of large gulls. (4) These gulls are highly tolerant of humans and thrive on human garbage. (5) Sea turtles and the horseshoe crab, dependent on sandy beaches for nesting sites, find themselves evicted. (6) _____, they are declining rapidly. (7) Furthermore, each incoming tide brings onto the beaches feces-contaminated water that makes them unhealthy for humans and wildlife alike. (8) This contaminated water comes from a number of different sources, such as sewer overflows, failing private and commercial septic systems, animal and wildlife waste, and swimmers' illnesses. (9) The oceans have become dumping grounds. (10) Major chronic pollutants are oil that is released from tanker accidents, seepage from offshore drilling and other sources, toxic materials such as pesticides and heavy metals from industrial, urban, and agricultural sources. (11) The most devastating human activity in reefs is overfishing, especially in the Philippines and the Caribbean. (12) Tides also carry in old fishing lines, plastic debris, and other wastes hazardous to wildlife. (Adapted from Robert Leo Smith and Thomas M. Smith, *Elements of Ecology*, 5th ed., San Francisco: Benjamin Cummings, 2003.)

6. Which word or phrase, if inserted in the blank in sentence 6, would make the relationship of the ideas clear?
   A. For example,
   B. Finally,
   C. Similarly,
   D. Consequently,

PASSAGE #7

Read the passage and answer the question that follows.

(1) _____.
(2) About 21 million people trace their origin to Mexico, 3 million to Puerto Rico, 1 million to Cuba, and almost 5 million to Central or South America, primarily Venezuela or Colombia. (3) Officially tallied at 35 million in the year 2000 census, the actual number of Latinos is higher because, not surprisingly, many who are in the country illegally avoid contact with both public officials and census forms. (4) Each year, more than 1 million people are apprehended at the border or at points inland and are deported to Mexico. (5) Perhaps another million or so manage to enter the United States. (6) _____ many migrate for temporary work and then return to their homes and families. (7) To gain an understanding of how vast these numbers are, we can note that there are millions more Latinos in the United States than there are Canadians in Canada (31 million). (8) To Midwesterners, such a comparison often comes as a surprise, for Latinos are absent from vast stretches of mid-America. (9) Sixty-nine percent are concentrated in just four states: California, Texas, New York, and Florida. (10) In the next twenty-five years, changes in the U.S. racial-ethnic mix will be dramatic. (Adapted from James M. Henslin, *Sociology*, 6th ed., Boston: Allyn and Bacon, 2003.)

7. Which word or phrase, if inserted in the blank in sentence 6, would make the relationship of the ideas clear?
   A. Nevertheless,
   B. In addition,
   C. In other words,
   D. Nearby,

Answers and Explanations to Diagnostic: Transitional Devices

1. Answer   D

"For example" is the transition that makes the relationship between ideas clear. The sentence is an example of how an instructor's subject matter dictates how he or she teaches.

False choices

    Choice A, "Therefore," suggests a result, not an example.
    Choice B, "However," suggests a contrast, not an example.
    Choice C, "In contrast," suggests a contrast, not an example.

2. Answer   B

"Moreover" is the appropriate transition word to make the relationship of ideas clear. The sentence adds information about what the two bonobos learned. In the previous sentence, the reader learns that they learned symbols by watching people and other bonobos. This sentence adds that they can understand some spoken English.

False choices

    Choice A, "In contrast," suggests that a contrast is being made.
    Choice C, "Next," leads the reader to think that the sentence is part of a sequence.
    Choice D, "In conclusion," indicates that the sentence is providing a summary or a conclusion for the paragraph.

3. Answer   A

"On the other hand" is the appropriate transition for making the relationship of ideas clear. The sentence points out a contrast. Although people are more likely to assault when the weather is warm, in contrast, they are less likely to assault when the weather is hot.

False choices

    Choice B, "In fact," indicates that an example is being given.
    Choice C, "Now," is a word used to express time, not contrast.
    Choice D, "In conclusion," indicates that the sentence is providing a summary or a conclusion for the paragraph.

4. Answer   C

"First of all" is the appropriate transition for making the relationship of ideas clear. It indicates that the first supporting idea is being introduced. In the passage, the reader learns that dogs are economically useful for the Hare Indians.

False choices

    Choice A, "In contrast," indicates that a contrast is being made.
    Choice B, "Then," is used to express time.
    Choice D, "Nevertheless," expresses contrast.

5. Answer   C

"Therefore" is the appropriate transition word to make the relationship of ideas clear. "Therefore" expresses the effect of the robin's ignoring less valuable prey and preferring earthworms.

False choices

    Choice A, "However," suggests a contrast, not an effect.
    Choice B, "On the other hand," also suggests a contrast, not an effect.
    Choice D, "In conclusion," indicates that the sentence is providing a summary or a conclusion for the paragraph.

6. Answer   D

"Consequently" is the appropriate transition word to make the relationship of ideas clear. "Consequently" expresses a result or effect. The sentence explains the effect of the loss of habitat of sea turtles and horseshoe crabs.

False choices

    Choice A, "For example," indicates that the sentence will provide an example.

    Choice B, "Finally," is used to express the last item in a sequence or the last idea.

    Choice C, "Similarly," suggests that a comparison is being made.

7. Answer   B

"In addition" is the appropriate transition for making the relationship of ideas clear. "In addition" tells the reader that another detail is being added. The sentence provides more supporting information for the fact that there are more Latinos in the U.S. than the 2000 census indicates.

False choices

    Choice A, "Nevertheless," expresses a contrast.

    Choice C, "In other words," is used to restate a point or give a conclusion.

    Choice D, "Nearby," is used when describing a spatial relationship.

SECTION 5 ◆ EXERCISES: TRANSITIONAL DEVICES

PASSAGE #1

Read the passage and answer the question that follows.

¹_____.
²First of all, because e-mail messages are informal and quick, writers may be sloppy in transferring their thoughts to the screen. ³Misspellings and ungrammatical sentences can project a negative image if users do not take time to edit what they write on e-mail. ⁴Second, the messages are sent and read online, often leaving no paper trail at all. ⁵As a result, some important messages are forgotten or lost. ⁶It is easy to read your electronic mail and delete it instead of printing out a copy of the message to keep in a file or filing the message electronically in your e-mail file folder. ⁷Although generally thought of as a quick method of communication, e-mail's efficiency is only as good as the recipient's care in routinely checking e-mail messages. ⁸Electronic communication can be slow if people don't check their messages. ⁹Moreover, you have no privacy. ¹⁰Another disadvantage is the increasing use of e-mail as a replacement for personal contact of a phone call or face-to-face meeting. ¹¹The 1986 Electronic Communications Privacy Act considers e-mail to be the property of the company paying for the mail system. ¹²_____, writing on a computer screen often encourages people to drop inhibitions and write things in e-mail that they would never write in a paper letter or say over the telephone. (Adapted from Kristin R. Woolever, *Writing for the Technical Professions*, 2nd ed., New York: Longman, 2002.)

1. Which word or phrase, if inserted in the blank in sentence 12, would make the relationship of the ideas within the sentence clear?
    A. In contrast
    B. In conclusion
    C. Finally
    D. For example

PASSAGE #2

Read the passage and answer the question that follows.

1 _____.

2Although women have served in every branch of the armed services since World War II, two differences between the treatment of men and women in the military persist. 3First, only men must register for the draft when they turn eighteen. 4In 1981, the Supreme Court ruled that male-only registration for the military did not violate the Fifth Amendment. 5Second, statutes and regulations also prohibit women from serving in combat. 6A breach exists between policy and practice, however, as the Persian Gulf War showed. 7Women piloted helicopters at the front and helped to operate antimissile systems; some were taken as prisoners of war. 8_____, women are not permitted to serve as combat pilots in the navy and air force and to serve on navy warships. 9They are still not permitted to serve in ground combat units in the army or marines. 10These actions have reopened the debate over whether women should serve in combat. 11Others argue that men will not be able to fight effectively beside wounded or dying women. 12Critics of these views point out that some women surpass men in body strength and that we do not know how well men and women will fight together. 13Some experts insist that because women, on the average, have less body strength than men, they are less suited for combat. 14This debate is not only a controversy about ability, but it also touches on the question of whether engaging in combat is a burden or a privilege. (Adapted from George C. Edwards, Martin P. Wattenberg, and Robert L. Lineberry, *Government in America*, 9th ed., New York: Longman, 2000.)

2. Which word or phrase, if inserted in the blank in sentence 8, would make the relationship of the ideas within the sentence clear?
   A. Therefore
   B. In conclusion
   C. For example
   D. However

PASSAGE #3

Read the passage and answer the question that follows.

1 _____.

2Jaime Escalante taught calculus in an East Los Angeles inner-city school that was plagued with poverty, crime, drugs, and gangs. 3As a result of his methods, his students earned the highest Advanced Placement scores in the city. 4_____, Escalante had to open his students' minds to the possibility of success in learning. 5Most Latino students were tracked into craft classes where they made jewelry and birdhouses. 6Escalante felt that his students were talented and needed an opportunity to show it. 7Also, the students needed to see learning as a way out of the barrio, as a path to good jobs. 8By arranging for foundations to provide money for students to attend colleges of their choice, Escalante showed students that if they did well, their poverty would not stop them. 9When Escalante first came to the United States, he worked as a busboy and attended Pasadena Community College. 10Escalante also changed the system of instruction. 11Before class, his students did "warm-ups," hand clapping and foot stomping to a rock song. 12To foster team identity, students wore team jackets, caps, and T-shirts with logos that identified them as part of the math team. 13He had his students think of themselves as a team, of him as the coach, and the national math exams as a sort of

Olympics for which they were preparing. [14]Escalante thought it was important to teach his classes in English, not Spanish. [15]Escalante demonstrated that a teacher can motivate students to believe in their ability to achieve at high levels, no matter how great their problems. (Adapted from James M. Henslin, *Sociology*, 6th ed., Boston: Allyn and Bacon, 2003.)

3. Which word or phrase, if inserted in the blank in sentence 4, would make the relationship of the ideas within the sentence clear?
   A. First
   B. Then
   C. Next
   D. Consequently

PASSAGE #4

Read the passage and answer the question that follows.

1 _____ .

[2]Anorexia nervosa literally means loss of appetite, but this is a misnomer. [3]The anorexic individual approaches weight loss with a fervor, convinced that her body is too large. [4]A person with anorexia nervosa is hungry, but he or she denies the hunger because of an irrational fear of becoming fat. [5]Therefore, the first characteristic is a significant weight loss due to a relentless drive for thinness. [6]She is unable to recognize that her appearance is abnormal. [7]She will insist that her emaciated figure is just right or is too fat. [8]There is a strong argument that eating disorders are a form of addiction. [9]This condition is more than a simple eating disorder. [10]_____, anorexia is a distinct psychological disorder with a wide range of psychological disturbances. [11]Anorexics are typically compulsive, perfectionistic, and very competitive. [12]Food preoccupation and rituals and compulsive exercising are other characteristics. [13]The anorexic sometimes suffers from low self-image due to a feeling of incompetence, so she becomes consumed with losing weight to demonstrate to herself and others that she is in total control. [14]Additional features of the disease develop from the effects of starvation over time. [15]Untreated anorexia can be fatal. [16]Causes of death include starvation, infections due to poor nutrition, irregular heartbeat due to potassium deficiency, and suicide due to depression. (Adapted from David J. Anspaugh and Gene Ezell, *Teaching Today's Health*, 7th ed., San Francisco: Pearson, 2004.)

4. Which word or phrase, if inserted in the blank in sentence 10, would make the relationship of the ideas within the sentence clear?
   A. Consequently
   B. In fact
   C. Meanwhile
   D. However

PASSAGE #5

Read the passage and answer the question that follows.

1 _____ .

[2]Bare-knuckle boxing, the forerunner of modern boxing, was a brutal, bloody sport. [3]Two men fought bare-fisted until one could not continue. [4]A round lasted until one of the men knocked or threw down his opponent. [5]At that point, both men rested for thirty seconds and

then started to fight again. [6]Fights often lasted over one hundred rounds and as long as seven or eight hours. [7]After such a fight, it took months for the fighters to recover. [8]During the 1800s, boxing underwent a series of reforms. [9]There have been periodic efforts to outlaw the sport. [10]The challenge system was replaced by modern promotional techniques. [11]Fighters deserted bare-fisted combat and started wearing gloves. [12]Most importantly, professional boxers adopted the Marquis of Queensberry Rules, which standardized a round at three minutes, allowing a one-minute rest period between rounds, and outlawed all wrestling throws and holds. [13]_____, the fight to the finish was replaced with a fight to a decision over a specified number of rounds. [14]A bell and a referee told fighters when to fight and when to rest. [15]Currently there are eight major professional divisions. [16]Although the new rules did not reduce the violence, they did provide for more orderly bouts. (Adapted from James Kirby Martin et al., *America and Its Peoples*, 5th ed., New York: Longman, 2003.)

5. Which word or phrase, if inserted in the blank in sentence 13, would make the relationship of the ideas within the sentence clear?
   A. In short
   B. Specifically
   C. However
   D. In addition

PASSAGE #6

Read the passage and answer the question that follows.

[1]_____.
[2]For example, with eye movements you can seek feedback. [3]In talking with someone, you look at her or him intently, as if to say, "Well, what do you think?" [4]Your pupils enlarge when you are interested or emotionally aroused. [5]You can also inform the other person that the channel of communication is open and that he or she should now speak. [6]You see this in the college classroom, when the instructor asks a question and then locks eyes with a student. [7]Without saying anything, the instructor expects that student to answer the question and the student knows it. [8]Eye movements may also signal the nature of a relationship, whether positive (an attentive glance) or negative (eye avoidance). [9]_____, you can signal your power through visual dominance behavior. [10]The average speaker, for example, maintains a high level of eye contact while listening and a lower level while speaking. [11]When people want to signal dominance, they may reverse this pattern: maintaining a high level of eye contact while talking but a lower level while listening. [12]Eye contact can also change the psychological distance between yourself and another person. [13]When you catch someone's eye at a party, for example, you become psychologically close even though far apart. [14]By avoiding eye contact—even when physically close as in a crowded elevator—you increase the psychological distance between you. (Adapted from Joseph A. DeVito, *Essentials of Human Communication*, 3rd ed., New York: Longman, 1999.)

6. Which word or phrase, if inserted in the blank in sentence 9, would make the relationship of the ideas within the sentence clear?
   A. However
   B. Afterwards
   C. Moreover
   D. As a result

PASSAGE #7

Read the passage and answer the question that follows.

1 _____.

^{2}It even drinks seawater, which is much saltier than its body fluids. ^{3}Few animals can tolerate such salty liquid because the salt draws water out of their tissues, and they become severely dehydrated. ^{4}An albatross can thrive on salt water because it has special salt-excreting glands in its nostrils. ^{5}The glands dispose of excess salts, allowing the bird to eat salty fish and squid and drink all it needs without ever visiting land. ^{6}Their scientific name, *Diomedea exulans*, means exiled warrior in Greek. ^{7}_____ its remarkable salt tolerance, the wandering albatross has extraordinary flight abilities specially suited to its seafaring life. ^{8}Its wingspan is greater than that of any other bird—about 3.6 meters (nearly twelve feet). ^{9}Most birds have to flap their wings to stay up in the air very long, but the albatross's long wings provide so much lift that the bird can stay aloft for hours by gliding up and down on wind currents. ^{10}The wandering albatross spends most of its time in an area of high winds and rough seas, far from land, often alone on the open ocean. ^{11}The winds carry it from west to east, and in a year's time, an albatross may circle the globe, seeing little land except New Zealand and the tip of South America. (Adapted from Neil A. Campbell, Lawrence G. Mitchell, and Jane B. Reece, *Biology*, 3rd ed., San Francisco: Benjamin Cummings, 2000.)

7. Which word or phrase, if inserted in the blank in sentence 7, would make the relationship of the ideas within the sentence clear?
   A. In contrast to
   B. Along with
   C. Finally
   D. Because of

PASSAGE #8

Read the passage and answer the question that follows.

1 _____.

^{2}Testosterone is a male hormone that causes a general buildup in muscle and bone mass during puberty in males and maintains masculine traits throughout life. ^{3}Anabolic steroids are synthetic variants of the male hormone testosterone. ^{4}Pharmaceutical companies first produced and marketed anabolic steroids in the early 1950s as a treatment for certain diseases that destroy body muscle. ^{5}About a decade later, some athletes began using anabolic steroids to build up their muscles quickly and enhance their performance with less hard work. ^{6}It is not surprising that some of the heaviest users are weight lifters, football players, and body builders. ^{7}Today, anabolic steroids, along with other drugs, are banned by most athletic organizations. ^{8}Black market sales bring in up to $400 million a year. ^{9}Medical research indicates that these substances can cause serious physical and mental problems. ^{10}Overdosing in males can cause acne, baldness, and breast development. ^{11}Mental effects can range from mood swings to deep depression. ^{12}Internally, there may be liver damage leading to cancer. ^{13}_____, anabolic steroids can make blood cholesterol levels rise, perhaps increasing a user's chances of developing serious cardiovascular problems. ^{14}Heavy users may also experience a reduced sex drive and become infertile because anabolic steroids often make the body reduce its normal output of sex hormones. (Adapted from Neil A. Campbell, Lawrence G. Mitchell, and Jane B. Reece, *Biology*, 3rd ed., San Francisco: Benjamin Cummings, 2000.)

8. Which word or phrase, if inserted in the blank in sentence 13, would make the relationship of the ideas within the sentence clear?
   A. Moreover
   B. Consequently
   C. However
   D. Nevertheless

PASSAGE #9

Read the passage and answer the question that follows.

1 _____.

2In most cases, the child continually learns from the parent. 3In the area of computer and Internet-mediated communication, however, the child may be able to teach the parent. 4_____, one five-year-old learned a graphics program before she could read. 5The child taught herself how to operate the rather intuitive program. 6Not only did the computer provide the child with a valuable learning process, but the parents totally depended on the child when they wanted to use the program she knew. 7In another case, a young boy taught his parents how to use PowerPoint. 8The examples are endless. 9Children are more apt to interact with the computer as if it were alive. 10A child may be able to understand a concept differently from the parent, and the role reversal of the child-as-teacher can be an important way the computer and the Internet can enhance a child's self-esteem. 11The child and parent alike may feel positive toward themselves when they are able to learn new things, master a program, or win an Internet game. 12Their self-confidence may increase when others seek their advice, for example, because they are the family computer experts. (Adapted from Leonard J. Shedletsky and Joan E. Aitken, *Human Communication on the Internet*, Boston: Allyn and Bacon, 2004.)

9. Which word or phrase, if inserted in the blank in sentence 4, would make the relationship of the ideas within the sentence clear?
   A. Then
   B. Nevertheless
   C. Meanwhile
   D. For example

PASSAGE #10

Read the passage and answer the question that follows.

1 _____.

2Highlighting is a strategy for condensing textbook material and emphasizing what is important. 3_____, the process of highlighting forces you to sift through what you have read to identify important information. 4This sifting or sorting is an active thought process; you are forced to weigh and evaluate what you read. 5One mistake to avoid is highlighting almost every idea on a page. 6Another benefit of highlighting is that it keeps you physically active while you are reading. 7In addition, highlighting can help you discover the organization of facts and ideas as well as their connections and relationships. 8Highlighting demonstrates to you whether you have understood a passage you have just read. 9When combined with annotation, highlighting is a quick and easy way to review so that you do not have to reread everything when studying for an exam. 10If you highlight 20 percent of a chapter, you will be able to avoid rereading 80 percent of the material. 11If it normally takes two hours to read a chapter, you should be able to review a highlighted chapter in less than a half hour. [12]Highlighting has many benefits, but it is not by itself a sufficient study method; you must process the information by organizing it, expressing it in your own words, and testing yourself periodically. (Adapted from Kathleen T. McWhorter, *Study and Critical Thinking Skills in College*, 5th ed., New York: Longman, 2003.)

10. Which word or phrase, if inserted in the blank in sentence 3, would make the relationship of the ideas within the sentence clear?
    A. Besides
    B. Thus
    C. First
    D. Also

Chapter 2: Language Skills

Competency 2.1	Word Choice Skills
Skill Tested	Chooses the appropriate word or expression in context

The Skill

This item tests your knowledge of the meanings of a variety of vocabulary words and their use within a sentence. You are being asked to choose the word that is used accurately and correctly.

For example, in the following sentence, which word is the best choice?
- Memorial Day is a day of **commendation** for those who have died in our nation's service.
- Memorial Day is a day of **remembrance** for those who have died in our nation's service.

Remembrance is the most accurate word choice. "Remembrance" is the act of honoring the memory of a person or event. "Commendation" means praise of someone's abilities or an award given to someone in recognition of an outstanding achievement.

The Test Question

The test question consists of a sentence that contains a missing word. You will be given three words to choose from; only one of the words is correct. Two of the three words may be similar in meaning. In that case, pick the one that expresses the meaning most accurately. One of the word choices may be clearly incorrect, and you can eliminate it immediately. If you are not sure which word is correct, look at the words surrounding the word in question. Use those words for clues to help you figure out the meaning.

Which word would you choose in the following sample question?

Although Jemi was a _____ tennis player, she quickly developed a strong backhand during her very first match.

     A. mediocre   B. novice   C. courageous

The sentence sets up a contrast. You know that Jemi developed a strong backhand during her first tennis match. Therefore, she must be a new player. "Novice," which means beginner, is the correct answer. "Mediocre," meaning not exceptional in ability, is not appropriate because the sentence tells you that she had not played tennis before, so she has not previously showed her ability. "Courageous" suggests that she showed bravery, but the rest of the sentence does not support this.

A careful reading of the sentence and the use of context clues will help you choose the correct answer.

For each of the following questions, choose the most effective word or phrase based on the context suggested by the sentence(s). When you are done, check your work with the answers immediately following the diagnostic. Even if you get a perfect score here, go ahead and complete the exercises in this section; they are designed to help build confidence and to give you practice for future test success.

1. Gabriella was uncomfortable about giving her presentation in front of the class because she was _____ about her accent.
   - A. apprehensive
   - B. self-conscious
   - C. arrogant

2. My favorite teachers are the ones who _____ me to do my best, not the ones who discourage me.
   - A. instigate
   - B. administer
   - C. inspire

3. The boss was _____ because three of the five servers scheduled to work last Saturday night called in sick, and he could not find anyone to cover for them.
   - A. elated
   - B. irate
   - C. indifferent

4. Although the instructor warned Kenny about the effects of _____, he waited until the night before the project was due to begin working on it.
   - A. procrastination
   - B. tenacity
   - C. cowardice

5. The _____ effects of smoking cigarettes is well known, but some people smoke anyway.
   - A. derogatory
   - B. innocuous
   - C. adverse

6. Despite the extremely hot summer temperatures, the tomato plants _____, supplying us with ripe, tasty tomatoes throughout the season.
   - A. thrived
   - B. languished
   - C. gesticulated

7. Some people at the gym are so _____ that they spend most of their time posing in front of the mirror and staring at themselves.
   - A. modest
   - B. crude
   - C. vain

Answers and Explanations to Diagnostic: Choosing Proper Expressions

1. Answer   B
"Self-conscious" means ill at ease.

False choices
   - A "Apprehensive" means fearful or uneasy.
   - C "Arrogant" means displaying a sense of superiority.

2. Answer   C

"Inspire" means to motivate.

False choices
    A   "Instigate" means to provoke or stir up.
    B   "Administer" is to manage, to take charge of.

3. Answer   B

"Irate" means extremely angry, enraged.

False choices
    A   "Elated" is proud, joyful.
    C   "Indifferent" means having no interest or concern.

4. Answer   A

"Procrastination" means to put off doing something.

False choices
    B   "Tenacity" is persistent determination.
    C   "Cowardice" means lack of courage.

5. Answer   C

"Adverse" means harmful or unfavorable.

False choices
    A   "Derogatory" means expressing a low opinion.
    B   "Innocuous" means harmless, having no adverse effects.

6. Answer   A

"Thrived" means to grow vigorously.

False choices
    B   "Languished" is to lose strength or vigor.
    C   "Gesticulated" means to say or express by making gestures.

7. Answer   C

"Vain" means excessively proud of one's appearance.

False choices
    A   "Modest" means having or showing a moderate estimation of one's own talents or abilities.
    B   "Crude" means blunt or offensive.

SECTION 1 ◆ EXERCISES: CHOOSING PROPER EXPRESSIONS

DIRECTIONS: *For each of the following questions, choose the most effective word or phrase based on the context suggested by the sentence(s).*

    1. Good vision helps animals _____ their prey or predators from a distance.
        A. realize
        B. detect
        C. ignore

    2. Although the computer has become _____ into our daily lives, most of us never think about it.

A. integrated
B. forced
C. combined

3. Sleep enables the body to _____ itself by repairing the body.
   A. revise
   B. relieve
   C. restore

4. Research _____ that students who become involved with college activities tend to be more successful than those who do not.
   A. warns
   B. reveals
   C. conceals

5. An essential part of critical thinking is _____ fact from opinion.
   A. observing
   B. describing
   C. distinguishing

6. The movement for African-American pride found its cultural _____ in the Harlem Renaissance, which was a literary and artistic movement.
   A. expression
   B. explanation
   C. publication

7. While the September 11, 2001, attacks produced a surge of patriotism, national unity, and pride, they also _____ a new era of vulnerability.
   A. motivated
   B. created
   C. discouraged

8. Social scientists have seen a _____ amount of change in marriage practices in the past fifty years.
   A. huge
   B. lavish
   C. significant

9. Body odor is only a problem if the culture defines it as such; if a person believes body odor is a problem, he or she will do something to _____ it.
   A. invalidate
   B. eradicate
   C. restore

10. Test stress may _____ itself in distinct physical symptoms, such as a speeded-up heart rate, sweaty palms, and clouded thinking.
    A. present
    B. flaunt
    C. mask

Competency 2.2	Word Choice Skills
Skill Tested	Recognizes commonly confused or misused words or phrases

The Skill

This item tests your ability to distinguish among words or phrases that are commonly misused or confused. Words that are often misused or confused may sound alike or look alike, but their spellings or meanings are different.

For example, **affect** and **effect** sound alike and are almost spelled alike; however, they have different meanings.

Affect can be a verb meaning "to influence."
Your speech affected me deeply.

Effect is a noun meaning "result."
The effect of my friends is strong.

Another trouble spot is confusing **it's** and **its**. **It's** is the contracted form of "it is," while **its** is a possessive pronoun.

It's a perfect day to go to the beach.

The sea gull caught a fish in **its** beak.

Here is a list of words most often confused:

a, an	hole, whole	than, then
accept, except	idea, ideal	there, their, they're
alot, a lot	its, it's	to, two, too
already, all ready	lose, loose	through, threw
among, between	passed, past	thorough, though
are, our	personnel, personal	waist, waste
breath, breathe	principle, principal	weather, whether
capital, capitol	quit, quite, quiet	were, where
cite, site, sight	receipt, recipe	who, whose
choose, chose	right, rite, write	your, you're
coarse, course	rain, reign, rein	
complement, compliment	sense, since	
explicit, implicit	set, sit	
good, well	should of, should have	

The Test Question

The test question consists of a sentence containing three underlined words or phrases. You must choose the answer that corrects an error in one of the underlined portions.

SECTION 2 ◆ DIAGNOSTIC: CONFUSED OR MISUSED WORDS/PHRASES

Choose the most effective word or phrase within the context suggested by the sentence(s). If no error exists, choose "No change is necessary." When you are done, check your work with the answers immediately following the diagnostic. Even if you get a perfect score here, go ahead and complete the exercises in this section; they are designed to help build confidence and to give you practice for future test success.

1. At the Halloween party, the host, who wore a ghost <u>costume</u>, told a scary <u>tale</u>

A
B

   about a <u>statute</u> that came alive and wreaked havoc on a small town in Idaho.

C

   A. custom
   B. tail
   C. statue
   D. No change is necessary.

2. Mark was able to <u>bear</u> the discomfort of getting a tattoo of an American eagle

A

   on his back, but after it was done, he was not <u>quite</u> sure <u>whether</u> he liked it.

B
C

   A. bare
   B. quiet
   C. weather
   D. No change is necessary.

3. The children were <u>all together</u> surprised when they received <u>their</u> <u>presents</u>.

A
B
C

   A. altogether
   B. they're
   C. presence
   D. No change is necessary.

4. The <u>council</u> <u>ascented</u> to <u>proceed</u> with its plans.

A
B
C

   A. counsel
   B. assented
   C. precede
   D. No change is necessary.

5. After his <u>fourth</u> movie, the actor knew that he had a <u>flair</u> for his craft because

A
B

   he was receiving offers for better <u>rolls</u>.

C

   A. forth
   B. flare
   C. roles
   D. No change is necessary.

6. As Joy began her <u>decent</u> from the <u>peak</u> of the mountain, she could see the

A
B

   <u>whole</u> canyon below her.

C

   A. descent
   B. peek
   C. hole
   D. No change is necessary.

7. The writer was so stubborn that he would not follow the editor's suggestion to

    <u>alter</u> the end of the book so that the hero would make it <u>through</u> enemy territory
    A   B

and successfully cross the <u>border</u>.
                                   C

    A. altar
    B. threw
    C. boarder
    D. No change is necessary.

Answers and Explanations to Diagnostic: Confused or Misused Words/Phrases

1. Answer   C

A "statue" is a three-dimensional form that is sculpted, modeled, or carved in a material such as clay, bronze, stone, or wood. A "statute" is an established rule or law.

False choices
    A "Custom" is a practice followed by a particular group or region; a "costume" is an outfit or disguise.
    B A "tale" is a story, and a "tail" is a posterior part of an animal.

2. Answer   D

In the context of the sentence, "bear" means to endure while "bare" means naked.

False choices
    B "Quite" means to the greatest extent. "Quiet" is free of noise.
    C "Whether" means if; "weather" refers to conditions such as temperature, wind, clouds, and rain.

3. Answer   A

"Altogether" means entirely. "All together" means at the same time.

False choices
    B "Their" is the possessive form of they used as a modifier before a noun. "They're" is the contracted form of "they are."
    C "Presents" are gifts. "Presence" means the immediate proximity of someone or something or the state of being present.

4. Answer   B

"Assented" means agreed. "Ascent" means a climb.

False choices
    A "Counsel" is to advise, whereas "council" is a group that advises.
    C "Proceed" means to go forward; "precede" is to come before.

5. Answer   C

A "role" is the part of a character in a play. A "roll" has many definitions, such as a list of names or a small rounded form of bread.

False choices
    A "Fourth" is something that follows third in order, place, rank, or quality. "Forth" means to move forward.
    B "Flair" means a natural talent; a "flare" is a device for producing a bright light.

6. Answer   A

"Descent" means the act of moving downward. "Decent" means appropriate, in good taste.

False choices

   B A "peak" is the highest point of a mountain; "peek" means a brief look.

   C "Whole" means all, the full extent, and "hole" is a hollowed place in something solid.

7. Answer   D

No change is necessary.

False choices

   A "Alter" means to change; "altar" is a platform where religious ceremonies are enacted.

   B "Through" is a preposition meaning in one side and out the other. "Threw" is the past tense of the verb "throw," which means to hurl through the air.

   C A "border" is a part that forms the edge of something. A "boarder" is one who pays a fee for room and board.

SECTION 2 ◆ EXERCISES: CONFUSED OR MISUSED WORDS/PHRASES

DIRECTIONS: *Choose the most effective word or phrase within the context suggested by the sentence(s).*

 ### Test Taking Hint

Pay particular attention to the way these questions are made. Notice that there are three words underlined in the stem of the question. Each of these underlined words is labeled in alphabetical order "A" through "C." Notice that each of the answer options is also labeled "A" through "C." The labels in the question are directly matched to the answer options. So the option labeled "A" is only going to replace the word in the question labeled "A." The same is true for "B" and "C." This labeling system means that word "A" does not have any-thing to do with option "B" or "C." Just be aware of this as you take the test.

---

1. All students are <u>supposed to</u> get <u>advice</u> from a counselor before pre-registration
                   A   B

    <u>has past</u>.
      C

    A. suppose to
    B. advise
    C. has passed

2. The <u>desserts</u> looked so <u>good</u> that I could not choose <u>among</u> the chocolate fudge brownie
           A   B   C
    and the strawberry cheesecake.

    A. deserts
    B. well
    C. between

3. I like to <u>sit</u> the TV remote control <u>right</u> next to my chair so I always know <u>where</u> it is.
              A   B   C

    A. set
    B. rite
    C. were

4. At the masquerade party, Derek received a large <u>amount</u> of <u>compliments</u> on his
                                                    A   B

   imaginative <u>costume</u>.
                  C

   A. number
   B. complements
   C. custom

5. I would like to take the Introduction to Psychology <u>course</u>, but <u>it's</u> <u>all ready</u> full.
                                                          A   B   C

   A. coarse
   B. its
   C. already

6. <u>Stationary</u> sales have decreased <u>since</u> many people use e-mail to <u>write</u> to each other.
        A   B   C

   A. Stationery
   B. sense
   C. right

7. You <u>should have</u> tried to <u>except</u> <u>their</u> point of view.
            A   B   C

   A. should of
   B. accept
   C. they're

8. When I graduated from high school, my <u>principal</u> told me to always keep my <u>ideal</u> in <u>site</u>.
                                            A   B   C

   A. principle
   B. idea
   C. sight

9. Watching <u>too</u> many violent movies can <u>effect</u> <u>your</u> attitude toward violence.
                A   B   C

   A. to
   B. affect
   C. you're

10. <u>A lot</u> of people <u>loose</u> money <u>through</u> bad investments.
        A   B   C

   A. alot
   B. lose
   C. though

Chapter 3: Sentence Skills

SECTION 1 ◆ MODIFIERS	
Competency 3.1	Sentence Structure Skills
Skill Tested	**Uses modifiers correctly**

The Skill

This item tests your ability to correctly place modifiers next to the word(s) they modify. A *modifier* is a word or phrase that describes another word. When the modifier is in the wrong position in the sentence, it is misplaced. A modifier should be placed as close as possible to the word it modifies.

The two types of errors using modifiers are the **dangling modifier** and the **misplaced modifier**.

The **dangling modifier** is a word or group of words that has nothing to describe, as in the following sentence:

Typing all night, the paper was finished in time.

Typing all night is a phrase that is supposed to describe another word in the sentence. Who was typing the paper? The phrase does not modify **the paper** because the paper cannot type itself. Here is the correct sentence in which the modifier describes **I**:

Typing all night, I finished the paper in time.

The **misplaced modifier** is a word or group of words that is simply in the wrong place (*misplaced*) in the sentence. Other words separate it from the word it is describing, as in this sentence:

Bob takes a towel to the gym that is ragged and stained.

The phrase **that is ragged and stained** is the misplaced modifier. The way the sentence is written, the gym is ragged and stained. Even though you may know what the writer intended, the sentence is still wrong. The towel is ragged and stained.

Bob takes a ragged and stained towel to the gym.

The Test Question

You will be given three versions of one sentence; two will have misplaced modifiers. You must choose the sentence in which the modifier is correctly placed.

    A. Catching the can of soda before it fell over, a messy spill was avoided.
    B. Catching the can of soda before it fell over, Jose avoided a messy spill.
    C. Catching the can of soda avoided a messy spill.

The modifier **Catching the can of soda before it fell over** is correctly placed in sentence B. Jose is the person who caught the can of soda.

Choose the sentence in which the modifier is correctly placed. When you are done, check your work with the answers immediately following the diagnostic. Even if you get a perfect score here, go ahead and complete the exercises in this section; they are designed to help build confidence and to give you practice for future test success.

1.
   A. Arriving home after two years of service in the navy, Turrell's family gave a surprise party for him.
   B. Arriving home after two years of service in the navy, Turrell was given a surprise party.
   C. Arriving home after two years of service in the navy, a big surprise party was given for Turrell.

2.
   A. While I was walking on the beach, a fishing boat came too close to shore and got stuck in the sand.
   B. While walking on the beach, a fishing boat came too close to shore and got stuck in the sand.
   C. While walking on the beach, a fishing boat got stuck in the sand because it came too close to shore.

3.
   A. Being sleepy, my sociology project did not get finished.
   B. Because I was sleepy, I did not finish my sociology project.
   C. Because of sleepiness, my sociology project did not get finished.

4.
   A. We ate a bucket, which were too spicy for me, of barbequed wings during the game.
   B. We ate a bucket of barbequed wings during the game, which were too spicy for me.
   C. During the game, we ate a bucket of barbequed wings, which were too spicy for me.

5.
   A. The pen ran out of ink that I just bought to write my essay.
   B. To write my essay, the pen ran out of ink that I just bought.
   C. The pen that I just bought to write my essay ran out of ink.

6.
   A. The palmetto bug that startled the students flew onto the teacher's head.
   B. The palmetto bug flew onto the teacher's head that startled the students.
   C. Onto the teacher's head that startled the students flew the palmetto bug.

7.
   A. The bottle of milk that was grabbed by the baby was hungry.
   B. The baby that was hungry grabbed the bottle of milk.
   C. The baby grabbed the bottle of milk that was hungry.

Answers and Explanations to Diagnostic: Modifiers

For each of these questions, to avoid needless repetition of information, only the correct option is explained. The type of error is also identified: dangling modifier or misplaced modifier.

1. Answer   B   Dangling Modifier
The modifier "Arriving home after two years of service" should be followed by the word it modifies, which is Turrell. In Choice A, the modifier modifies Turrell's family. In Choice C, the modifier is placed before "a surprise party," which indicates that the surprise party arrived home.

2. Answer   A   Dangling Modifier
The modifier "While I was walking on the beach" correctly identifies who was walking. In the false choices, it seems that the fishing boat was walking on the beach.

3. Answer   B   Dangling Modifier
The correct choice, "Because I was sleepy," identifies the person who did not finish the sociology project. In false choices A and C, the sociology project follows the modifier, making it seem as if the sociology project was sleepy.

4. Answer   C   Misplaced Modifier
The modifier "which were too spicy for me" must follow the words it modifies, "barbequed wings." In false choice A the modifier modifies "bucket," and in false choice C it modifies "game."

5. Answer   C   Misplaced Modifier
The modifier "that I just bought" must modify "pen." In the false choices, the modifier modifies "ink."

6. Answer   A   Misplaced Modifier
"That startled the students" is the modifier, which modifies "palmetto bug." In the false choices, the modifier modifies "head."

7. Answer   B   Misplaced Modifier
The modifier "that was hungry" modifies "baby," not "the bottle of milk" as in the false choices.

SECTION 1 ◆ EXERCISES: MODIFIERS

DIRECTIONS: *Choose the sentence in which the modifier is correctly placed.*

1.
   A. Having entered the gym, the screams of the crowd were overwhelming.
   B. Having entered the gym, the crowd's screams overwhelmed me.
   C. Having entered the gym, I was overwhelmed by the screams of the crowd.

2.
   A. To revise my paper, I need to rewrite it.
   B. To revise my paper, it needs to be rewritten.
   C. To revise my paper, rewriting is necessary.

3.
   A. While watching a movie on television, my friend called and asked me to go out.
   B. While I was watching a movie on television, my friend called and asked me to go out.
   C. My friend called and asked me to go out while watching a movie on television.

4.
   A. My dad, at the age of five, taught me to ride my bicycle without training wheels.
   B. My dad taught me to ride my bicycle without training wheels when I was five.
   C. At the age of five, my dad taught me to ride my bicycle without training wheels.

5.

    A. Riding on the escalator, I caught the heel of my shoe on one of the steps.

    B. Riding on the escalator, the heel of my shoe got caught on one of the steps.

    C. The heel of my shoe riding on the escalator got caught on one of the steps.

6.

    A. As a foreign student studying in the U.S., my mother does not get the chance to see me very often.

    B. My mother does not get the chance to see me very often as a foreign student studying in the U.S.

    C. As a foreign student studying in the U.S., I do not get the chance to see my mother very often.

7.

    A. After writing a check and signing the documents, we now owned the house.

    B. After writing a check and signing the documents, the house was now ours.

    C. The house, after writing a check and signing the documents, was now ours.

8.

    A. While fishing on the ocean with my friend, a barracuda jumped onto the boat.

    B. A barracuda jumped onto the boat while I was fishing on the ocean with my friend.

    C. A barracuda jumped onto the boat while fishing on the ocean with my friend.

9.

    A. Removing the label at the neckline, the T-shirt felt more comfortable.

    B. The T-shirt felt more comfortable at the neckline after removing the label.

    C. After I removed the label at the neckline, the T-shirt felt more comfortable.

10.

    A. Having run the red light, I got a ticket from the police officer.

    B. Having run the red light, the police officer gave me a ticket.

    C. The police officer, having run the red light, gave me a ticket.

SECTION 2 ◆ COORDINATION AND SUBORDINATION

Competency 3.2	Sentence Structure Skills
Skill Tested	**Uses coordination and subordination effectively**

The Skill

This item tests your ability to combine sentences effectively by using coordination and subordination. Coordination and subordination are both methods of combining ideas. A sentence using coordination is called a compound sentence; a sentence using subordination is called a complex sentence.

Coordination

Coordination is the combination of two simple sentences, also called independent clauses. The ideas that are joined are equal in that they are both complete sentences. Also, the ideas expressed in each of the sentences are related. Two independent clauses can be coordinated in three different ways. In the explanation that follows, you will see the same sentence combined by each of the three methods.

Method 1

| Independent clause | + | , coordinating conjunction | + | independent clause. |

Sandra is training to run a ten-mile race on the beach, **so** she is running every evening to build up endurance.

In this method, you add a comma and a coordinating conjunction to combine the two simple sentences. There are seven **coordinating conjunctions**, which are simple to remember by using this mnemonic: FANBOYS. Each letter represents one of the coordinating conjunctions.

for	to give a reason
and	to add
nor	to give a negative choice
but	to show a contrast
or	to show a choice
yet	to show a contrast
so	to give a result

Method 2

| Independent clause | + | ; | + | independent clause. |

Sandra is training to run a ten-mile race on the beach; she is running every evening to build up endurance.

To use this method, place a semicolon between the two independent clauses.

Method 3

| Independent clause | + | ; conjunctive adverb, | + | independent clause. |

Sandra is training to run a ten-mile race on the beach; therefore, she is running every evening to build up endurance.

Method 3 combines the two independent clauses by using an appropriate conjunctive adverb. Conjunctive adverbs are words that work as transitions from one sentence to the next. They help you make the connection between the two ideas. The punctuation of this sentence is different from the others. After the first independent clause, place a semicolon before the appropriate conjunctive adverb. Follow the conjunctive adverb with a comma and add the other independent clause.

The following is a list of some of the most commonly used conjunctive adverbs and their meanings.

in addition also furthermore moreover	to add

however in contrast	to contrast
therefore consequently thus as a result	to give a result
meanwhile then	to show time
on the other hand in contrast	to give an alternative

Subordination

Subordination is the joining of two ideas that are so closely related that one completely depends upon the other to make sense. The type of sentence that is formed from this combination is called a complex sentence. To use subordination, follow these steps:

1. Start with two independent clauses that express ideas that are closely related.
2. Decide which independent clause you want to make more important.
3. Add an appropriate subordinating conjunction to the other independent clause.

Let's change the example sentence already used in this section:

Original: Sandra is in training for the ten-mile run on the beach, so she is running every evening to build up her endurance.

Revised using subordination: Sandra is running every evening to build up her endurance **because** she is in training for the ten-mile race on the beach.

This formation of the sentence follows this model:

$$\boxed{\text{Independent clause}} + \boxed{\text{subordinating conjunction}} + \boxed{\text{independent clause.}}$$

When you add a subordinating conjunction to an independent clause, you have changed that clause to a dependent clause. It is no longer considered a complete sentence.

$$\boxed{\text{Independent clause}} + \boxed{\text{dependent clause.}}$$

A comma is used to punctuate a complex sentence only if the dependent clause begins the sentence:

$$\boxed{\text{Dependent clause,}} + \boxed{\text{independent clause.}}$$

Here is a list of the most commonly used subordinating conjunctions:

after	even if	since	whenever
although	if	so that	where
as	if only	than	whereas
as if	in order that	though	wherever
as soon as	now that	unless	
as much as	once	while	
as though	provided that	whether	
because	rather than	when	

Another way to create a complex sentence is to use one of the relative pronouns: who, whom, which, that, whoever, whomever. The dependent clause that you make will modify one of the words in the sentence.

Sandra, **who runs every evening to build up her endurance**, is training to run a ten-mile race on the beach.

Sandra is in training for the ten-mile race **that is going to be held on the beach.**

The Test Question
You can be tested on your ability to use subordination and coordination in two different ways:

1. You may be given a sentence from which a conjunction has been omitted. You must choose the most effective word or phrase suggested by the context of the sentence.
2. You may be given three versions of the same sentence and asked to pick the one that best expresses the relationship between ideas within the sentence.

SECTION 2 ◆ DIAGNOSTIC: COORDINATION AND SUBORDINATION

For each of the following questions, choose the most effective word or phrase within the context suggested by the sentence. When you are done, check your work with the answers immediately following the diagnostic. Even if you get a perfect score here, go ahead and complete the exercises in this section; they are designed to help build confidence and to give you practice for future test success.

1. Matt was going to major in electrical engineering, _____ when he found out the number of math courses he would have to take, he changed his mind.
   A. or
   B. for
   C. nor
   D. but

2. My mother, _____ was the oldest of five siblings, had to quit school and get a job to help the family financially.
   A. which
   B. who
   C. that
   D. what

3. The homes in our neighborhood were badly damaged from the hurricane last year; _____, this year we bought hurricane shutters for all of our windows.
   A. next
   B. likewise
   C. on the other hand
   D. consequently

4. _____ the lines to buy tickets for the movie at Muvico were so long, Dad used the automated ticket machine.
   A. Although
   B. Unless
   C. Because
   D. Until

5.

    A. Since I had not played football in high school and spent most of my time in practice, I would have ended up going out and getting in trouble.

    B. As long as I had not played football in high school and spent most of my time in practice, I would have ended up going out and getting in trouble.

    C. If I had not played football in high school and spent most of my time in practice, I would have ended up going out and getting in trouble.

6.

    A. Danielle has been able to rise above her drug addiction and financial instability although it is an ongoing battle for her.

    B. Danielle has been able to rise above her drug addiction and financial instability because it is an ongoing battle for her.

    C. Danielle has been able to rise above her drug addiction and financial instability so that it is an ongoing battle for her.

7.

    A. I do not have a car, but I have to depend on other people and public transportation to get me where I need to go.

    B. I do not have a car, so I have to depend on other people and public transportation to get me where I need to go.

    C. I do not have a car, or I have to depend on other people and public transportation to get me where I need to go.

Answers and Explanations to Diagnostic: Coordination and Subordination

For each of the following questions, the correct definition for each transitional phrase is provided, and the correct relationship between ideas is explained; however, only the definitions for the false choices are given.

1. Answer   D

But: contrast. The first independent clause tells what Matt had planned to study. The second independent clause sets up the contrast between his original plan and his decision to change that plan.

    A. Or   choice between two persons, places, things, or ideas

    B. For   reason/cause

    C. Nor   negative choice

2. Answer   B

Who: relative pronoun used at the beginning of the adjective clause "who was the oldest of five siblings." "Who" is the word used to refer to a person.

    A. Which   relative pronoun used at the beginning of an adjective clause to describe a place, thing, or animal

    C. That   relative pronoun used at the beginning of an adjective clause to describe a place, thing, or animal; can be used to refer to people in general

    D. What   pronoun meaning "that which"

3. Answer   D

Consequently: result. The second independent clause gives the result of the first.

    A. Next   transition word meaning immediately following, as in time, order, or sequence

    B. Likewise   transition word meaning similarly, in the same way

    C. On the
        other hand   transition phrase indicating contrast

4. Answer   C

Because: reason. The dependent clause that begins the sentence gives the reason for the independent clause that follows it.

    A. Although   subordinating conjunction indicating contrast

    B. Unless   subordinating conjunction meaning except on the condition that

    D. Until   subordinating conjunction meaning before or up to the time that

5. Answer   C

If: cause and effect. The dependent clause that begins the sentence sets up the condition necessary for a result.

    A. Since   subordinating conjunction indicating reason

    B. As long as subordinating conjunction meaning during the time that or on the condition that

6. Answer   A

Although: contrast meaning regardless of the fact that. The dependent clause that follows the independent clause sets up a contrast.

    B. Because   subordinating conjunction indicating a reason for something

    C. So that   subordinating conjunction meaning in order that

7. Answer   B

So: result or effect. The first independent clause establishes the cause; the second independent clause is the effect.

    A. But   coordinating conjunction meaning however

    C. Or   coordinating conjunction indicating a choice

SECTION 2 ◆ EXERCISES: COORDINATION AND SUBORDINATION

DIRECTIONS: *For each of the following questions, choose the most effective word or phrase within the context suggested by the sentence.*

    1. _____ having a baby can be a joyous event for a couple, it can cause a strain on their relationship.

        A. Although

        B. Whenever

        C. Besides

        D. If

2. Our class plan to study Spanish at the University of Seville during the summer; _____, we intend to see the famous historical sites.
   A. therefore
   B. finally
   C. conversely
   D. moreover

3. Surfing the Internet has increased in popularity among teens and young adults, _____ they spend less time watching television.
   A. yet
   B. nor
   C. so
   D. or

4. The telemarketing company is looking for a person _____ can work on weekends.
   A. which
   B. who
   C. that
   D. what

5. Andrea's job as a nurse's aid at the hospital is very demanding; _____, she can take only two college classes each semester.
   A. however
   B. therefore
   C. finally
   D. certainly

DIRECTIONS: *For each of the following questions, choose the sentence that expresses the thought most clearly and effectively and that has no error in structure.*

6.
   A. Because the bus was late, I missed my first class.
   B. Although the bus was late, I missed my first class.
   C. While the bus was late, I missed my first class.

7.
   A. Whereas I receive my two-year degree from the community college, I plan to transfer to a four-year university.
   B. Since I receive my two-year degree from the community college, I plan to transfer to a four-year university.
   C. After I receive my two-year degree from the community college, I plan to transfer to a four-year university.

8.
   A. The pilot who is flying this airplane served in the Air Force before becoming a commercial pilot.
   B. The pilot which is flying this airplane served in the Air Force before becoming a commercial pilot.
   C. The pilot that is flying this airplane served in the Air Force before becoming a commercial pilot.

9.
   A. In my reading class, I have to learn fifty new words every week where I can improve my vocabulary.
   B. In my reading class, I have to learn fifty new words every week so that I can improve my vocabulary.
   C. In my reading class, I have to learn fifty new words every week since I can improve my vocabulary.

10.
   A. My friends and I like to eat fast food whereas most of the choices are high in calories.
   B. My friends and I like to eat fast food so that most of the choices are high in calories.
   C. My friends and I like to eat fast food even though most of the choices are high in calories.

SECTION 3 ◆ PARALLEL STRUCTURE

| Competency 3.3 | Sentence Structure Skills |
| Skill Tested | **Recognizes parallel structure** |

The Skill

This item tests your ability to recognize parallel structure. When you place two or more words, phrases, or clauses together and connect them, each of those words, phrases, or clauses should be in the same grammatical form. An easy way to visualize this skill is to think of ideas as running on tracks, like a train. The tracks must be even, equal, parallel to each other to avoid a wreck. This balance occurs through repetition of the grammatical pattern. Read the following examples:

| Not Parallel | I love thinking, writing, and to speak. |
| Parallel | I love thinking, writing, and speaking. |

In the first sentence, three items are listed after the verb "love." The grammatical pattern of the third one, "to speak," is different from the first and second ones. Change "to speak" to "speaking" so that all are in the same form.

Here are examples of sentences that correctly use parallel words, phrases, or clauses:

| Parallel words: | Writing includes **drafting, editing,** and **revising.** |
| | At the mall, we bought **shoes, shirts,** and **sneakers.** |

Parallel phrases:	Writing enables students **to record information, to learn concepts,** and **to share knowledge.**
	Watching a concert in person is more fun than **watching a concert on television.**
	This summer, I will either **visit my relatives in North Carolina** or **take classes at my college.**

| Parallel clauses: | Many students learn to write well **because they want knowledge** and **because they value high grades.** |

The Test Question

You can be tested on your ability to recognize parallel structure in two different ways:

1. You may be given a sentence containing a blank. You must choose the correct word or phrase within the context suggested by the sentence that makes it grammatically parallel.
2. You may be given three versions of one sentence. You must choose the sentence that has no error in parallelism.

SECTION 3 ◆ DIAGNOSTIC: PARALLEL STRUCTURE

For each of the following questions, choose the sentence that has no error in structure. When you are done, check your work with the answers immediately following the diagnostic. Even if you get a perfect score here, go ahead and complete the exercises in this section; they are designed to help build confidence and to give you practice for future test success.

1.
   A. To surprise me, my husband placed all the dirty clothes in the hamper, organizing the shoes in the closet, and changed the sheets on the bed.
   B. To surprise me, my husband placed all the dirty clothes in the hamper, organized the shoes in the closet, and the sheets on the bed.
   C. To surprise me, my husband placed all the dirty clothes in the hamper, organized the shoes in the closet, and changed the sheets on the bed.

2.
   A. As she walked closer to the village, to her amazement, she could see candlelight, she could hear adults conversing, and she could sense their happiness.
   B. As she walked closer to the village, to her amazement, she could see candlelight, was hearing adults conversing, and she could sense their happiness.
   C. As she walked closer to the village, to her amazement, she could see candlelight, she could hear adults conversing, and sensing their happiness.

3.
   A. Phillipe enjoys his new job at the stadium because he can see all the games for free, meeting some of the players, and get discount tickets for family and friends.
   B. Phillipe enjoys his new job at the stadium because he can see all the games for free, meet some of the players, and discount tickets are available for family and friends.
   C. Phillipe enjoys his new job at the stadium because he can see all the games for free, meet some of the players, and get discount tickets for family and friends.

4.
   A. I broke up with my boy friend because he did not respect me, verbally abusive, and unfaithful.
   B. I broke up with my boy friend because he was disrespectful, verbally abusive, and unfaithful.
   C. I broke up with my boy friend because he was disrespectful, verbally abusive, and his unfaithful behavior.

DIRECTIONS: *For each of the following questions, choose the correct word or phrase within the context suggested by the sentence.*

5. Now that Javier is a college student, he worries about doing well on tests, _____ to class on time, and keeping up with assignments.

A. get
B. he gets
C. got
D. getting

6. The neighborhood in Detroit where I grew up has changed; the park has been converted to a zoo, my favorite gathering place has become a tattoo shop, and my neighbors _____ moved away.
   A. having
   B. they have
   C. have
   D. will have

7. I lost my volleyball scholarship because I _____ too many classes, I had a bad attitude, and I failed all my tests.
   A. missed
   B. am missing
   C. would miss
   D. miss

Answers and Explanations to Diagnostic: Parallel Structure

For each of these questions, to avoid needless repetition of information, only the correct option is explained.

1. Answer   C

At the end of each sentence is a series of verb phrases. The verbs that begin each of the phrases must be in the same verb tense, as they are in Choice C: placed, organized, and changed.

2. Answer   A

This sentence contains a series of independent clauses. Each of them should begin with "she could" and the base verb, as in Choice A: she could see the candlelight, she could hear adults conversing, and she could sense their happiness.

3. Answer   C

The series of details is contained in a dependent clause beginning with "because." The subject of that clause is "he," which is followed by the helping verb "can." These two words are not repeated in the series but are understood to apply to each word group. Each verb must be in its base form because it follows the helping verb "can." The detail that comes after each of the verbs has been formed with a direct object and a prepositional phrase.

4. Answer   B

The dependent clause that ends the sentence contains a list of words all of which must be adjectives to maintain parallel structure, as in Choice B: disrespectful, verbally abusive, and unfaithful.

5. Answer   D

To make the phrases that follow "he worries about" parallel, the verbs must be in the –ing form. Therefore, "getting" matches the verbs "doing" and "keeping."

6. Answer   C

This second part of this compound sentence contains a series of three independent clauses. In each of these clauses, the verbs must be in the present perfect tense. Each verb will contain both the present tense of have (has for singular and have for plural) and the past participle form of the verb. The correct answer, Choice C, supplies "have" to form the present perfect tense "have moved."

7. Answer   A

In this sentence, a series of clauses follows "because." Each of the clauses should be in the simple past tense to be parallel. Therefore, "missed," Choice A is correct.

SECTION 3 ◆ EXERCISES: PARALLEL STRUCTURE

DIRECTIONS: *For each of the following questions, choose the sentence that has no error in structure.*

1.
   A. Scott inserted his credit card in the slot, selected the grade of gas he wanted, and filled the gas tank.
   B. Scott inserting his credit card in the slot, selected the grade of gas he wanted, and filled the gas tank.
   C. Scott inserted his credit card in the slot, selecting the grade of gas he wanted, and filled the gas tank.

2.
   A. To plan their Saturday night at the movies, Gina and Andres look at the movie listings online, read the reviews, and they buy their tickets with a credit card.
   B. To plan their Saturday night at the movies, Gina and Andres look at the movie listings online, reading the reviews, and buying their tickets with a credit card.
   C. To plan their Saturday night at the movies, Gina and Andres look at the movie listings online, read the reviews, and buy their tickets with a credit card.

3.
   A. While studying for her psychology test, Francena had trouble concentrating because her friends were calling her, her brother's blasting stereo, and her dad mowing the lawn.
   B. While studying for her psychology test, Francena had trouble concentrating because her friends were calling her, her brother was blasting his stereo, and her dad was mowing the lawn.
   C. While studying for her psychology test, Francena had trouble concentrating because of phone calls from her friends, noise from her brother's stereo, and her dad was mowing the lawn.

4.
   A. Shiva's family follows three traditions when they enter their house: they take their shoes off, say hello to every person in the house, and hugging and kissing their elders.
   B. Shiva's family follows three traditions when they enter their house: they take their shoes off, they say hello to every person in the house, and they hug and kiss their elders.
   C. Shiva's family follows three traditions when they enter their house: taking their shoes off, say hello to every person in the house, and hugging and kissing their elders.

5.
   A. Every morning when Paulette wakes up, she brushes her teeth, takes a shower, and then she will walk the dog.
   B. Every morning when Paulette wakes up, she is brushing her teeth, takes a shower, and then will be walking the dog.
   C. Every morning when Paulette wakes up, she brushes her teeth, takes a shower, and then walks the dog.

6. Some methods students use to cheat are storing information on their cell phones, _____ answers on the inside of bottled water, and writing answers on the bottoms of their sneakers.
   A. tape
   B. taping
   C. they tape
   D. will tape

7. While taking a pleasurable swim in the ocean, Casey got stung by a Portuguese Man of War, _____ out in agony, and raced to the shore.
   A. is crying
   B. cries
   C. cried
   D. wanted to cry

8. After accumulating credit card debt I could not pay, I now pay for everything with cash and _____ a credit card for emergencies only.
   A. using
   B. used
   C. by using
   D. use

9. I am able to attend college full-time because of _____, a loan from the bank, and a monthly allowance from my parents.
   A. a tuition scholarship
   B. my ability to win a scholarship for tuition
   C. a scholarship for tuition
   D. receiving a scholarship for tuition

10. The dangers of the waves at Teahapoo, a surf spot off the coast of Tahiti, are the volume of the wave and _____.
    A. that the water is shallow
    B. the shallowness of the water
    C. shallow water
    D. water that is shallow

SECTION 4 ◆ FRAGMENTS, COMMA SPLICES, AND FUSED SENTENCES (RUN-ONS)

Competency 3.4	Sentence Structure Skills
Skills Tested	**Avoids fragments**
	Avoids comma splices
	Avoids fused sentences

The Skills

This item tests your ability to recognize three sentence errors: fragments, comma splices, and fused sentences. These errors occur when the rules of punctuation or structure are ignored or broken.

Fragments

A fragment may look like a sentence because it begins with a capital letter and ends with a period, but if you read the word group more carefully, you'll notice that the thought is incomplete. Fragments are often pieces of information that were separated from an independent clause. The most common types of fragments are as follows.

1. No verb: The old movie on television last night about an alien invasion.
   Revised: The old movie on television last night was about an alien invasion.

2. No subject: Passed the test on her first try.
   Revised: Monique passed the test on her first try.

3. Dependent clause: Because James lost his keys.
   Revised: Because James lost his keys, he could not drive home after class.

4. –ing phrase: Trying to lift the weight.
   Revised: Trying to lift the weight, Brian pulled a muscle.

5. Lists that follow the words "such as" or "for example": Such as pizza, chocolate candy, and ice cream.
   Revised: I had to give up my favorite foods when I went on a diet, such as pizza, chocolate candy, and ice cream.

Comma Splices

A comma splice is an error in which a comma by itself is used to join two independent clauses. The following sentence is an example of the comma splice and its correction.

Paul did not have his own **car, he** had to share a car with his sister.
Correction: Paul did not have his own car. He had to share a car with his sister.

Fused Sentence (Run-on)

A fused sentence consists of two independent clauses with no punctuation to indicate where the one ends and the second one begins. Read the following example and its correction.

In the summer, afternoon thunderstorms are common driving in heavy rain on the highway can be dangerous.
Correction: In the summer, afternoon thunderstorms are common. Driving in heavy rain can be treacherous.

The Test Question

You can be tested on your ability to recognize fragments, comma splices, and fused sentences in two different ways.

1. You will be given a set of ideas with one underlined portion that indicates a possible error. The error may include a sentence fragment, a comma splice, or a fused sentence. You will be asked to choose the option that corrects the underlined portion.
2. You will be given a set of ideas with three underlined portions that could contain a possible fragment, comma splice, or fused sentence. Check each one of them for possible errors.

Keep in mind the possibility that the sentence is correct.

For each of the following questions, choose the option that corrects an error in the underlined portion(s). If no error exists, choose "No change is necessary." When you are done, check your work with the answers immediately following the diagnostic. Even if you get a perfect score here, go ahead and complete the exercises in this section; they are designed to help build confidence and to give you practice for future test success.

1. When we go to the <u>mall, we</u> buy just about anything we <u>like, for example,</u> we buy

                 A   B

   clothes, hats, shoes, and <u>jewelry, anything</u> that catches our eye.

                                C

   A. mall. We
   B. like; for example,
   C. jewelry. Anything
   D. No change is necessary.

2. My grandparents and parents lived in <u>Colombia when</u> it was a safe <u>country, but</u>

                                      A   B

   this country has changed <u>dramatically, now</u> it is not safe to be anywhere outside

                                      C

   of one's own house.

   A. Colombia. When
   B. country; but
   C. dramatically. Now
   D. No change is necessary.

3. At my cousin's fifteenth birthday party, while I was dancing to a bachata song

   with a handsome <u>guest. I</u> suddenly fell to the <u>floor. When</u> I stood <u>up, I</u> saw that

                            A   B   C

   the heel of my favorite shoe had broken off completely.

   A. guest, I
   B. floor, when
   C. up; I
   D. No change is necessary.

4. I chose to attend a community <u>college, because</u> I do not <u>think that</u> I should pay

                                   A   B

   more money at a university for the same books and classes offered at the

   community <u>college. Also,</u> I can save money on gas and living expenses by living

                              C

   at home to attend school.

   A. college because
   B. think. That
   C. college, also,
   D. No change is necessary.

5. During our vacation, the weather was not very <u>cooperative it</u> rained most of the time.
   A. cooperative, it
   B. cooperative; it
   C. cooperative and, it
   D. No change is necessary.

6. As a student, I need a flexible work <u>schedule however</u> my boss schedules me to work when I have classes.
   A. schedule, however,
   B. schedule, however;
   C. schedule; however,
   D. No change is necessary.

7. If a police officer suspects that you have been driving while <u>drunk, the</u> officer has the right to pull you over and give you a breath test.
   A. drunk. The
   B. driving; the
   C. driving, and the
   D. No change is necessary.

Answers and Explanations to Diagnostic: Fragments, Comma Splices, and Fused Sentences (Run-ons)

1. Answer   B

Choice B places a semicolon after "like." This corrects the comma splice in the sentence. Two independent clauses cannot be connected with a comma alone.

False choices

  A An introductory subordinate clause is followed by a comma. Placing a period after "mall" would make the introductory subordinate clause into a fragment.

  C Placing a period after "jewelry" would create a fragment of the modifier, "anything that catches our eye."

2. Answer   C

Replacing the comma with a period and capitalizing "Now" corrects the comma splice error.

False choices

  A The subordinate clause "when it was a safe country" belongs with the independent clause that begins the sentence. The logic of the sentence is lost if that clause is placed at the beginning of the next sentence.

  B "But" is a coordinating conjunction used to join two independent clauses. The punctuation rule requires a comma before "but," not a semicolon.

3. Answer   A

Choice A corrects the fragment error in the sentence. The sentence begins with a prepositional phrase followed by a dependent clause.

False choices

  B Placing a comma after "floor" would create a comma splice error.

  C Placing a semicolon after the word "up" would create a fragment of the introductory dependent clause "When I stood up."

4. Answer   A

No comma is necessary when the dependent clause follows the independent clause.

False choices

    B   Placing a period after "think" creates a dependent clause fragment of the rest of the sentence "that I should pay more money at a university for the same books and classes offered at the community college."

    C   Placing a comma after "college" creates a comma splice.

5. Answer   B

The semicolon placed after "cooperative" corrects the fused sentence.

False choices

    A   Placing a comma after "cooperative" creates a comma splice.

    C   The comma should be placed before the coordinating conjunction, in this case "and," when used to join two independent clauses.

6. Answer   C

This choice corrects the fused sentence by adding a semicolon, a conjunctive adverb, and a comma.

False choices

    A   A comma placed after "schedule" creates a comma splice.

    B   The semicolon is misplaced; it belongs before "however," which should be followed by a comma.

7. Answer   D

This sentence is correctly punctuated.

False choices

    A   Placing a period after "drunk" makes the introductory dependent clause into a fragment.

    B   Placing a semicolon after "drunk" makes the introductory dependent clause into a fragment.

    C   Adding a comma and the word "and" to the sentence changes the sentence into a fragment.

SECTION 4 ◆ EXERCISES: FRAGMENTS, COMMA SPLICES, AND FUSED SENTENCES (RUN-ONS)

 Test Taking Hint

Remember this hint from an earlier chapter? Pay particular attention to the way these questions are made. Notice that there are three words underlined in the stem of the question. Each of these underlined words is labeled in alphabetical order "A" through "C." Notice that each of the answer options is also labeled "A" through "C." The labels in the question are directly matched to the answer options. So the option labeled "A" is only going to replace the word in the question labeled "A." The same is true for "B" and "C." This labeling system means that word "A" does not have anything to do with option "B" or "C." Just be aware of this as you take the test.

DIRECTIONS: *For each of the following questions, choose the option that corrects an error in the underlined portion(s). If no error exists, choose "No change is necessary."*

  1. Some people do not have the patience to revise their writing, so they just recopy their rough <u>draft; and</u> hand it in to the instructor.
      A. draft. And
      B. draft and

C. draft, and,
D. No change is necessary.

2. While walking on the <u>beach I</u> saw a lone sea gull with a fish hook through its jaw.
A. beach; I
B. beach. I
C. beach, I
D. No change is necessary.

3. My dial-up Internet connection was <u>slow, so</u> I switched my service to cable
A

<u>modem now</u> searching <u>online is</u> quick and easy.
B   C
A. slow; so
B. modem; now
C. online, is
D. No change is necessary.

4. Last Tuesday night, two servers did not show up at the <u>restaurant, therefore</u> I had to take on extra tables.
A. restaurant; therefore,
B. restaurant, therefore;
C. restaurant, therefore,
D. No change is necessary.

5. Because I could not catch the <u>cockroach that</u> ran under my <u>bed, I was</u> too nervous
A   B

to go to <u>sleep and</u> decided to wait up for it to come out of its hiding place.
C
A. cockroach, that
B. bed. I
C. sleep, and
D. No change is necessary.

6. Although Azaleas is a full-time college <u>student; she</u> has a <u>husband and</u> two young
A   B

children to take <u>care of, which</u> takes up much of her time.
C
A. student, she
B. husband, and
C. care of; which
D. No change is necessary.

7. I used to play basketball every night with my <u>friends studying</u> is my evening activity now that I am in college.
A. friends, studying
B. friends. Studying
C. friends, studying;
D. No change is necessary.

8. After sitting through three classes in a <u>row, I</u> get very hungry and <u>sleepy. As a result,</u> all I
   $\qquad$ A $\qquad$ B

   think about is <u>food, not</u> the content of the lectures.
   $\qquad$ C

   A. row. I
   B. sleepy, as a result;
   C. food; not
   D. No change is necessary.

9. Jon used to be very <u>skinny, but</u> since he joined a <u>gym, he</u> has put on significant muscle
   $\qquad$ A $\qquad$ B

   <u>mass, and</u> likes to wear muscle shirts to show off.
   $\qquad$ C

   A. skinny, but,
   B. gym; he
   C. mass and
   D. No change is necessary.

10. Danielle spends all the money that she earns at her job on designer clothes, shoes, and
    <u>purses, for example</u> last week she spent $350 on a pair of faded, worn-out looking jeans
    with holes cut out of the knees.
    A. purses; for example,
    B. purses, for example,
    C. purses, for example;
    D. No change is necessary.

11. I do not have a printer at <u>home, so</u> I saved my essay on a <u>disk, when</u> I tried to open the
    $\qquad$ A $\qquad$ B

    disk in the lab at <u>school, I</u> discovered that I had saved my work in a different program than
    $\qquad$ C

    the one used by the lab.
    A. home so,
    B. disk; when
    C. school. I
    D. No change is necessary.

12. Don bought a new hybrid <u>car, he</u> claims that he gets 45 miles per <u>gallon unlike</u> his old
    $\qquad$ A $\qquad$ B

    <u>car that</u> got 19 miles per gallon.
    $\qquad$ C

    A. car; he
    B. gallon; unlike
    C. car, that
    D. No change is necessary.

13. Now that my best friend has become a <u>vegetarian, she</u> does not want <u>to go to</u> any of the
    $\qquad$ A $\qquad$ B

    <u>restaurants where</u> we used to eat.
    $\qquad$ C

    A. vegetarian; she
    B. to go, to

C. restaurants, where
D. No change is necessary.

14. Whenever the people who live in the apartment above mine have a <u>party. They</u> play their music so loudly that my walls vibrate to the beat.
    A. party, they,
    B. party, they
    C. party, and they
    D. No change is necessary.

15. Every Saturday, each of the children in Tamika's family has chores <u>to do such as</u> cleaning the bathrooms, changing the sheets, and doing the laundry.
    A. to do, such as
    B. to do; such as,
    C. to do. Such as
    D. No change is necessary

16. Marcellus left his English <u>book in</u> the <u>classroom, when</u> he came back to get <u>it, the</u>
                                       A   B   C

    book was gone.
    A. book. In
    B. classroom; when
    C. it. The
    D. No change is necessary.

17. After Annabelle <u>graduates, she</u> plans to look for a nursing position in a <u>hospital rather</u>
                                      A   B

    than in a nursing <u>home, the salary</u> is better at a hospital.
                                          C

    A. graduates; she
    B. hospital. Rather
    C. home. The
    D. No change is necessary.

18. At our college, students may not withdraw from more than three <u>courses during</u> their
                                                                       A

    <u>enrollment, this</u> does not include courses dropped during the drop and add <u>period at</u> the
            B   C

    beginning of the semester when students can drop classes without penalty.
    A. courses. During
    B. enrollment; this
    C. period. At
    D. No change is necessary.

19. In order to pay for my car <u>expenses, which</u> <u>include: insurance</u>, gas, and
                                              A   B

    <u>repairs, I</u> must have a part-time job.
        C
    A. expenses; which
    B. include insurance
    C. repairs. I
    D. No change is necessary.

20. The United States culture, through images in the print and electronic media, promotes

    slimness in <u>women as</u> the <u>ideal; to</u> try to attain that <u>appearance; some</u> young women
                   A   B   C

    become anorexic.
    A. women, as
    B. ideal, to
    C. appearance, some
    D. No change is necessary.

Chapter 4: Grammar Skills

SECTION 1 ◆ STANDARD VERB FORMS	
Competency 4.1	Grammar, Spelling, Capitalization, and Punctuation Skills
Skill Tested	Uses standard verb forms

The Skill

This item tests your ability to use standard forms of regular and irregular verbs. A standard form is one that is considered correct in standard written English.

The difference between regular and irregular verb forms is that regular verbs follow specific rules to show tense whereas irregular verbs do not. Therefore, irregular verb forms must be memorized.

To prepare for this skill, you need to know the regular and irregular forms for the present tense, past tense, and past participle. The following chart shows the differences in their formations:

	Present	Past	Past Participle
Regular	-s or -es is added to the end of the verb when the subject is he, she, it, or a noun	-ed is added to the end of the verb	-ed is added to the end of the verb
Irregular	-s or -es is added to the end of the verb when the subject is he, she, it, or a noun	form must be memorized	form must be memorized

Regular and Irregular Verbs in the Present Tense

With the exception of the verb **be**, regular and irregular verbs form their present tenses in the same way. The first chart shows the forms of the regular verb **attend** in the present tense. The second chart shows the irregular verb **do** in the present tense.

	Singular Forms	Plural Forms
First person	I attend college at night.	We attend college at night.
Second person	You attend college at night.	You attend college at night.
Third person	He **attends** college at night. She **attends** college at night. The secretary **attends** college at night.	They attend college at night.

	Singular Forms	Plural Forms
First person	I do every assignment on time.	We do every assignment on time.
Second person	You do every assignment on time.	You do every assignment on time.
Third person	He **does** every assignment on time. She **does** every assignment on time. Brandon **does** every assignment on time.	They do every assignment on time.

Regular and Irregular Verbs in the Past Tense

In the past tense, regular verbs are formed by adding –ed to the end of the verb. However, irregular verb forms do not follow a specific rule and must be memorized. In the previous example, you saw how the present tense of the regular verb **attend** and the irregular verb **do** were formed. Look at how the past tense is formed for the same verbs.

Past tense of regular verb **attend**	Add –ed	attended
Past tense of irregular verb **do**	No rule	does

Regular and Irregular Verbs in the Past Participle

The past participle is used to form the present perfect and past perfect verb tenses. These verb tenses help to show the time relationship between two events. The past participles of regular verbs are formed the same way that their past tenses are formed; however, past participle forms of irregular verbs do not follow any specific rule. Therefore, you must memorize the irregular verb past participles.

The following charts show how the present perfect and past perfect tenses are formed with regular and irregular verbs.

	Formation with regular verb	Use in sentence
Present Perfect	has/have + past participle has attended, have attended	He **has attended** college since he moved to Florida.
Past Perfect	had + past participle had attended	She **had attended** a college in New Jersey before she moved to Florida.

	Formation with irregular verb	Use in sentence
Present Perfect	has/have + past participle has done, have done	He **has done** every assignment on the syllabus.
Past Perfect	had + past participle had done	She **had done** every assignment on the syllabus before it was due.

Here is a list of commonly used irregular verbs for you to study. Three forms are listed: the base form, the past tense form, and the past participle form

Base Form	Past Tense	Past Participle (following has/have/had)
be	was/were	been
become	became	become
break	broke	broken
bring	brought	brought
choose	chose	chosen
come	came	come
do	did	done
draw	drew	drawn
eat	ate	eaten
fall	fell	fallen
forget	forgot	forgotten
freeze	froze	frozen

Base Form	Past Tense	Past Participle (following has/have/had)
give	gave	given
go	went	gone
grow	grew	grown
have	had	had
hide	hid	hidden
know	knew	known
ride	rode	ridden
rise	rose	risen
run	ran	run
see	saw	seen
steal	stole	stolen
take	took	taken
tell	told	told
throw	threw	thrown
wear	wore	worn
write	wrote	written

The Test Question

You will be given a sentence with one or three underlined sections that may have an error in the use of standard verb forms. If the original sentence contains an error, you must choose the answer that corrects an error in the underlined section. If the verbs are used correctly, choose the option "No change is necessary."

SECTION 1 ◆ DIAGNOSTIC: STANDARD VERB FORMS

For each of the following questions, choose the option that corrects an error in the underlined portion(s). If no error exists, choose "No change is necessary." When you are done, check your work with the answers immediately following the diagnostic. Even if you get a perfect score here, go ahead and complete the exercises in this section; they are designed to help build confidence and to give you practice for future test success.

1. After Ashley <u>finished</u> her shopping at the mall, she could not <u>find</u> her car, and she
             A   B

   realized that it was <u>stole</u>.
                   C

   A. finish
   B. finds
   C. stolen
   D. No change is necessary.

2. Last year, I <u>come</u> to Florida to <u>study</u> and <u>gain</u> independence.
                   A   B   C

   A. came
   B. studied
   C. gaining
   D. No change is necessary.

3. Our dog <u>ran</u> into the yard during the rainstorm; when he <u>came</u> back in, he
         A   B

   <u>drug</u> in mud all over the house.
     C
   A. had ran
   B. had came
   C. dragged
   D. No change is necessary.

4. Loretta <u>had gone</u> without breakfast, so her stomach <u>be</u> rumbling all morning
            A   B

   until she <u>ate</u>.
         C
   A. had went
   B. was
   C. eat
   D. No change is necessary.

5. Allen Iverson, the well-known basketball player, <u>has</u> great power; he <u>could go</u>
                                           A   B

   anywhere he wants and <u>does</u> not have to wait to get in to restaurants,
                     C

   movies, and parties.
   A. have
   B. can go
   C. do
   D. No change is necessary.

6. Joe jumped into the lake where he <u>had swam</u> many times before, but he did not know that
   an alligator had made that same lake his new home.
   A. had swum
   B. had swimmed
   C. swum
   D. No change is necessary.

7. In London, some people <u>weeped</u> when they heard of the terrorist bombings on a bus and
   in the underground railway.
   A. weep
   B. wept
   C. wepted
   D. No change is necessary.

Answers and Explanations to Diagnostic: Standard Verb Forms

1. Answer   C
The past participle form of the verb "steal" is "stolen."

2. Answer   A
"Last year" calls for the simple past tense. "Come" must be changed to "came."

3. Answer   C
The simple past tense of the verb "drag" is "dragged," not "drug."

4. Answer   B

The verb "be" in the sentence is the base form of the verb; the sentence requires the past tense form of "be," which is "was."

5. Answer   B

The helping verb should be in the present tense, "can."

6. Answer   A

The past participle form of the verb "swim" is "swum" and it should be accompanied by "had" in this sentence.

7. Answer   B

The past form of the verb "weep" is "wept."

SECTION 1 ◆ EXERCISES: STANDARD VERB FORMS

DIRECTIONS: For each of the following questions, choose the option that corrects an error in the underlined portion(s). If no error exists, choose "No change is necessary."

1. I <u>slammed</u> on my brakes and <u>come</u> inches from being <u>hit</u> by the car that sped out of control.
      A   B   C
   A. have slammed
   B. came
   C. hitted
   D. No change is necessary.

2. While the guerillas interrogated my grandfather, my grandmother <u>took</u> all the children,
                                                           A
   <u>hid</u> them under the bed in one of the rooms, and <u>locked</u> the door.
    B   C
   A. taked
   B. hided
   C. lock
   D. No change is necessary.

3. As she <u>started</u> to climb the steps to reach the stage, Melissa <u>slipped</u> and <u>falled</u>, splashing
              A   B   C
   the cranberry juice all over our vice president's new suit.
   A. start
   B. slips
   C. fell
   D. No change is necessary.

4. As soon as I <u>had approach</u> the dark street corner, I <u>heard</u> a strange noise and then
                         A   B
   <u>felt</u> a heavy blow to the back of my head, knocking me off my bicycle.
    C
   A. had approached
   B. herd
   C. feel
   D. No change is necessary.

5. One night in the discount clothing store where I <u>worked</u>, a group of five people <u>came</u> in;
                                                              A   B
   ...asked sales associates for help, and the other two <u>stealed</u> clothing by hiding
                                                            C
   ...coats.

   ...ge is necessary.

   ...er for my two toddlers <u>was</u> late, the dog <u>dug</u> a huge hole under the fence,
                             A   B
   ...under the sink <u>bursted</u>.
                       C

   ...ge is necessary.

   ...as a ghost in her apartment: one night while we were watching television, a stack
   ...had been piled up on a bookshelf <u>flown</u> across the room, hit the wall, and
   ...he floor.

   ...nge is necessary.

   ...<u>forgotten</u> her sunscreen, so she <u>had become</u> very badly sunburned the day she
              A   B
   ...r kayak down the river.

   ...got

   ...nge is necessary.

   ...day, Jodi <u>lays</u> on the beach soaking in the sun and listening to the waves break
   along the shore.
   A. laid
   B. layed
   C. lay
   D. No change is necessary.

10. We thought we <u>had brought</u> enough food to the barbeque, but some of the relatives
                    A
    <u>took</u> such huge portions that most of the ribs and chicken <u>had been ate</u> before all the
     B   C
    guests arrived.
    A. had brung
    B. had took

It's easy to draw comparisons of *Taken to Ransom*, *The Bourne Supremacy*, or *24*, and *Hardcore*, a shocking 1979 Paul Schrader a father's search for his runaway daughter in the L.A. porn scene. But that's fine. This isn't a film that's trying to shatter the mold; on the contrary, it's playing on your familiarity with this type of story, filling it with superb action and a solitary hero who is always one step ahead even though he's fighting from behind.

C. had been eaten

D. No change is necessary.

SECTION 2 ◆ SHIFTS IN VERB TENSE

Competency 4.2	Grammar, Spelling, Capitalization, and Punctuation Skills
Skill Tested	**Avoids inappropriate shifts in verb tenses**

The Skill

This item tests your ability to recognize when verb tenses have shifted. Verb tense expresses the time frame of a piece of writing. Usually, you select one time frame as a point of reference for your discussion, such as the present or past tense. Once you have selected that tense, use it consistently. When it is necessary to change the time frame, you then shift to another verb tense. If you change the time frame unnecessarily, then you have inappropriately shifted verb tenses. Here are pointers to help you avoid verb tense shifts.

1. Keep verb tenses consistent when talking about the same time frame.

   Incorrect: We all **decided** to go to the movies, but then Jean **says** he **wants** to play miniature golf.

In this example, the sentence first uses the past tense, then unnecessarily shifts to the present. To correct the sentence, you would put both verbs in the past tense.

   Correct: We all **decided** to go to the movies, but then Jean **said** he **wanted** to play miniature golf.

2. Coordinate past actions.

Here is an instance in which a change in verb tense is necessary. Sometimes you have a sentence in which two actions occur in the past. To show that one of the actions happened before the other, use the past perfect tense for the earlier action.

   Incorrect: She **had gone** to the bookstore after she **had registered** for her classes.

   Correct: She **went** to the bookstore after she **had registered** for her classes.

The correct version shows that registering for class happened before she went to the bookstore.

Review these verb tenses to avoid inappropriate verb tense shifts.

Verb Tense	Time Frame	Example
Present	Shows an action or state of being that is now taking place or takes place on a regular basis	Anthony lifts weights every morning.
Past	Shows an action or state of being that has already happened	Anthony lifted weights every morning for the past year.
Future	Shows an action or state of being that is to come	Anthony will lift weights every morning for the next six months.
Present Perfect	Shows an action or state of being that began in the past and continues into the present	Anthony has lifted weights for five years.

| Past Perfect | Shows a past action or state of being that happened before another past action | Anthony had lifted weights for two months before he began to enjoy it. |
| Future Perfect | Shows an action or state of being that will be completed before a specific time in the future. | Anthony will have lifted weights for six years when he turns twenty-one. |

The Test Question

You will be given one or two sentences in which one or three underlined parts may have an error in verb tense. If the original sentence contains an error, you must choose the answer that corrects an error in the underlined part. If the verbs are used correctly, choose the option "No change is necessary."

SECTION 2 ◆ DIAGNOSTIC: SHIFTS IN VERB TENSE

Choose the option that corrects an error in the underlined portion(s). If no error exists, choose "No change is necessary." When you are done, check your work with the answers immediately following the diagnostic. Even if you get a perfect score here, go ahead and complete the exercises in this section; they are designed to help build confidence and to give you practice for future test success.

1. Shortboards are very fast, so they <u>gain</u> speed quickly, and when the surfer <u>made</u> a turn,
                                             A   B

   called a cutback, the board <u>slashes</u> through the wave, ripping it and creating spray.
                                 C

   A. gained
   B. makes
   C. slashed
   D. No change is necessary.

2. Gabriel Garcia Marquez <u>wrote</u> about the rural areas of Colombia and <u>describes</u> the
                                       A   B

   places and people in so much detail that the reader <u>thinks</u> he or she is there.
                                           C

   A. writes
   B. described
   C. thought
   D. No change is necessary.

3. After Rasheed Wallace <u>play</u> basketball in college for two years, he <u>got drafted</u> into the
                                       A   B

   NBA to play for Portland; six years later, he <u>was transferred</u> to the Detroit Pistons.
                                                    C

   A. played
   B. gets drafted
   C. is transferring
   D. No change is necessary.

4. Several years ago, Jamie <u>was living</u> out of his truck, which frequently <u>broke</u> down,
                                       A   B

   and eating the unwanted leftovers from customers at the restaurant where he <u>works</u>.
                                                                   C

A. is living
B. breaks
C. worked
D. No change is necessary.

5. Gonzalo likes to make people laugh, and he <u>enjoyed</u> the time they are with him.
A. was enjoying
B. would enjoy
C. enjoys
D. No change is necessary.

6. My cousin Derreck has planned his future step-by-step; so far, he <u>has completed</u> his goals of attending college and playing football.
A. complete
B. had completed
C. was completing
D. No change is necessary.

7. Dr. Mark, a physician who is on the admissions board of a prestigious medical university, <u>had activated</u> my aspiration to be a doctor because he is an African-American who has achieved success despite many setbacks in his life.
A. had been activating
B. was activating
C. has activated
D. No change is necessary.

Answers and Explanations to Diagnostic: Shifts in Verb Tense

1. Answer   B
All of the ideas in the sentence are expressed in the present tense; "made" should be changed to "makes" to correct the shift.

2. Answer   A
All of the ideas in the sentence are expressed in the present tense. "Wrote" should be changed to "writes" to correct the shift.

3. Answer   A
The verb "play" in the sentence is missing –ed to show that the verb expresses the past tense.

4. Answer   C
To correct the verb tense shift, "works" should be changed to "worked," the past tense form of the verb "work."

5. Answer   C
The correct verb form is "enjoys" because the ideas in the sentence are expressed in the present tense.

6. Answer   D
There are no verb shifts in this sentence.

7. Answer   C
The present perfect form of the verb "has activated" is required in this sentence. "Had activated" is the past perfect form.

DIRECTIONS: Choose the option that corrects an error in the underlined portion(s). If no error exists, choose "No change is necessary."

1. Whenever I take a test, I <u>become</u> so nervous that I <u>forgot</u> everything that I <u>know.</u>
                                     A   B   C
   - A. became
   - B. forget
   - C. knew
   - D. No change is necessary.

2. After being punched on the back of his head by his opponent, the ice hockey player
   <u>fell</u> onto his face on the ice and <u>suffered</u> a broken neck; right after it happened, the
    A   B
   coach <u>suspends</u> the opponent.
            C
   - A. falls
   - B. is suffering
   - C. suspended
   - D. No change is necessary.

3. A woman <u>is trying</u> to pay for eight hundred dollars worth of household items at a
                    A
   discount store with a counterfeit million dollar bill, but the cashier <u>alerted</u> the
                                                             B
   manager, who <u>called</u> the police.
                C
   - A. tried
   - B. alerts
   - C. had called
   - D. No change is necessary.

4. Every day before I leave for school, I feed the dog and then <u>am taking</u> him for a walk.
   - A. would take
   - B. took
   - C. take
   - D. No change is necessary.

5. When Michael gets his college degree, he <u>worked</u> as an accountant in his father's company.
   - A. does work
   - B. will work
   - C. would work
   - D. No change is necessary.

6. When Carlos <u>has flown</u> his first solo flight as a pilot, he <u>forgot</u> his flight plan,
                          A   B
   <u>entered</u> the airspace of the wrong airport, and had to call his instructor to help him get back.
     C

A. flew
B. was forgetting
C. has entered
D. No change is necessary.

7. Bruce <u>started</u> to wash his truck after the rain had stopped.
A. had started
B. will start
C. is starting
D. No change is necessary.

8. While Mark <u>sleeps</u>, his younger brother threw a glass of cold water on him.
A. is sleeping
B. was sleeping
C. would be sleeping
D. No change is necessary.

9. If I <u>have seen</u> William tomorrow, I will tell him about our plans for the weekend.
A. did see
B. would see
C. see
D. No change is necessary.

10. Suzanne <u>does not work</u> at the bakery anymore; she <u>finds</u> a new job at a clothing store
                A   B
that she <u>likes</u> better.
           C
A. did not work
B. found
C. would like
D. No change is necessary.

SECTION 3 ◆ SUBJECT AND VERB AGREEMENT

Competency 4.3	Grammar, Spelling, Capitalization, and Punctuation Skills
Skill Tested	**Maintains agreement between subject and verb**

The Skill
This item tests your ability to identify and correct an error in subject-verb agreement when the subject is **simple** or **compound**. The subject of a sentence is the person, thing, idea, or place that is the topic of the statement. The simple subject is the subject without any modifiers. A compound subject is two or more simple subjects joined by the word "and."

Example of simple subject: The well-built, muscular **athlete** plays on his high school football team.

Athlete is the simple subject of the sentence.

Example of compound subject: The steamed **vegetables** and grilled **salmon** are healthy food choices.

The verb tells what the subject is or does. It must agree in number with its subject. Like subjects, verbs can be singular or plural in form. (You may want to go back to the section on regular and irregular verb forms to review the formation of verbs in the present, past, and past participle forms.)

Here is the sentence used to show a simple subject. Notice how the verb, "plays," agrees with the subject, "athlete."

> The well-built, muscular **athlete** <u>plays</u> on his high school football team.

Study these sentence structures in which subject-verb agreement errors sometimes occur.

1. Compound subjects
In a sentence with a compound subject, use a plural verb. In the sentence below, "are" is the plural form of the verb "be."

> The steamed **vegetables** and grilled **salmon** <u>are</u> healthy food choices.

Sometimes a subject looks like it is compound, but actually both words describe one person, place, thing, or idea, as in this sentence:

> My best **friend** and **husband** <u>loves</u> me very much.

Also, certain foods may look like two subjects but are actually considered one:

> **Peanut butter and jelly** <u>tastes</u> delicious on a bagel.

2. Inverted word order
Inverted word order occurs when the verb comes before the subject. Inverted means that the words are not placed in the basic subject first, verb next order. This happens in these situations:

Question	<u>Is</u> **Melissa** in school right now?
	<u>Are</u> **you** taking the test today?
Here/There + Be verb	Here <u>are</u> your **keys**.
	There <u>is</u> a **fly** in my soup.

3. Words that come between subjects and verbs
Prepositional phrases often come between a subject and a verb in the sentence. Neither a subject nor a verb will be found in a prepositional phrase. A prepositional phrase begins with a preposition and ends with a noun or pronoun. Some common prepositions are:

of	into	without
in	about	within
to	like	during
for	between	toward
on	after	off
with	through	upon
at	over	among
by	under	around
from	against	across
as	before	behind

Example: The **shows** *on television during the summer* <u>are</u> poor replacements for my favorites.

In this sentence, two prepositional phrases come between the subject and the verb: "on television" and "during the summer."

4. Indefinite pronouns
Indefinite pronouns are words that replace nouns, like other pronouns do; however, they do not specify the nouns that they are replacing. Some indefinite pronouns take singular verbs and others take plural verbs.

Example: **Everyone** <u>thinks</u> about the future once in a while.
  Each of the dogs at the pound <u>wants</u> a home.
  Some of the best beaches in the United States <u>are</u> in Florida.

Here is a chart for your review.

Singular or Plural	Indefinite Pronoun		

Always singular	Body words:
	  anybody
	  everybody
	  nobody
	  somebody
	
	  each
	  every
		Thing words:
		  anything
		  everything
		  nothing
		  something
		
		  either
		  neither
			One words:
			  anyone
			  everyone
			  no one
			  someone
			  one
			  another

Always plural	both few many others several		
Singular or plural depending on the context	some any none all more most		

The Test Question
You will be given a sentence with three underlined parts, which may contain a subject-verb agreement error. If the original sentence contains an error, you must choose the answer that corrects the error in the underlined portion. If the sentence is correct, choose "No change is necessary."

SECTION 3 ◆ DIAGNOSTIC: SUBJECT AND VERB AGREEMENT

In each of the following questions, choose the option that corrects an error in the underlined portion(s). If no error exists, choose "No change is necessary." When you are done, check your work with the answers immediately following the diagnostic. Even if you get a perfect score here, go ahead and complete the exercises in this section; they are designed to help build confidence and to give you practice for future test success.

1. Under the stack of papers and books on my desk <u>is</u> my homework assignment, but my wallet
                                                    A
   as well as my driver's license <u>are</u> missing, and my friends <u>expect</u> me to drive to school today.
                                   B   C

   A. are
   B. is
   C. expects
   D. No change is necessary.

2. There <u>is</u> some chips on the kitchen counter, and other snacks <u>are</u> in the cabinet;
       A   B

   also, if anyone <u>wants</u> soda, we only have cola.
                     C

   A. are
   B. is
   C. want
   D. No change is necessary.

3. At graduation, the audience <u>disrespect</u> the speaker by talking during his speech;
                              A

   no one <u>seems</u> to dignify the event or <u>shows</u> respect for the people being honored.
             B   C

   A. disrespects
   B. seem
   C. show
   D. No change is necessary.

4. Neither your ear mitts nor your knit cap <u>are</u> warm enough to keep your head warm
                                     A

   while you are in Alaska, so you should buy a fake fur hat that <u>covers</u> your ears;
                                        B

   a warm pair of boots <u>is</u> another item you should take with you.
                   C

   A. is
   B. cover
   C. are
   D. No change is necessary.

5. A carrying case and an A/C adaptor <u>are</u> included with your portable DVD player;
                               A

   not only do you get these items, but for no extra charge <u>are</u> the remote control and
                                            B

   headphones, so the only thing left to buy <u>are</u> batteries.
                           C

   A. is
   B. is
   C. is
   D. No change is necessary.

6. One of my favorite television shows <u>is</u> *CSI Las Vegas* because Grissom's
                               A

   team <u>works</u> so well together, and the crimes <u>are</u> difficult for me to figure out.
         B   C

   A. are
   B. work
   C. is
   D. No change is necessary.

7. Every meal at our favorite Thai restaurant <u>is</u> not only delicious to eat, but also
                                                A

   beautiful to look at; every entrée <u>have</u> a unique presentation with vegetables that
                                                         B

   <u>are</u> cut into shapes of leaves and flowers.
   C
   A. are
   B. has
   C. is
   D. No change is necessary.

Answers and Explanations to Diagnostic: Subject and Verb Agreement

1. Answer   B

The subject of the clause after "but" is "wallet," which is singular. Don't be fooled by thinking "as well as" is the same as "and."

False choices

   A   The sentence begins with a series of prepositional phrases and, therefore, does not follow the usual subject-verb sentence pattern. The subject and verb are inverted; in other words, the subject comes after the verb. "My homework assignment" is the subject, so the verb must be singular, not plural.

   C   The subject of the verb "expect" is plural ("friends"), so the verb must be in the third person plural form.

2. Answer   A

The word "there" does not function as a subject. Therefore, in this sentence, the subject and verb are inverted. The subject is "chips," so to agree, the verb must be the plural "are."

False choices

   B   The subject "snacks" is plural and does not agree with the singular verb form "is."

   C   The subject "anyone" is singular and does not agree with plural verb form "want."

3. Answer   A

The subject "audience" is acting as a group, so the correct verb form is "disrespects," third person singular.

False choices

   B   In the second main clause of the sentence, the subject is "no one." Because "no one" is singular, it does not agree with the plural verb form "seem."

   C   The subject of the verb is "no one," which does not agree with the plural verb form "show."

4. Answer   A

With a "neither-nor" compound subject, the subject closest to the verb determines the form of the verb. In this sentence, "cap" follows "nor," so the verb must be singular, "is."

False choices

   B   The dependent clause beginning with "that" modifies "hat." Therefore, the verb should agree with the singular "hat." "Cover" is the plural form.

   C   The verb should agree with "pair," not "boots." "Boots" is in the prepositional phrase and in this case does not affect the subject-verb agreement. The verb form should not be "are," which is plural.

5. Answer   C

The verb "are" does not agree with the singular subject "thing."

False choices
    A   The verb form "is" does not agree with the two subjects "carrying case" and "A/C adaptor."
    B   The two subjects "remote control" and "headphones" follow the verb in this part of the sentence, so the verb must be plural, "are."

6. Answer   D
All of the subjects and verbs in the sentence agree.

False choices
    A   The subject "one" is singular, so the verb must be singular, not plural.
    B   The subject of the verb "works" is "team," which is singular.
    C   The subject of the verb "are" is "crimes," which is plural.

7. Answer   B
The verb "has" agrees with the singular subject "entrée."

False choices
    A   The singular subject "meal" requires a singular verb "is," not "are."
    C   In this sentence, the verb follows the relative pronoun "that." The relative pronoun refers to a noun that comes before it in the sentence, "vegetables." Since the noun is plural, the verb form must also be plural, "are." (The dependent clause modifies "vegetables.")

SECTION 3 ◆ EXERCISES: SUBJECT AND VERB AGREEMENT

DIRECTIONS: *In each of the following questions, choose the option that corrects an error in the underlined portion(s). If no error exists, choose "No change is necessary."*

1. Neither my keys nor my MP3 player <u>were</u> on the counter; maybe my roommates,
                                A

    who <u>have been</u> home all afternoon, know where either of them <u>is</u>.
           B   C
    A. was
    B. has been
    C. were
    D. No change is necessary.

2. The committee <u>disagree</u> on the dates we <u>have</u> chosen for our yearly event; we must
                   A   B

    decide soon because each of the speakers <u>need</u> two months' notification.
                                     C
    A. disagrees
    B. has
    C. needs
    D. No change is necessary.

3. The Golden Cockatoo is one of the few stores in town that <u>specializes</u> in selling
                                                A

    tropical birds; my family <u>enjoys</u> going there because each of the birds on display
                        B

    <u>have</u> its own perch outside its cage.
      C

A. specialize
B. enjoy
C. has
D. No change is necessary.

4. The Department of Science and Engineering library <u>sponsors</u> a lecture series that

                                                           A

  <u>have become</u> so popular that none of the people I know <u>have been</u> able to get tickets.

            B   C

A. sponsor
B. has become
C. has been
D. No change is necessary.

5. There <u>are</u> many different food options to choose from for lunch, but Joe, along

          A

  with his brother, <u>prefers</u> peanut butter and jelly, which <u>are</u> his favorite.

                    B   C

A. is
B. prefer
C. is
D. No change is necessary.

6. *Stand and Deliver* <u>tell</u> a story of a dedicated math teacher; the movie <u>focuses</u> on his

                            A   B

  work with students who <u>come</u> from poor backgrounds.

                            C

A. tells
B. focus
C. comes
D. No change is necessary.

7. Diseases such as mumps and measles <u>have</u> been almost completely eradicated; however,

                                            A

  AIDS scientists from all over the world, who <u>performs</u> research every day, <u>have</u> not been

                                          B   C

  able to find a cure.

A. has
B. perform
C. has
D. No change is necessary.

8. The number of students in my class <u>has</u> dropped from thirty to nine; anatomy and

                                          A

  physiology <u>is</u> a difficult subject, and few <u>passes</u> the course.

                B   C

A. have
B. are
C. pass
D. No change is necessary.

9. The slaughter of elephants for their tusks <u>has</u> caused a decline in the elephant
   A

   population; the tusks <u>are</u> used to make jewelry and other precious items on
   B

   which artisans <u>carve</u> intricate designs.
   C

   A. have
   B. is
   C. carves
   D. No change is necessary.

10. Shelters for abused women <u>offers</u> a place where single women or mothers and
    A

    children <u>go</u> to escape the person who <u>wants</u> to harm them.
    B   C

    A. offer
    B. goes
    C. want
    D. No change is necessary.

11. Refreshments on short flights <u>are</u> inadequate; a beverage and a small package of salted
    A

    peanuts <u>does</u> not satisfy the hunger that most travelers <u>experience</u>.
    B   C

    A. is
    B. do
    C. experiences
    D. No change is necessary.

12. Briana, along with her family, <u>have</u> recently moved to this area; she <u>wants</u> to buy a large
    A   B

    piece of property in the country where she <u>plans</u> to build a large home and barn.
    C

    A. has
    B. want
    C. plan
    D. No change is necessary.

13. My new glasses <u>hurt</u> my nose, my blue jeans with the red stitching <u>are</u> too tight, but
    A   B

    every one of my tattoos <u>look</u> just fine.
    C

    A. hurts
    B. is
    C. looks
    D. No change is necessary.

14. Our accommodations at the hotel <u>has</u> been confirmed, so now one of us <u>needs</u> to
    A   B

    book our flight; then we can figure out how much money the trip <u>costs</u>.
    C

A. have
B. need
C. cost
D. No change is necessary.

15. Although statistics <u>are</u> difficult for me, mathematics <u>seems</u> easy; languages, like
                      A   B

Spanish or French, <u>present</u> no problem at all since I lived in Venezuela and Paris.
                      C

A. is
B. seem
C. presents
D. No change is necessary.

16.   Many students from the Bahamas <u>have come</u> to study in South Florida because the
                                  A

weather is similar; in addition, there <u>are</u> a variety of schools that <u>offer</u> college degrees.
                        B   C

A. has come
B. is
C. offers
D. No change is necessary.

17. Many foods and beverages that we enjoy today <u>come</u> from other countries; for example,
                                    A

the French, who <u>is</u> known for their cuisine, <u>have</u> given us café au lait, soufflés,
                 B   C

baguettes (French bread), petit fours, and fondue.

A. comes
B. are
C. has
D. No change is necessary.

18. The news of your accomplishments <u>make</u> us very proud; Automaticlabs <u>is</u> a new company
                                  A   B

with enormous potential, and with you as president, the future of the business <u>looks</u> bright.
                                                         C

A. makes
B. are
C. look
D. No change is necessary.

19. A number of squirrels <u>live</u> in my neighborhood, and many of the neighbors <u>enjoy</u>
                            A   B

watching them; unfortunately, a few of them <u>gets</u> run over by cars.
                                            C

A. lives
B. enjoys
C. get
D. No change is necessary.

20. On July 4th, most of the country <u>celebrates</u>; outdoor picnics and barbeques <u>are</u> popular

                                      A   B

daytime activities while at night, fireworks displays <u>attract</u> people of all ages.

                                                 C

A. celebrate
B. is
C. attracts
D. No change is necessary.

SECTION 4 ◆ PRONOUN AND ANTECEDENT AGREEMENT

Competency 4.4	Grammar, Spelling, Capitalization, and Punctuation Skills
Skill Tested	**Maintains correct agreement between pronoun and antecedent**

The Skill

This item tests your ability to identify and correct errors in pronoun and antecedent agreement. A pronoun is a word that is used to replace a noun or another pronoun. When the pronoun refers to a word that appears earlier in a sentence, that word is called the pronoun's antecedent.

    Example: Linda agreed to lend me **her** Bob Marley albums.

The pronoun "her" refers to Linda. "Linda" is the antecedent. If we were to replace the pronoun with a noun, the sentence would read: Linda agreed to lend me Linda's Bob Marley albums.

1. Pronouns must agree with their antecedents in number.

If the antecedent is singular, the pronoun must be singular.
If the antecedent is plural, the pronoun must be plural.

Example: My little brother never cleans **his** room.

The pronoun **his** is singular to match its antecedent, the singular subject "brother."

    Example: My younger brothers never clean **their** rooms.
                 My sister and brother never clean **their** rooms.

In the first sentence, the antecedent of the pronoun **their**, which is plural, is the plural subject "brothers." The second sentence has two subjects, so the pronoun **their** must also be plural.

    Example: Everyone in the class typed **his or her** essay.

The pronoun combination **his or her** is singular, matching the singular indefinite pronoun subject "Everyone." Some indefinite pronouns are always singular, some are always plural, and some are sometimes singular and sometimes plural. (Refer to the chart of indefinite pronouns in the previous section.)

    Example: The jury reached a guilty verdict unanimously and was pleased with **its** decision.

The pronoun **its** is singular to match the antecedent "jury." The word "jury" is called a collective noun because it refers to a group of people as a single unit. When the group works together as one entity, the pronoun will be singular, as in this sentence. However, if the group works as individuals, the pronoun will be plural.

> Example: The jury disagreed on the guilt and innocence of the defendant, so they were not pleased with **their** inability to decide.

In this sentence, the jury is not working as a unit because its members disagreed. Therefore, the pronoun must be **their**.

2. Pronouns must agree with their antecedents in person. Person has to do with whether the writer refers to himself or to someone else.

> Examples: I always bring **my** lunch to work.
> You have three more writing courses to take to complete **your** requirement.
> Erin rides **her** motorcycle whenever she gets the chance.

3. Pronouns must agree with their antecedents in gender.

> Example: The boa constrictor seizes **its** prey in **its** jaws and then wraps itself around the victim to suffocate it.
> My dog Charlie chewed on **his** bone for an hour last night.
> The children hung up **their** drawings in the hallway for all the students to see.

The Test Question

You will be presented with one or two sentences that have one or three underlined parts that may reflect a pronoun-antecedent agreement error. If the original sentence contains an error, you must choose the option that corrects the error in an underlined part. If the sentence is correct, choose "No change is necessary."

SECTION 4 ◆ DIAGNOSTIC: PRONOUN AND ANTECEDENT AGREEMENT

For each of the following questions, choose the option that corrects an error in the underlined portion(s). If no error exists, then choose "No change is necessary." When you are done, check your work with the answers immediately following the diagnostic. Even if you get a perfect score here, go ahead and complete the exercises in this section; they are designed to help build confidence and to give you practice for future test success.

1. Each group will have three minutes for <u>their</u> presentation.
   A. our
   B. your
   C. its
   D. No change is necessary.

2. A student should register early to get the courses at the times <u>you</u> would like.
   A. they
   B. he or she
   C. we
   D. No change is necessary.

3. The jury in the Michael Jackson case took <u>their</u> time to come to a unanimous verdict.
   A. its
   B. his

C. our

D. No change is necessary.

4. When lifting heavy weights, Joe must maintain his concentration so <u>you</u> won't get hurt.
   A. one
   B. we
   C. he
   D. No change is necessary.

5. Each year, the teens in the neighborhood stockpile fireworks to create <u>their</u> own display;

                                                                               A

   however, <u>they</u> do not realize that <u>we</u> could get hurt.

            B   C

   A. you
   B. you
   C. they
   D. No change is necessary.

6. Any woman who purchased a knock-off designer purse wasted <u>their</u> money; <u>its</u> stitching

                                                                            A   B

   easily comes loose, and <u>its</u> zippers get stuck or break.

                                    C

   A. her
   B. their
   C. your
   D. No change is necessary.

7. Our culture stresses the importance of physical perfection in women, so <u>they</u> try many

                                                                                 A

   different kinds of diets and get plastic surgery to alter <u>our</u> looks; few seem to appreciate

                                                                         B

   <u>their</u> inner beauty.

     C

   A. she
   B. their
   C. her
   D. No change is necessary.

Answers and Explanations to Diagnostic: Pronoun and Antecedent Agreement

1. Answer   C

The correct pronoun is the singular "its," which agrees with the singular antecedent "each group." The antecedent is third person singular, so the matching pronoun must also be a third person singular form. Choice A is second person plural, and Choice B is second person singular.

2. Answer   B

In this sentence, the pronoun "he or she" agrees with its antecedent "student." Both are third person singular. Choice A, "they" is a third person plural pronoun, and Choice C, "we" is a second person plural pronoun.

3. Answer   A

The pronoun "its" agrees with the antecedent "jury." "Jury" is a collective noun that can be singular or plural depending on its use. When referring to the individuals of the jury acting as a unit, the pronoun should be singular. Since the gender of the jury is unknown, "his" would be an inappropriate choice. Choice C, "our," is second person plural.

4. Answer   C

The pronoun "he" refers to the antecedent "Joe." Since Joe is male, we can use "he" rather than "one." "We" is a second person plural pronoun.

5. Answer   C

All of the pronoun choices in the sentence refer to the antecedent "teens." Therefore, they should all be third person plural forms.

6. Answer   A

The pronoun for choice A should agree with the antecedent "woman," so "her" is the correct choice. The second two pronouns in the sentence both refer to "purse," so they are the same, "its."

7. Answer   B

The pronoun "their" agrees with its antecedent, "women." All of the choices refer to "women" and, therefore, should be third person plural forms.

SECTION 4 ◆ EXERCISES: PRONOUN AND ANTECEDENT AGREEMENT

DIRECTIONS: *For each of the following questions, choose the option that corrects an error in the underlined portion(s). If no error exists, choose "No change is necessary."*

1. Each passenger wanting to board the plane to Tampa must present their identification to the airline representative.
   A. her
   B. its
   C. our
   D. No change is necessary.

2. Either the band or the choir will give its performance first.
   A. their
   B. her
   C. his
   D. No change is necessary.

3. The company gives each of their employees a bonus at the end of the year.
   A. his
   B. its
   C. her
   D. No change is necessary.

4. Even though the weather conditions were not optimal, neither the surfers nor the boater changed its plans for a day on the ocean.
   A. their
   B. our
   C. his
   D. No change is necessary.

5. Pete has a successful landscaping business because the employees work hard, and its prices are fair.

A. their
B. his
C. our ✓
D. No change is necessary.

6. Andrea and Sebastian do not seem to understand the concepts presented in <u>their</u>
                                                         A

   algebra class. They have gone for tutoring in the math lab, but <u>it</u> has not helped <u>him.</u>
                                                     B   C

A. his   ✓
B. he
C. them
D. No change is necessary.

7. The downtown improvement committee has presented <u>their</u> decision to tear down the
                                                     A

   existing strip mall and build a park. <u>It</u> wanted to give each child a place where <u>he</u>
                                      B   C

   could play.
A. its
B. They
C. they
D. No change is necessary.

8. The neighbor's pool was crowded with children who came to celebrate Brian's third
   birthday party with <u>him</u>. Each child was given an inflated toy to help <u>him</u> float in the
                       A   B

   water; as well, each child's parent went in the pool with <u>their</u> child.
                                                  C

A. them
B. them
C. his or her   ✓
D. No change is necessary.

9. The professor was angry with the class because no one brought <u>his or her</u> book to
                                                           A

   class; therefore, neither the students nor the professor could do <u>their</u> lesson for the
                                                         B

   day. As a result, the professor gave <u>them</u> a lengthy homework assignment.
                                          C

A. their
B. his
C. him or her
D. No change is necessary.

10. If anyone wants tickets to the game, <u>he or she</u> can buy <u>his or hers</u> online, at a ticket outlet,
                                      A   B

   or at the stadium. Because the tickets are selling fast, buy <u>them</u> as soon as possible.
                                                  C

A. they
B. them
C. it
D. No change is necessary.

SECTION 5 ◆ PRONOUN SHIFTS

| Competency 4.5 | Grammar, Spelling, Capitalization, and Punctuation Skills |
| Skill Tested | **Avoids inappropriate pronoun shifts in person** |

The Skill

This item tests your ability to identify and correct pronoun shifts in person. Person as it is used in grammar separates nouns and pronouns into groups:

	Subject Pronouns		Object Pronouns	
Person	**Singular**	**Plural**	**Singular**	**Plural**
First	I	we	me	us
Second	you	you	you	you
Third	he, she, it	they	him, her, it	them

Nouns are third person singular or plural.

A shift in person in a sentence occurs when the main pronoun in the sentence is replaced by another. This changes the point of view.

> Example: When one travels to San Antonio, you should take their comfortable walking shoes.

The pronouns in this sentence are incorrect. In this example, the subject is "one." However, the writer shifts to "you" and "their" in the same sentence, thus confusing the reader.

> Example: When one travels to San Antonio, they should take their comfortable walking shoes.

This sentence also shifts pronouns. Like the previous sentence, the subject is "one." Then the writer shifts from "one" to "they" and "their."

There are three ways to correct the example sentences. Each option uses the same pronoun throughout the sentences to maintain consistency.

> Option 1: When one travels to San Antonio, he or she should take his or her comfortable walking shoes.
> Option 2: When they travel to San Antonio, they should take their comfortable walking shoes.
> Option 3: When you travel to San Antonio, you should take your comfortable walking shoes.

> Example: When a **tourist** travels to San Antonio, **he or she** should take her comfortable walking shoes.

This sentence is correct. The word "tourist" is a third person singular noun. "He or she" is used because the writer does not say whether the subject "tourist" is male or female.

The Test Question

You will be given one or two sentences with one or three underlined parts that may contain an inappropriate pronoun shift. If the original sentence contains an error, you must choose the answer that corrects the error in an underlined part. If the sentence is correct, choose "No change is necessary."

SECTION 5 ◆ DIAGNOSTIC: PRONOUN SHIFTS

For each of the following questions, choose the option that corrects an error in the underlined portion(s). If no error exists, choose "No change is necessary." When you are done, check your work with the answers immediately following the diagnostic. Even if you get a perfect score here, go ahead and complete the exercises in this section; they are designed to help build confidence and to give you practice for future test success.

1. Some people are not satisfied with what <u>they</u> have; <u>you</u> want more material things
                                    A   B

   or <u>they</u> wish to be like someone else.
      C
   A. you
   B. they
   C. we
   D. No change is necessary.

2. I would like to be Oprah Winfrey for a brief time because <u>you</u> would have a chef
                                                      A

   making all <u>my</u> meals and <u>my</u> own personal hair, nail, and makeup artist.
              B   C
   A. I
   B. your
   C. her
   D. No change is necessary.

3. When I shop at the mall, <u>I</u> wear comfortable clothes because <u>you</u> need to be able to
                             A   B

   easily slip my clothes off and on as <u>I</u> am constantly changing in the dressing rooms.
                                           C
   A. you
   B. you
   C. I
   D. No change is necessary.

4. This summer, <u>she</u> started looking for work as soon as the semester ended, and in
                    A

   no time <u>she</u> found a job; taking this approach gave <u>one</u> an advantage over people
            B   C

   who waited several weeks.
   A. they
   B. they
   C. her
   D. No change is necessary.

5. To avoid theft, <u>one</u> should never leave <u>your</u> valuable possessions in plain view
                                   A   B

   in a car; also, <u>you</u> should never leave a wallet or a purse inside the vehicle.
                       C

   A. you
   B. his or her
   C. one
   D. No change is necessary.

6. <u>You</u> can get rid of ants without <u>their</u> having to use pesticides by putting baking
    A   B

   soda in the places where they are entering <u>your</u> house.
                                  C

   A. One
   B. your
   C. one's
   D. No change is necessary.

7. Every Sunday afternoon, Tamika does her laundry at her mother's house, so <u>she</u> can
                                                           A

   save money, <u>she</u> can spend time with her brother and sister, and she can help cook the
                    B

   family dinner; Tamika feels that it is important to spend time with <u>your</u> family.
                                                     C

   A. they
   B. you
   C. her
   D. No change is necessary.

Answers and Explanations to Diagnostic: Pronoun Shifts

1. Answer   B
The third person plural is established with the pronoun "they." To correct the shifted pronoun "you," replace it with "they."

2. Answer   A
The first person "I" is established in the sentence. "I" corrects the shifted pronoun "you."

3. Answer   B
The first person singular pronoun form is established with the use of "I." The shifted pronoun "you" can be corrected by replacing it with "I."

4. Answer   C
The third person pronoun "she" is established in the sentence. Replacing "one" with "her" corrects the shift in person.

5. Answer   A
The second person is established with "you" and "your." The shifted pronoun "one" can be corrected by replacing it with "you."

6. Answer   B
The pronoun "you" determines second person. Replacing the shifted pronoun "their" with "your" corrects the error.

7. Answer   C

The noun "Tamika" establishes third person in the sentence. The shifted pronoun "your" can be corrected by replacing it with "her."

SECTION 5 ◆ EXERCISES: PRONOUN SHIFTS

DIRECTIONS: *For each of the following questions, choose the option that corrects an error in the underlined portion(s). If no error exists, choose "No change is necessary."*

1. If <u>you</u> want to succeed in college, <u>one</u> must set aside sufficient time to study; also,
      A   B

   <u>you</u> should not take too many credits each semester.
   C
   A. one
   B. you
   C. they
   D. No change is necessary.

2. Professor Morrison told <u>us</u> that <u>we</u> have to turn in <u>your</u> research papers on Friday.
                             A   B   C
   A. me
   B. you
   C. our
   D. No change is necessary.

3. Teenagers enjoy trying out a variety of changes to <u>their</u> appearance; <u>they</u> may get a tattoo,
                                             A   B

   or sometimes <u>one</u> may try out a new hairstyle or hair color.
               C
   A. one's
   B. he
   C. they
   D. No change is necessary.

4. When my brother was in high school, <u>you</u> were required to do thirty hours of service
                                     A

   learning; <u>he</u> did <u>his</u> hours by volunteering at the computer lab in the library.
           B   C
   A. he
   B. one
   C. our
   D. No change is necessary.

5. A full-time student who also works has to budget <u>his</u> time so that <u>you</u> can make <u>his</u>
                                   A   B   C

   education a priority.
   A. their
   B. he
   C. you
   D. No change is necessary.

6. The furniture deliverymen are coming this morning, so <u>we</u> have to make room in
                                                                A

   <u>our</u> den for the new sofa and chairs; now, when <u>he</u> invites friends over, we will not have
    B   C

   to bring in chairs from the kitchen to sit on.
   A. they
   B. your
   C. we
   D. No change is necessary.

7. Some people who participate in extreme sports put <u>their</u> lives in danger, but <u>they</u> like the
                                                      A   B

   rush <u>you</u> get.
        C
   A. your
   B. you
   C. they
   D. No change is necessary.

8. Many people I know are a little nervous about flying even though <u>we</u> realize that airport
                                                                     A

   security has improved; however, this has not stopped <u>them</u> from flying for business or for
                                                         B

   <u>their</u> vacation.
    C
   A. they
   B. him
   C. his
   D. No change is necessary.

9. Many college students know more about using computers than <u>their</u> parents do; it is
                                                               A

   not unusual for <u>them</u> to get a phone call from a parent asking for <u>their</u> help.
                   B   C
   A. one's
   B. I
   C. your
   D. No change is necessary.

10. My truck is <u>my</u> most prized possession, but <u>you</u> have to work so that <u>I</u> can pay for
                A   B   C

    the insurance and maintenance.
    A. one's
    B. I
    C. you
    D. No change is necessary.

Competency 4.6	Grammar, Spelling, Capitalization, and Punctuation Skills
Skill Tested	**Makes clear pronoun references**

The Skill

This item tests your ability to identify unclear pronoun reference and to recognize that a pronoun refers to a specific word or phrase, not a whole idea. A pronoun can refer to only one antecedent and must do so clearly without any confusion.

There are two instances in which errors are made in pronoun reference.

1. The pronoun does not refer to a specific word or phrase

> Example: At the flea market, **they** have bargains on many different kinds of products.

Who is **they** referring to? The shoppers? The vendors? The owners? You aren't told. To correct the sentence, you will have to replace the pronoun with a noun describing who **they** are.

> Correction: At the flea market, **the vendors** have bargains on many different kinds of products.

2. The pronoun may refer to more than one person, place, or thing in a sentence.

> Example: Heather told Kimberly that **she** should ask Ryan out for a date.

Who is the pronoun **she** referring to, Heather or Kimberly? You might interpret the sentence to mean that Heather states that Kimberly should ask Ryan out. However, the sentence could just as easily mean that Heather thinks she, herself, should ask Ryan out. To make pronoun reference clear, you need to find a way to let the reader know which person the pronoun refers to. On the test, you may see one option which suggests this correction:

> Correction: Heather told Kimberly that **she, Heather,** should ask Ryan out for a date.

This is an acceptable answer because by adding the specific name after the pronoun, you know exactly who the pronoun refers to. You may think that this sentence sounds strange, but it is probably going to be your best choice for correcting the sentence.

The Test Question

You will be presented with one or two sentences with one or three underlined parts that may contain a pronoun reference error. If the original sentence passage contains an error, you must choose the option that corrects an underlined part. If the sentence is correct, choose "No change is necessary."

SECTION 6 ◆ DIAGNOSTIC: CLEAR PRONOUN REFERENCE

For each of the following questions, choose the option that corrects an error in the underlined portion(s). If no error exists, then choose "No change is necessary." When you are done, check your work with the answers immediately following the diagnostic. Even if you get a perfect score here, go ahead and complete the exercises in this section; they are designed to help build confidence and to give you practice for future test success.

1. Greg beat Brandon at basketball when <u>he</u> had not even played for several months.
   A. the team
   B. he, Greg,
   C. the coach
   D. No change is necessary.

2. Melissa, whose book was stolen, told the instructor that <u>she</u> should report the theft.
   A. the class
   B. she, Melissa,
   C. the thief
   D. No change is necessary.

3. While I was carrying my essay to English class during the rainstorm, <u>it</u> made the ink run, and as a result, the essay was unreadable.
   A. the weather
   B. the essay
   C. the rain
   D. No change is necessary.

4. On the radio, <u>it</u> said that traffic on I-75 would be backed up for miles.
   A. the radio
   B. the traffic report
   C. the traffic reporter
   D. No change is necessary.

5. Sean had to take the CD player out of the car and fix <u>it</u>.
   A. the CD player
   B. the car
   C. the CD
   D. No change is necessary.

6. Halfway through the movie, the bucket of popcorn was empty, but we were tired of eating <u>it</u> anyway.
   A. the bucket
   B. the popcorn
   C. the movie
   D. No change is necessary.

7. Caroline called Pat, <u>her</u> boss, to explain why <u>she</u> did not come to the meeting
   A   B
   yesterday and was sorry to have missed <u>it</u>.
   C
   A. their
   B. she, Caroline,
   C. them
   D. No change is necessary.

Answers and Explanations to Diagnostic: Clear Pronoun Reference

1. Answer   B

Two males are mentioned in the sentence, and although the reader may know that Greg is the one who had not played recently, there is no clue to that fact in the sentence as it is written. Repeating the name of the person intended clarifies any possible confusion.

2. Answer   B

Two people are mentioned in the sentence, Melissa and the instructor. The reader does not know to whom the pronoun "she" refers. Repeating the name of the person intended clarifies any possible confusion.

3. Answer   C

The use of the pronoun "it" is confusing because the pronoun does not appear to refer to anything in the sentence. The pronoun refers to the rain from the storm.

4. Answer   C

The use of the pronoun "it" does not specify who said the traffic would be backed up. "The traffic reporter" specifies what is meant by "it."

5. Answer   A

Although the reader may know that Sean was going to fix the CD player, not the car, there is no clue to that fact as the sentence is written. Therefore, replacing "it" with "the CD player" clarifies any confusion.

6. Answer   B

Although the reader may realize that "it" refers to the popcorn, not the bucket, there is no clue to that fact in the sentence as written; therefore, replacing "it" with "the popcorn" corrects any confusion.

7. Answer   B

The reader may realize that the pronoun "she" refers to Caroline, but there is no clue to that fact in the sentence as it is written. Repeating the name of the person next to the pronoun, "she, Caroline" helps to correct any confusion.

SECTION 6 ◆ EXERCISES: CLEAR PRONOUN REFERENCE

DIRECTIONS: For each of the following questions, choose the option that corrects an error in the underlined portion(s). If no error exists, choose "No change is necessary."

1. Yesterday, when I went for my job interview at the bank, <u>they</u> asked me difficult questions.
    A. he
    B. the manager
    C. the bank
    D. No change is necessary.

2. After carefully measuring the wall for a spot to hang the poster, Steve hammered the hook into the wall, and now <u>it</u> is crooked.
    A. the wall
    B. the hook
    C. the poster
    D. No change is necessary.

3. Tavar's phone rang ten times, but <u>it</u> did not answer.
   A. Tavar
   B. the phone
   C. they
   D. No change is necessary.

4. In the newspaper, <u>it</u> says that one lane of the Interstate will be closed for repairs for a year.
   A. the newspaper
   B. the reporter
   C. the article
   D. No change is necessary.

5. When Josh put the television on the table, <u>it</u> collapsed.
   A. the television
   B. Josh
   C. the table
   D. No change is necessary.

6. In the writing lab, <u>they</u> showed me how to edit my paper; <u>this</u> was helpful to me because
                            A   B
   now I know how to do <u>it</u>.
                        C
   A. the lab assistants
   B. the lab
   C. them
   D. No change is necessary.

7. Augusto had to take so many college preparatory courses that he thought he would
   never finish <u>it</u>; <u>they</u> frustrated him because <u>they</u> were not interesting.
                      A   B   C
   A. them
   B. it
   C. it was
   D. No change is necessary.

8. The boss told <u>her</u> employee, Doreen, that <u>she</u> was the best worker <u>she</u> had.
                             A   B   C
   A. their
   B. she, Doreen,
   C. they
   D. No change is necessary.

9. Mr. Linger instructed Jim, his reference specialist, to develop a virtual library tour for
   <u>his</u> new students even if the tour took less than an hour.
   A. Jim's
   B. their
   C. Mr. Linger's
   D. No change is necessary.

10. Learning how to lift weights properly is important; <u>it</u> requires concentration because the
                                                      A

   lifter can accidentally lose <u>his</u> grip and drop the weight on <u>himself</u>.
                                      B   C

   A. they require
   B. its
   C. itself
   D. No change is necessary.

SECTION 7 ◆ PRONOUN CASE FORM

Competency 4.7	Grammar, Spelling, Capitalization, and Punctuation Skills
Skill Tested	Uses proper case forms

The Skill

This item tests your ability to use subjective, objective, and possessive case forms according to the context of the sentence. The form of a pronoun used in a sentence depends on its function: subject of a verb, object of a verb, or ownership.

1. Subject of a verb

Use subject pronouns as subjects of verbs. The pronouns that are used as subjects of verbs are **I, you, he, she, it, we, they.**

     Example: **We** are learning to be good writers.

The pronoun **we** is the subject of the verb "are learning." Be careful to choose the correct form of pronoun when you have more than one pronoun as a subject or when you have a noun and a pronoun as subject. The following sentences show the incorrect use of subject pronouns, then their corrections.

     Example: **My friends and me** are going to play basketball.

This is incorrect. The pronoun must be selected from the list of subject pronouns.

     Correction: **My friends and I** are going to play basketball.

Here is an example of two pronouns as subjects that are used incorrectly:

     Example: **Her and me** go to the same nail salon.

     Correction: **She and I** go to the same nail salon.

There is one exception to this rule. Subject pronouns follow the verb **be.**

     Example: The person who won the race was **he.**

In conversational English, you will hear people use the pronoun **him;** however, in standard written English, **he** is the correct pronoun.

---

2. Object of a verb, object of a preposition

Use object pronouns as objects of verbs or objects of prepositions. The pronouns that are used as objects of verbs or objects of prepositions are **me, you, him, her, it, us, them.**

Object of a verb

Example: The boss gave **me** a raise.

The pronoun comes after the verb "gave," so it must be an object pronoun—in this sentence, **me.**

Example: The boss gave **him** and **me** a raise.

In this sentence, two pronouns come after the verb "gave." They both must be in the objective case.

Object of a preposition

Prepositional phrases often end with pronouns. A prepositional phrase is a word group that begins with a preposition and ends with a noun or pronoun. It does not have a subject or verb. When the prepositional phrase ends with a pronoun, it should be an object pronoun.

Example: The dog brought the Frisbee to **me.**

The prepositional phrase is "to me." **Me** is the object of the preposition.

Example: The dog placed the ball between my friend and **me.**

The prepositional phrase is "between my friend and me." You may have heard people say "between my friend and I," but this is not correct. You must choose an object pronoun.

3. Possessive pronouns

Possessive pronouns show ownership. Some are used alone: **mine, ours, yours, his, hers, theirs, whose.** Others are used as adjectives: **my, our, your, his, her, its, whose.**

Example: That motorcycle must be **yours.**
That must be **your** motorcycle.

Problems with Who and Whom

The correct use of **who** and **whom** can be confusing. **Who** is a subject pronoun, and **whom** is an object pronoun.

Who or whom in sentences that are questions

Who is at the door?	**Who** is the subject of the question.
For **whom** is this package?	**Whom** is the object of the preposition "for."

Who or whom in sentences that are statements

Mr. Sterling is the person **who** manages the store.	**Who** is the subject of the dependent clause "who manages the store."
Mr. Sterling, **whom** I told you about, manages the store.	**Whom** is the object of the preposition "about." The dependent clause has a subject, "I."

The Test Question

You will be presented with three underlined pronouns in a sentence. You must determine if the sentence is correct as written or choose the answer that corrects the underlined part. If the sentence is correct, choose "No change is necessary."

SECTION 7 ◆ DIAGNOSTIC: PRONOUN CASE FORM

For each of the following questions, choose the option that corrects an error in the underlined portion. If no error exists, then choose "No change is necessary." When you are done, check your work with the answers immediately following the diagnostic. Even if you get a perfect score here, go ahead and complete the exercises in this section; they are designed to help build confidence and to give you practice for future test success.

1. My reading class started out with twenty-five students, but by midterm, only <u>me</u> and
   A

   ten other students remained; even though the class is small, the instructor can give

   <u>me and them</u> more individual attention, which is better for <u>us</u>.
   B   C

   A. I
   B. I and they
   C. we
   D. No change is necessary.

2. Every Saturday, my dad makes <u>my brother and I</u> mow the lawn and trim any
                                   A

   overgrown plants; in the summer, <u>he and I</u> jump in the pool to cool off when
                                      B

   <u>he and I</u> are finished doing yard work.
       C

   A. my brother and me
   B. him and me
   C. him and me
   D. No change is necessary.

3. James and <u>I</u> both like wrestling; although James has been wrestling longer than I have,
               A

   he was surprised when the coach picked <u>me</u> instead of <u>he</u> to be captain of the team.
                                            B   C

   A. me
   B. I
   C. him
   D. No change is necessary.

4. The art appreciation lecture class is so long that <u>we</u> students <u>whom</u> sit in the back
                                                        A   B

   of the lecture hall tend to lose concentration; those of <u>us</u> who want to learn try to
                                                             C

   get to class early to sit in the front.

A. us
B. who
C. we
D. No change is necessary.

5. Three players, Tania, Abbey, and <u>me</u>, will be able to play on the team if we
                                            A

    pass this course; the semester has been tough for <u>them and me</u>, but <u>they and I</u>
                                                         B   C

    feel confident of our success.
    A. I
    B. they and I
    C. them and me
    D. No change is necessary.

6. When Bob Dole was shot during World War II, <u>he</u> and the other wounded men
                                                        A

    lay in a field until the medics found <u>them</u>; Dole was paralyzed from the neck
                                       B

    down, and doctors had given up on <u>him</u>.
                                 C
    A. him
    B. they
    C. he
    D. No change is necessary.

7. Come to Spanish River Park with my girl friend and <u>I</u>; <u>you and I</u> can take a swim
                                                 A   B

    in the ocean while she grills some chicken and ribs for <u>us</u> hungry men.
                                           C

    A. me
    B. you and me
    C. we
    D. No change is necessary.

Answers and Explanations to Diagnostic: Pronoun Case Form

1. Answer   A
"I" as well as "ten other students" is the subject of the verb remained.

False choices
    A "Me and them" are the objects of the verb "can give."
    B "Us" is the object of the preposition "for."

2. Answer   A
"My brother and me" are objects of the verb "makes."

False choices
    B "He and I" is the subject of the verb "jump."
    C "He and I" is the subject of the verb "are finished."

3. Answer   C

"Him" is the object of the preposition "of."

False choices

A   "James and I" is the subject of the verb "like."

C   "Me" is the object of the verb "picked."

4. Answer   B

"Who" is the subject of the verb "sit."

False choices

A   "We" is a subject pronoun that is part of the subject "students."

C   "Us" is the object of the preposition "of."

5. Answer   A

"Tania, Abbey, and I" renames the subject "players." The pronoun "I" is a subject pronoun.

False choices

B   "Them and me" are objects of the preposition "for."

C   "They and I" are subjects of the verb "feel."

6. Answer   D

All of the pronouns are properly used in the sentence. "He" is one of the compound subjects of "lay." "Them" is the object of the verb "found." "Him" is the object of the preposition "on."

7. Answer   A

"Me" is the object of the preposition "with."

False choices

B   "You and I" is the subject of "take a swim," not "you and me."

C   "Us" is the object of the preposition "for," not "we."

SECTION 7 ◆ EXERCISES: PRONOUN CASE FORM

DIRECTIONS: *For each of the following questions, choose the option that corrects an error in the underlined portion(s). If no error exists, choose "No change is necessary."*

1. Between you and <u>I</u>, I would rather go to the football game with you and <u>her</u> because <u>we</u>
                            A   B   C
    get along so well.
    A. me
    B. she
    C. us
    D. No change is necessary.

2. My dad, <u>who</u> helps me out with some of my expenses, gave fifty dollars to my brother
                   A
    Ben and <u>I</u>; both <u>he</u> and I appreciate the help.
                   B   C
    A. whom
    B. me
    C. him
    D. No change is necessary.

3. We took our midterms last week. Between the two of us, Jeff did better in chemistry;
   A

   however, English and math were easy for him and I.
                                                B   C

   A. us
   B. he
   C. me
   D. No change is necessary.

4. Curly, our new puppy, enjoyed the new ball that Pete and he brought her; she and the
                                                                  A   B

   boys played together until the dog and them were exhausted.
                                            C

   A. him
   B. her
   C. they
   D. No change is necessary.

5. The police stopped me and Alex and found some pills in the car. The pills belonged to
                        A

   Alex, who has epilepsy and must be on medication. Unfortunately, the officers did not
         B

   believe him or I.
                   C

   A. I
   B. whom
   C. me
   D. No change is necessary.

6. My parents are planning a trip to Alaska, for the two of them have not had a vacation in
                                                            A

   several years. They both could use some time away from us children.
                  B   C

   A. they
   B. Them
   C. we
   D. No change is necessary.

7. Tom and me will be the first to test the new lightweight training shoes on the track;
          A

   the coach chose him and me because he knew our times would improve with them.
                    B   C

   A. I
   B. he and I
   C. they
   D. No change is necessary.

8. Since <u>they</u> both have long blond hair, from a distance I could not tell whether Shannon or
        A

   <u>her</u> was walking across campus. <u>They</u> look like sisters.
    B   C
   A. them
   B. she
   C. Them
   D. No change is necessary.

9. The teachers told <u>us</u> students that we must not bring beverages into the computer lab;
                      A

   anyone of <u>us</u> <u>who</u> does will be asked to leave.
             B   C
   A. we
   B. ourselves
   C. whom
   D. No change is necessary.

10. In our department at work, anyone <u>who</u> wants to can contribute a dollar a week to our
                                       A

    lottery pool. This way <u>us</u> employees have a better chance of winning when all of <u>us</u> chip in.
                            B   C
    A. whom
    B. we
    C. we
    D. No change is necessary.

SECTION 8 ◆ ADJECTIVES AND ADVERBS

| Competency 4.8 | Grammar, Spelling, Capitalization, and Punctuation Skills |
| Skill Tested | **Uses adjectives and adverbs correctly** |

The Skill
This item tests your ability to understand the difference between the adjective and the adverb and to recognize which to use in the context of a sentence. Adjectives and adverbs are both modifiers, but they modify different types of words.

> **Adjectives** modify nouns and pronouns.
> **Adverbs** modify verbs, adjectives, and other adverbs.

The following sentences illustrate how adjectives and adverbs are used.

Adjectives	Adverbs
My grandpa is a **slow** driver.	My grandpa drives **slowly**.
Slow modifies the noun "driver."	**Slowly** modifies the verb "drives."
Her boy friend gave her a **real** diamond ring.	The diamond ring her boy friend gave her is **really** pretty.
Real modifies the noun "diamond ring."	**Really** modifies the adjective "pretty."

When the verb is a linking verb, use an adjective, not an adverb. Here is a list of some of the common linking verbs:

appear	seem	become	remain
feel	taste	smell	turn
sound	look	am, is, are, was, were	

Examples: The math test seemed **difficult**, but I realized that I understood all the questions.
Sal always feels **sleepy** after a big dinner at Arturo's Italian restaurant.
My sister's dog is **happy** when she gets her treats.

Using good and well, bad and badly

Good and **bad** are both adjectives; **well** and **badly** are adverbs.

Which of these two sentences is correct?
Dan played his guitar well.
Dan played his guitar good.
The first sentence is correct. The adverb **well** modifies the verb "played."

Before he took guitar lessons, Dan played bad.
Before he took guitar lessons, Dan played badly.
The second sentence is correct. The adverb **badly** modifies the verb "played."

The only instance in which you use **well** as an adjective is to refer to health.

After having been sick for several weeks, Angel felt **well** enough to play volleyball again.

The Test Question
You will be presented with a sentence that contains one or three underlined adjectives and/or adverbs. You must decide if the sentence is correct as written or choose the answer that corrects an underlined part. If the sentence is correct, choose "No change is necessary."

SECTION 8 ◆ DIAGNOSTIC: ADJECTIVES AND ADVERBS

For each of the following questions, choose the option that corrects an error in the underlined portion(s). If no error exists, then choose "No change is necessary." When you are done, check your work with the answers immediately following the diagnostic. Even if you get a perfect score here, go ahead and complete the exercises in this section; they are designed to help build confidence and to give you practice for future test success.

1. My friend drove his <u>enormous</u> monster truck with 40-inch tires to the movie
                        A
theatre; when the movie was over, a man in a Porsche would not let him out
because the man was waiting for a <u>real</u> good parking space nearby, so my friend
                                    B
put the truck in reverse and backed <u>directly</u> onto the Porsche, then drove away.
                                     C

   A. enormously
   B. really
   C. direct
   D. No change is necessary.

2. If a sky diver is not experienced and is not aware of how to breathe <u>correctly</u>,
                                                                   A

   he or she can pass out in mid air; if this happens, the sky diver will fall

   <u>unconscious</u> through the air and, therefore, will not be able to open the
        B

   parachute <u>quickly</u>.
            C

   A. correct
   B. unconsciously
   C. quick
   D. No change is necessary.

3. After three months of attending GED classes <u>regularly</u> and studying <u>diligently</u>,
                                             A   B

   Elizabeth passed the GED test <u>easy</u>.
                             C

   A. regular
   B. diligent
   C. easily
   D. No change is necessary.

4. The streets in my neighborhood in Venezuela were not maintained <u>good</u>; driving
                                                                      A

   was <u>perilous</u> because of the jagged holes, which led to <u>recurring</u> automobile accidents.
         B   C

   A. well
   B. perilously
   C. recurrently
   D. No change is necessary.

5. The Christmas celebrations in Puerto Rico include foods that are prepared <u>special</u>
                                                                   A

   for this holiday, traditional music played <u>continuously</u> by radio stations, and
                                                B

   "parrandas," songs sung after midnight by <u>joyous</u> friends and neighbors.
                                                C

   A. specially
   B. continuous
   C. joyously
   D. No change is necessary.

6. While growing up in <u>imperfect</u> conditions, I made trips <u>frequent</u> to the
                                  A   B

   pediatrician's office with my brother since he was <u>constantly</u> ill.
                                                  C

   A. imperfectly
   B. frequently
   C. constant
   D. No change is necessary.

7. My cousin Cameron grew up without water, heat, or electricity, the <u>mere</u>
                                                                        A
necessities that we take for granted; his apartment smelled <u>badly</u> from sewage
                                                                        B
because a pipe had exploded <u>unexpectedly</u>, and the landlord never fixed it.
                                        C

A. merely
B. bad
C. unexpected
D. No change is necessary.

Answers and Explanations to Diagnostic: Adjectives and Adverbs

1. Answer   B
"Really" is an adverb that modifies the adjective "good." "Real" is an adjective.

False choices
   A "Enormous" is an adjective modifying "truck." "Enormously" is an adverb.
   C "Directly" is an adverb modifying the verb "backed." "Direct" is an adjective, which does
      not modify a verb.

2. Answer   B
"Unconsciously" is an adverb modifying the verb "will fall." "Unconscious" is an adjective.

False choices
   A "Correctly" is an adverb modifying the verb "breathe." "Correct" is an adjective.
   C "Quickly" is an adverb modifying "open." "Quick" is an adjective.

3. Answer   C
"Easily" is an adverb modifying the verb "passed." "Easy" is an adjective.

False choices
   A "Regularly" is an adverb modifying the verb "attending." "Regular" is an adjective.
   B "Diligently" is an adverb modifying the verb "studying." "Diligent" is an adjective.

4. Answer   A
"Well" is an adverb modifying the verb "maintained." "Good" is an adjective.

False choices
   B "Perilous" is an adjective, required after the linking verb "was." "Perilously" is an adverb.
   C "Recurring" is an adjective modifying "automobile accidents." "Recurrently" is an adverb.

5. Answer   A
"Specially" is an adverb modifying the verb "prepared." "Special" is an adjective.

False choices
   B "Continuously" is an adverb modifying the verb "played." "Continuous" is an adjective.
   C "Joyous" is an adjective modifying the nouns "friends and neighbors." "Joyously" is an
      adverb.

6. Answer   B
"Frequently" is an adverb modifying the verb "made." "Frequent" is an adjective.

False choices
   A "Imperfect" is an adjective modifying the noun "conditions." "Imperfectly" is an adverb.
   C "Constantly" is an adverb modifying the adjective "ill." "Constant" is an adjective.

7. Answer   B

"Bad" is an adjective following the linking verb "smelled." "Badly" is an adverb.

False choices

A   "Mere" is an adjective modifying the noun "necessities."

C   "Unexpectedly" is an adverb modifying the verb "had exploded." "Unexpected" is an adjective.

SECTION 8 ◆ EXERCISES: ADJECTIVES AND ADVERBS

DIRECTIONS: *For each of the following questions, choose the option that corrects an error in the underlined portion(s). If no error exists, choose "No change is necessary."*

1. The residents were asked to evacuate as <u>peaceful</u> and as <u>quietly</u> as possible to avoid
                                                      A   B

    <u>unnecessary</u> panic.
        C
    A. peacefully
    B. quiet
    C. unnecessarily
    D. No change is necessary.

2. Noel carried out the karate demonstration <u>flawlessly</u>; each move was executed
                                                   A

    <u>skillfully</u> and <u>artistic</u>.
        B   C
    A. flawless
    B. skillful
    C. artistically
    D. No change is necessary.

3. The contestants at the talent show performed <u>enthusiastically</u>, but Carrie sang her song
                                                      A

    so <u>good</u> she should have won. Unfortunately, the judges were <u>extremely</u> harsh.
        B   C
    A. enthusiastic
    B. well
    C. extreme
    D. No change is necessary.

4. The food odor coming from the refrigerator was so <u>awfully</u> bad that no one wanted to
                                                          A

    investigate, but we held our noses <u>tight</u> and opened the door to find a <u>disagreeably</u> sour
                                            B   C

    carton of milk.
    A. awful
    B. tightly
    C. disagreeable
    D. No change is necessary.

5. After Tiffany got her very <u>challenging</u> job at the insurance company, she enjoyed
        A

   <u>frequent</u> shopping trips to the mall, but she spent her money <u>frivolously</u>.
        B   C
   A. challenged
   B. frequently
   C. frivolous
   D. No change is necessary.

6. After the <u>disastrous</u> tropical storm, people came out of their homes to find fallen trees,
             A

   broken glass, and <u>severely</u> damaged roofs; the result was <u>real</u> bad.
                      B   C
   A. disaster
   B. severe
   C. really
   D. No change is necessary.

7. The actress looked <u>really</u> <u>well</u> in her <u>unusual</u> designer gown, diamond studded shoes,
                        A   B   C

   and exotic Tahitian pearl necklace.
   A. real
   B. good
   C. unusually
   D. No change is necessary.

8. Renzo felt <u>terribly</u> about having to miss several classes, but his mother was injured in
             A

   a <u>horrible</u> car accident, and he <u>quickly</u> took the first plane to Peru.
     B   C
   A. terrible
   B. horribly
   C. quick
   D. No change is necessary.

9. Although he gets sick <u>infrequently</u>, this year Matt got the flu; he recovered <u>slowly</u>, but
                          A   B

   after two weeks, he felt <u>good</u> enough to return to his normal routine.
                            C
   A. seldomly
   B. slow
   C. well
   D. No change is necessary.

10. The crowd <u>sure</u> enjoyed the singer who sang <u>forcefully</u> and reached the high notes <u>perfectly</u>.
             A   B   C
    A. surely
    B. forceful
    C. perfect
    D. No change is necessary.

Competency 4.9	Grammar, Spelling, Capitalization, and Punctuation Skills
Skill Tested	**Uses appropriate degree forms of adjectives and adverbs**

The Skill

This item tests your ability to recognize the difference between comparative and superlative forms of adjectives and adverbs and to use them correctly.

Comparative is the form used when comparing two things.

Adjective:	My mother is **shorter** than my sister.
	Your baked lasagna is **more delicious** than my aunt's lasagna.
Adverb:	Our flight arrived **later** than we expected.
	Erin's picture was **more carefully** drawn than Linda's.

Superlative is the form used when comparing three or more things.

Adjective:	My mother is the **shortest** person in the family.
	Your baked lasagna is the **most delicious** of all.
Adverb:	Our flight arrived the **latest** of all the flights scheduled that day.
	Erin's picture was the **most carefully** drawn of all.

How to Form Adjective Comparatives and Superlatives

To form comparatives and superlatives, you will need to know the number of syllables in the word you want to change. Syllables are units of sound in a word. A syllable can be one letter or a group of letters. When written, the letters are used to express the spoken sounds. This chart shows how to form adjective comparatives and superlatives.

Number of Syllables	Comparative	Superlative
1 syllable	1. Add –r to words ending in –e.	1. Add –st to words ending in –e.
ripe	■ riper	■ ripest
	2. Add –er to words with more than one vowel or more than one consonant at the end.	2. Add –est to words with more than one vowel or more than one consonant at the end.
bright	■ brighter	■ brightest
	3. Double the consonant and add –er to words ending in one vowel and one consonant.	3. Double the consonant and add –est to words ending in one vowel and one consonant.
big	■ bigger	■ biggest
	4. Add –er to words ending in two vowels and a consonant.	4. Add –est to words ending in two vowels and a consonant.
sweet	■ sweeter	■ sweetest
2 syllables	1. For words ending in –y, drop the –y and add –ier.	1. For words ending in –y, drop the –y and add –iest.
healthy	■ healthier	■ healthiest

Number of Syllables	Comparative	Superlative
	2. For words not ending in –y, add the word **more** before the adjective. ■ more fragrant	2. For words not ending in –y, add the word **most** before the adjective. ■ most fragrant
fragrant		
3 syllables	Add the word **more** in front of the adjective.	Add the word **most** in front of the adjective.
delicious	■ more delicious	■ most delicious
succulent	■ more succulent	■ most succulent
pleasurable	■ more pleasurable	■ most pleasurable

Irregular forms of adjectives
Some adjectives have irregular comparative and superlative forms. It's a good idea to memorize them.

Adjective	Comparative form	Superlative form
good	better	best
bad	worse	worst
far	farther	farthest
ill	worse	worst
little (amount)	less	least
many	more	most
much	more	most

How to Form Adverb Comparatives and Superlatives
This chart explains how to form comparatives and superlatives. Either change the ending of the adverb or add **more/most** or **less/least** in front of the adverb.

Number of Syllables	Comparative	Superlative
1 or 2 syllables **fast** **late** **soon**	Add –er **faster** **later** **sooner**	Add –est **fastest** **latest** **soonest**
2 or more syllables adverbs ending in –ly **proudly** **lovingly** **carefully**	Add the word *more* or the word *less* in front of the adverb. **more (less) proudly** **more (less) lovingly** **more (less) carefully**	Add the word *most* or the word *least* in front of the adverb. **most (least) proudly** **most (least) lovingly** **most (least) carefully**

Irregular Adverbs

Some adverbs have irregular comparative and superlative forms. It's a good idea to memorize them.

Adverb	Comparative	Superlative
well	better	best
badly	worse	worst
little	less	least
much	more	most
far	farther/further	farthest/furthest

SECTION 9 ◆ DIAGNOSTIC: DEGREE FORMS OF ADJECTIVES AND ADVERBS

Choose the option that best completes the sentence. When you are done, check your work with the answers immediately following the diagnostic. Even if you get a perfect score here, go ahead and complete the exercises in this section; they are designed to help build confidence and to give you practice for future test success.

1. Nick needs to learn to be _____ with his money.
   A. carefuller
   B. more carefuller
   C. carefullest
   D. more careful

2. Cats seem to be _____ than dogs.
   A. more curiouser
   B. more curious
   C. curiouser
   D. most curious

3. That was the _____ movie I have ever seen.
   A. worse
   B. worst
   C. worstest
   D. most worst

4. The weather was _____ this spring than it was in the spring of last year.
   A. cooler
   B. coolest
   C. more cool
   D. more cooler

5. Hernan bought his girl friend the _____ BMW on the lot.
   A. more expensive
   B. expensivest
   C. most expensive
   D. most expensivist

6. I could not tell if Mother was _____ at me for coming home late or at my brother
   for not coming home at all last night.
   A. more angrier
   B. most angry
   C. angriest
   D. angrier

7. Although Helen likes her job at Chili's, she liked working at Applebee's _____.
   A. better
   B. best
   C. more better
   D. bestest

Answers and Explanations to Diagnostic: Degree Forms of Adjectives and Adverbs

1. Answer   D
The comparative "more careful" is the required form. Two-syllable adjectives not ending in –y often
require the addition of "more" before the word for the comparative form.

2. Answer   B
The comparative "more curious" is required to compare cats to dogs. Adjectives of more than three
syllables form the comparative by adding "more" before the word.

3. Answer   B
"Worst" is the superlative adjective form required because more than two movies are being compared, "the worst movie I have ever seen."

4. Answer   A
The spring weather in two different years is being compared in the sentence. One-syllable adjectives
form the comparative by adding –er to the end of the word.

5. Answer   C
The superlative form "most expensive" is required. Adjectives of more than three syllables form the
superlative by adding "most" before the word.

6. Answer   D
The comparative "angrier" is required. Two-syllable adjectives ending in –y form the comparative
by adding –ier.

7. Answer   A
The comparative "better" is required to compare the two jobs. "Better" is the comparative form
of the adjective "good."

SECTION 9 ◆ EXERCISES: DEGREE FORMS OF ADJECTIVES AND ADVERBS

DIRECTIONS: *For each of the following questions, choose the option that corrects an error in the
underlined portion(s). If no error exists, choose "No change is necessary."*

1. Ronnie is the _____ of the two guitar players in the band.
   A. best
   B. more better
   C. better
   D. bestest

2. The Blue Ridge Mountains are among the _____ mountain ranges in the United States.
   A. more beautiful
   B. most beautiful
   C. beautifullest

3. Last year was the <u>worse</u> year since 1992 for the number of hurricanes in our state.
   A. worst
   B. most worst
   C. more worst
   D. No change is necessary.

4. My sister thinks that Brad Pitt is the <u>handsomest</u> actor in movies today.
   A. more handsome
   B. most handsome
   C. most handsomest
   D. No change is necessary.

5. Josh works out _____ than I do.
   A. most effectively
   B. more effective
   C. more effectively
   D. most effective

6. My house is _____ from the college than your house is.
   A. farthest
   B. more far
   C. most farthest
   D. farther

7. Debbie plans to study <u>more diligent</u> for the final than she did for the midterm.
   A. more diligently
   B. most diligently
   C. most diligent
   D. No change is necessary.

8. Hai performed his routine <u>more enthusiastically</u> than Kim.
   A. most enthusiastically
   B. more enthusiastic
   C. most enthusiastic
   D. No change is necessary.

9. These exercises are _____ than I thought they would be.
   A. more hard
   B. hardest
   C. harder
   D. more harder

10. Math is <u>more easier</u> for her than English is.
    A. more easy
    B. easier
    C. easiest
    D. No change is necessary.

| Competency 4.10 | Grammar, Spelling, Capitalization, and Punctuation Skills |
| Skill Tested | Uses standard spelling |

The Skill

This item tests your knowledge of the rules for Standard American English spelling and your ability to apply them. The words used on the test will include words commonly misspelled and those requiring knowledge of spelling rules.

The best way to improve your spelling is to track your own misspellings and to learn to use your dictionary frequently. Many misspellings are the simple confusion of vowel sounds, such as substituting "a" and "e" for each other. Sometimes a word may be spelled correctly, but it may be the wrong word, like **their** for **there**. There are standard spelling rules that you should learn.

Five Basic Spelling Rules

1. The **ie** rule. You may have heard the rhyme "Put an *i* before *e* except after *c* or when sounded like *ay* as in *neighbor* and *weigh*."

achieve	believe	chief	relieve	mischievous
ceiling	deceive	perceive	receive	receipt
freight	neighbor	vein	weigh	heir

2. The **final e** rule. Drop a final silent *e* before an ending beginning with a vowel (*a, e, i, o, u,* and here, *y*).

   write + ing = writing   fame + ous = famous   scare + y = scary

   Exception: mileage

   Keep the e in these situations:

   - After **c** and **g** before an ending beginning with *a* or *o*:
     noticeable   courageous   outrageous   vengeance

   - To avoid confusion with other words:
     dye + ing = dyeing   singe + ing = singeing

3. The **final y** rule. Change a final *y* to *i* before any ending except *–ing*.

   happy + ness = happiness   lady + es = ladies   cry + ing = crying

   Ignore the rule if a vowel precedes the *y*.
   chimn*e*ys   anno*ye*d   monk*e*ys

   Exceptions: lay/laid   pay/paid   say/said

4. Double a final consonant before an ending that begins with a vowel (including *y*) if the original word does both of the following:

   - Ends in consonant-vowel-consonant
     drop/dropping   bat/batter

   - If more than one syllable is accented
     occur   occurred   occurrence
     begin   beginning   beginner

5. The let-it-alone rule. When adding beginnings or endings to words, do not add or drop letters unless you know that one of the spelling rules applies or that the word is irregular.

disappear   misspell   statement   achievement

(Adapted from Blanche Ellsworth and John A. Higgins, *English Simplified*, 9th ed., New York: Addison Wesley, 2001.)

Spelling Rules for Plurals

Making Nouns Plural. To form the plurals of most nouns, add an –s to the end of the word.

machine + s = machines
wave + s = waves
notebook + s = notebooks
Clark + s = Clarks

This general rule has several exceptions.

Exception 1: If the singular noun ends in –s, –ss, –sh, –ch, or –x, add –es to the end of the word.

| bus | buses | kiss | kisses | wish | wishes |
| fox | foxes | church | churches | witch | witches |

Exception 2: If the singular common noun ends in –o

- Add –s when the word ends in a vowel + –o

radio	radios
stereo	stereos
Soprano	Sopranos

- Add –es when the word ends in a consonant + –o

| tomato | tomatoes |
| veto | vetoes |

NOTE: A few words that end in a consonant + o do not change in this way.

solo	solos
piano	pianos
pro	pros
memo	memos

Exception 3: If the singular noun ends in a consonant and –y, change the –y to –i and add –es.

| salary | salaries |
| company | companies |

Exception 4: If the singular noun ends in a vowel and –y, add –s.

guy	guys
day	days
Gray	Grays

Exception 5: If the singular noun ends in –f or –fe, change the –f to a v and add –s or –es.

| knife | knives |
| self | selves |

NOTE: Some words ending in –f do not change:

belief	beliefs
chief	chiefs
staff	staffs

Exception 6: Some singular nouns have different plural forms and are considered irregular:

woman	women
man	men
child	children
foot	feet

Exception 7: With hyphenated nouns, add –s to the first word.

father-in-law	fathers-in-law
sister-in-law	sisters-in-law

100 Problem Words

absence	definite	management	pursue
acknowledge	description	maneuver	questionnaire
acquaintance	desperate	mathematics	reminisce
acquire	develop	meant	repetition
across	discipline	mischievous	restaurant
adolescence	doesn't	necessary	rhythm
amateur	eighth	ninety	ridiculous
analysis	erroneous	ninth	sacrifice
apologize	exaggerate	nucleus	schedule
apparent	excellent	omission	secretary
approximately	existence	opinion	sensible
argument	fascinating	opportunity	sincerely
article	forty	parallel	sophomore
auxiliary	fulfill	particularly	souvenir
business	guarantee	perform	supposed to
calendar	guidance	permanent	suppression
category	height	permissible	surprise
committee	hindrance	perseverance	synonym
competent	hypocrisy	persistent	tendency
condemn	independent	personally	tragedy
conscientious	indispensable	playwright	truly
courteous	irrelevant	prejudice	twelfth
criticism	irresistible	prevalent	unusually
criticize	knowledge	procedure	used to
curiosity	maintenance	psychology	vacuum

(From Blanche Ellsworth and John A. Higgins, *English Simplified*, 9th ed., New York: Addison Wesley, 2001.)

The Test Question

You will be presented with one or three underlined words in a sentence. In the sentence in which only one word is underlined, you must choose the correct spelling. If three words are underlined in the sentence, you must choose the option that is the correction for an error in one of the underlined portions. If the sentence is correct, choose "No change is necessary."

For each of the following questions, choose the option that corrects an error in the underlined portion(s). If no error exists, choose "No change is necessary." When you are done, check your work with the answers immediately following the diagnostic. Even if you get a perfect score here, go ahead and complete the exercises in this section; they are designed to help build confidence and to give you practice for future test success.

1. Gene was <u>transfered</u> to the company's corporate office in Tampa; this was a
               A

   <u>beneficial</u> move, for he gained a <u>substantial</u> raise.
     B   C
   A. transferred
   B. benificial
   C. substancial
   D. No change is necessary.

2. Jena refused to date men who <u>criticized</u> her <u>intelligence</u> and expected her to pay for <u>diner</u>.
                   A   B   C
   A. critisized
   B. inteligence
   C. dinner
   D. No change is necessary.

3. At the end of the semester, Kim was <u>exhausted</u> but <u>exhillarated</u> because she was now
             A   B

   <u>eligible</u> for a scholarship.
     C
   A. exausted
   B. exhilarated
   C. elligible
   D. No change is necessary.

4. The discovery of antibiotics has helped cure many <u>diseases</u>; however, some germ strains
                         A

   have become <u>resistent</u> to many antibiotics, and newer, stronger ones must be <u>developed</u>.
         B   C
   A. deseases
   B. resistant
   C. develloped
   D. No change is necessary.

5. When he was working out, Eric <u>accidentally</u> dropped a <u>dumbbell</u>, which greatly
                  A   B

   <u>embarassed</u> him.
     C

A. accidentaly
B. dumbell
C. embarrassed
D. No change is necessary.

6. Adnan worked on his English <u>pronunciation</u> on a daily basis.
   A. pronounciation
   B. pronountiation
   C. pronounsiation
   D. No change is necessary.

7. Tennessee Williams was a famous North American <u>playright</u>.
   A. playwright
   B. playwrite
   C. playrite
   D. No change is necessary.

Answers and Explanations to Diagnostic: Standard Spelling

1. Answer   A
"Transfer" contains two syllables and a single vowel precedes the final consonant, so the *r* is doubled before adding an ending, as in "transferred."
2. Answer   C
The correct spelling contains the double consonant "n" in "dinner."
3. Answer   B
The correct spelling contains a silent "h" and a single "l," "exhilarated."
4. Answer   B
The correct spelling contains an –ant ending, "resistant."
5. Answer   C
"Embarrassed" has two sets of double consonants, two r's and two s's.
6. Answer   D
The correct spelling has only two o's: "pronunciation."
7. Answer   A
The trouble spot in this word is its ending, "wright." This word must be memorized.

SECTION 10 ◆ EXERCISES: STANDARD SPELLING

DIRECTIONS: *For each of the following questions, choose the option that corrects an error in the underlined portion(s). If no error exists, choose "No change is necessary."*

1. Some day, I hope to become a <u>knowledgable</u> physician.
   A. knowledgible
   B. knowledgeable
   C. knowlegeable
   D. No change is necessary.

2. The most difficult <u>descision</u> Carla had to make was to come to the United States on her own to attend college.
   A. decision
   B. dicision

C. decishion

D. No change is necessary.

3. It was <u>truley</u> a <u>privilege</u> to hear the President's <u>speech</u> in person.
                  A   B   C

A. truly

B. priviledge

C. speach

D. No change is necessary.

4. Andy is <u>pursuing</u> a <u>career</u> as a <u>licenced</u> massage therapist.
                      A   B   C

A. persuing

B. carreer

C. licensed

D. No change is necessary.

5. When my sister went to see her favorite band in concert, she was in <u>extasy</u>.

A. exstasy

B. ecstacy

C. ecstasy

D. No change is necessary.

6. Although Jolie has become a vegetarian, she has to have a burger <u>occasionally</u>.

A. occassionally

B. occasionaly

C. occasinally

D. No change is necessary.

7. A brief afternoon shower is a common <u>occurence</u> in the summer.

A. occurrance

B. occurrence

C. ocurrence

D. No change is necessary.

8. The <u>committee</u> was able to <u>accomodate</u> visitors at the meeting without <u>noticeable</u>
            A   B   C

interruption.

A. comittee

B. accommodate

C. noticable

D. No change is necessary.

9. The team had an <u>arguement</u> about whether Edgar used good <u>judgment</u> when he
                          A   B

<u>interfered</u> with the coach's directions.
     C

A. argument

B. judgement

C. interferred

D. No change is necessary.

10. Luis had a guilty <u>conscience</u> after he saw how <u>embarassed</u> Natalie became when all the

                  A   B

servers at the restaurant sang "Happy Birthday" as a <u>surprise</u>.

                                                  C

    A. consience
    B. embarrassed
    C. suprise
    D. No change is necessary.

SECTION 11 ◆ STANDARD PUNCTUATION—COMMAS, SEMICOLONS, END MARKS, APOSTROPHES

| Competency 4.11 | Grammar, Spelling, Capitalization, and Punctuation Skills |
| Skill Tested | Uses standard punctuation |

The Skill

This item tests your ability to use standard punctuation: **periods, commas, semicolons,** and **apostrophes.** The punctuation rules for each of these skills are provided for you in this section.

Periods
- Place a period at the end of a sentence that makes a statement.

    Cell phone technology is constantly advancing.

- Place a period at the end of an indirect question.

    The instructor asked whose phone was beeping.

Commas
- Place a comma at the end of an introductory phrase.

    During our vacation at Disney World, we enjoyed going on the Twilight Zone Tower of Terror ride.

- Place a comma to separate elements in dates.

    Between the day and the year: October 26, 1972
    Between the day and the date: Monday, June 6, 2005
    On both sides of the year in a full date: Dan was born on October 26, 1972, in Philadelphia.

- Place a comma between items in a list or series. A series is made of three or more items; the items can be words, phrases, or clauses.

    We brought towels, water, chairs, and snacks to the beach but forgot sunscreen.
    Byron ate a tub of popcorn, drank an extra-large cola, and finished a box of chocolate-covered peanuts during the movie.

- Place a comma before the coordinating conjunction in a compound sentence. The coordinating conjunctions are **for, and, nor, but, or, yet, so.** These words are easy to remember by the mnemonic **FANBOYS;** each letter of this word is the first letter of one of the coordinating conjunctions.

    Josh would like to buy a new video game every month, **but** he doesn't have enough money.
    The bus was late, **so** I missed half of my English class.

- Place a comma after a dependent clause that begins a complex sentence.

    If I want to pass this test, I have to review grammar and do practice exercises.

    Do not place a comma after an independent clause that begins a complex sentence.

    I have to review grammar and do practice exercises if I want to pass this test.

- Place a comma before and after a nonessential dependent clause in a complex sentence.

    My treadmill, **which I bought online,** is my favorite piece of exercise equipment.

    In this sentence, the reader does not need to know where the treadmill was purchased to know that it is my favorite piece of exercise equipment. The next sentence is an example of an essential dependent clause in which no commas are used.

    The man who is wearing the red T-shirt is handing out free tickets to the game.

    You need to know which man is handing out free tickets, so the dependent clause is essential to the sentence; therefore, no commas are required.

- Use commas to set off words that interrupt a sentence. They may appear at the beginning, in the middle, or at the end of a sentence. Interrupters can be single words, phrases, or other clauses.

    Mr. Dupree, the papers are ready for you to sign.
    To avoid missing your exam, arrive early at the test site.
    The best student in class, **my friend Kimberly,** gets A's on all of her essays.
    Either the chocolate mousse or the cheesecake, **however,** is fine with me.
    Your outfit, **to be perfectly honest,** is not flattering on you.
    The cat, **racing across the tile floor to catch the catnip toy,** crashed into the wall.

- Use commas to set off geographical names.

    My family moved to Florida from **Atlanta, Georgia.**
    Atlanta, Georgia, is the place where I was born.

- Use commas to separate adjectives that modify the same noun.

    The **informative, dynamic** speaker captivated the audience.
    The **hungry, sneaky** dog ate an entire box of **rich, cream-filled, chocolate** cupcakes.

Semicolons

Semicolons are used to separate two independent clauses in two ways: with the semicolon alone or with the semicolon and a conjunctive adverb.

1. A semicolon may be used by itself to separate two independent clauses that are closely related in ideas.

    My two-year-old daughter doesn't like to take her **nap; she** doesn't want to miss out on our family activities.

2. A semicolon may be used to separate two independent clauses linked with conjunctive adverbs or transition words or phrases.

    My printer ran out of ink; **therefore,** I had to rush to the college computer lab to print my essay.

Apostrophes

Possession is the term used to show that something belongs to someone or something. In writing, we use the **apostrophe** to show possession of nouns and of indefinite pronouns. The rules for forming possessive nouns are summarized in this chart.

Singular noun not ending in –s	**Add apostrophe + s**
Dan	Dan's
week	week's vacation
university	university's policy
child	child's toy
Jamaica	Jamaica's population
Ft. Lauderdale	Rio de Janeiro's beaches
group	group's presentation
Singular noun ending in –s	**Add apostrophe (or apostrophe + s)**
Jarvis	Jarvis' new Honda
bus	bus' seats
class	class' assignment
Las Vegas	Las Vegas' casinos
United States	United States' laws

Note: the apostrophe + s can also be used if the extra syllable at the end of the word is pronounced.

Plural noun not ending in –s	**Add apostrophe + s**
children	children's programs
teeth	teeth's enamel
deer	deer's tracks
mice	mice's experiment results
Plural noun ending in –s	**Add apostrophe**
months	three months' summer vacation
glasses	glasses' lightweight frames
terrorists	terrorists' activities
countries	countries' attractions
Hyphenated words	**Add apostrophe + s to last word**
mother-in-law	mother-in-law's meatloaf
passer-by	passer-by's pink hair
Two nouns, joint owners	**Add apostrophe + s to last word**
Theo and Tamika	Theo and Tamika's computer
my sister and her son	my sister and her son's cell phone
Two nouns, individual owners	**Add apostrophe + s to each word**
Claudia and Mark	Claudia's and Mark's essays
the snake and the iguana	the snake's and the iguana's cages

Most of the time, apostrophes are not used to form plurals. The current trend is to add the *s* without the apostrophe, especially with acronyms, such as CD, VCR, NASA, MAAD, and NOW.

The Test Question

You will be given two types of questions.

1. You will be given a sentence with one or three underlined parts. You must choose the option that corrects the error.
2. You will be given three versions of one sentence. You must choose the sentence that is correctly punctuated.

SECTION 11 ◆ DIAGNOSTIC: STANDARD PUNCTUATION—COMMAS, SEMICOLONS, END MARKS, APOSTROPHES

For each of the following questions, choose the option that corrects an error in the underlined portion(s). If no error exists, choose "No change is necessary." When you are done, check your work with the answers immediately following the diagnostic. Even if you get a perfect score here, go ahead and complete the exercises in this section; they are designed to help build confidence and to give you practice for future test success.

1. Bimini is the most relaxing place to <u>fish; because,</u> Bimini is practically deserted most
                                     A

   of the <u>time, and</u> I can go out on my <u>boat and</u> fish for hours without being bothered.
          B   C
   A. fish because
   B. time and
   C. boat, and
   D. No change is necessary.

2. In the past five years, drug <u>dealer's</u> and <u>gangs have</u> taken over my <u>old neighborhood</u>.
                                A   B   C
   A. dealers
   B. gangs, have
   C. old, neighborhood
   D. No change is necessary.

3. When someone first walks into my room, he or she always <u>says, "Wow!</u> <u>That's</u>
                                                       A   B

   a nice <u>guitar"</u>.
           C
   A. says; "Wow!
   B. Thats'
   C. guitar."
   D. No change is necessary.

4. I enjoy playing <u>soccer for</u> a variety of <u>reasons, soccer</u> relieves my <u>stress, helps</u> me
                                A   B   C
   relax, and keeps me fit.
   A. soccer, for
   B. reasons; soccer
   C. stress. Helps
   D. No change is necessary.

5. A recent trip back to my old high <u>school revealed</u> a loss of <u>innocence as</u> I
                                       A   B
    retraced my wonderful teen <u>years, the</u> building was there, but the stone retaining
                                     C
    wall and the grand old oak tree were not.
    A. school. Revealed
    B. innocence, as
    C. years. The
    D. No change is necessary.

For each of the following options, choose the sentence that is correctly punctuated.

6.
    A. In his senior year of high school, Michael went to Los Angeles to play baseball on a minor
        league field; in college, he played on fields in Pensacola and St. Petersburg, where the
        Phillies have their spring training.
    B. In his senior year of high school; Michael went to Los Angeles to play baseball on a minor
        league field; in college, he played on fields in Pensacola and St. Petersburg where the
        Phillies have their spring training.
    C. In his senior year of high school, Michael went to Los Angeles to play baseball on a minor
        league field, in college, he played on fields in Pensacola and St. Petersburg where the
        Phillies have their spring training.
    D. In his senior year of high school, Michael went to Los Angeles to play baseball on a minor
        league field, in college, he played on fields in Pensacola and St. Petersburg, where the
        Phillies have their spring training.

7.
    A. At our football teams' annual awards dinner, the coach gave a speech about the player
        who had improved the most William Hawling.
    B. At our football team's annual awards dinner, the coach gave a speech about the player
        who had improved the most, William Hawling.
    C. At our football teams' annual awards dinner; the coach gave a speech about the player
        who had improved the most, William Hawling.
    D. At our football team's annual awards dinner, the coach gave a speech about the player,
        who had improved the most William Hawling.

Answers and Explanations to Diagnostic: Standard Punctuation

1. Answer   A

No punctuation is required before this dependent clause that follows an independent clause.

False choices
    B A comma and a coordinating conjunction are required to connect independent clauses.
    C A comma is not needed to separate the compound verbs "can go" and "fish." The "and"
       connects the two verbs.

2. Answer   A

"Dealers" is the correct plural form of the noun "dealer." "Dealer's" is the possessive form.

False choices
    B A comma is not used to separate a subject "gangs" from its verb, "have."
    C A comma is not used to separate an adjective placed right before a noun.

3. Answer   C
The period is placed inside the quotation mark at the end of a sentence.

False choices
    A A comma follows the signal verb introducing a direct quotation.
    B "That's" is the contracted form of "that is."

4. Answer   B
The semicolon after "reasons" corrects the fused sentence.

False choices
    A A comma is not required to separate a prepositional phrase from a direct object.
    C Placing a period after "stress" creates a fragment at the end of the sentence. The sentence contains a series of phrases: "relieves my stress, helps me relax, and keeps me fit."

5. Answer   C
Placing a period after "years" corrects a comma splice error.

False choices
    A Placing a period after "school" creates a fragment of the first part of the sentence; the sentence created following "school" would be awkward.
    B No comma is necessary before a dependent clause that follows an independent clause.

6. Answer   A
The first issue is the punctuation after the word "school." A comma is required after a long introductory phrase. The next point to consider is the punctuation mark after "field." The semicolon is required to separate two independent clauses. The last issue is the comma after the city St. Petersburg. A comma is used after geographical names.

7. Answer   B
The first issue is the apostrophe used with the word "team." In this sentence, the word "team" is singular, so to make it possessive, an apostrophe and an "s" are placed at the end of the word: "team's." The next issue is the punctuation mark after "dinner." A comma is used after a long introductory phrase. Finally, a comma is required after the word "most" to set off the appositive that follows.

SECTION 11 ◆ EXERCISES: STANDARD PUNCTUATION—COMMAS, SEMICOLONS, END MARKS, APOSTROPHES

DIRECTIONS: For each of the following questions, choose the option that corrects an error in the underlined portion(s). If no error exists, choose "No change is necessary."

1. Patrice, <u>who sits next to me in class,</u> called to find out if our professor assigned an
                                    A
   <u>essay or</u> a reading for <u>homework?</u>
        B   C
   A. who sits next to me in class
   B. essay, or
   C. homework.
   D. No change is necessary.

2. Magdalene <u>couldn't</u> attend her English <u>class, because</u> her son had to be rushed to
                     A   B
   the <u>hospital's</u> emergency room.
            C

A. could'nt
B. class because
C. hospitals'
D. No change is necessary.

3. Since <u>January 24, 1937</u> Bike Week has been held in Daytona <u>Beach; this</u> ten-day
                A   B

<u>festival includes</u> motorcycle races at Daytona International Speedway.
       C
A. January 24, 1937,
B. Beach, this
C. festival, includes
D. No change is necessary.

4. <u>Although Doris</u> likes to eat her favorite flavors of low-carb <u>bars, such as,</u> s'mores,
       A   B

cookie crunch, and chocolate peanut <u>butter,</u> she has trouble digesting them.
                                     C
A. Although, Doris
B. bars, such as
C. butter she
D. No change is necessary.

5. When Darryl received all <u>As</u> last <u>semester, he</u> made the <u>Dean's List</u> for the first time in
                                A   B   C

his life.
A. As'
B. semester; he
C. Deans' List
D. No change is necessary.

DIRECTIONS: *For each of the following questions, choose the sentence that is correctly punctuated.*

6.
A. As a student, Jessica was used to having summers and holidays off, so she was shocked to learn that she would get only two week's vacation on her first job after graduation.
B. As a student, Jessica was used to having summers and holidays off so she was shocked to learn that she would get only two week's vacation on her first job after graduation.
C. As a student, Jessica was used to having summers and holidays off so she was shocked to learn that she would get only two weeks' vacation on her first job after graduation.
D. As a student, Jessica was used to having summers and holidays off, so she was shocked to learn that she would get only two weeks' vacation on her first job after graduation.

7.
A. I can go to the movie but not dinner because somebody's coming to my house later.
B. I can go to the movie, but not dinner because somebody's coming to my house later.
C. I can go to the movie but not dinner because somebodys' coming to my house later.
D. I can go to the movie, but not dinner because somebodys' coming to my house later.

8.
A. Heather asked her boss if she could take a months' leave of absence to take care of her sick mother?

B. Heather asked her boss, if she could take a month's leave of absence to take care of her sick mother.

C. Heather asked her boss if she could take a month's leave of absence to take care of her sick mother.

D. Heather asked her boss if she could take a month's leave of absence to take care of her sick mother?

9.

A. Rabbits make wonderful pets and do not require much equipment; for example, a litter box, a hay manger, a food bowl, and a water bottle.

B. Rabbits make wonderful pets and do not require much equipment, for example, a litter box, a hay manger, a food bowl, and a water bottle.

C. Rabbits make wonderful pets, and do not require much equipment, for example, a litter box, a hay manger, a food bowl, and a water bottle.

D. Rabbits, make wonderful pets, and do not require much equipment; for example, a litter box, a hay manger, a food bowl, and a water bottle.

10.

A. The zircon gemstone was believed to have many powers, such as keeping evil spirits away and banishing grief and sadness from the mind.

B. The zircon gemstone was believed to have many powers, such as keeping evil spirits away, and banishing grief and sadness from the mind.

C. The zircon gemstone was believed to have many powers; such as, keeping evil spirits away and banishing grief and sadness from the mind.

D. The zircon gemstone was believed to have many powers, such as keeping evil spirits away, and, banishing grief and sadness from the mind.

SECTION 12 ◆ STANDARD CAPITALIZATION

Competency 4.12	Grammar, Spelling, Capitalization, and Punctuation Skills
Skill Tested	Uses standard capitalization

The Skill

This item tests your ability to apply basic capitalization rules. Always capitalize the first word of a sentence.

The following chart summarizes some of these rules.

People

Names	Martin Luther King, Jr., Amy Tan, Gabriel Garcia Marquez
Job titles or positions: Capitalize when they immediately precede the individual's name or when they are honorary titles.	Professor Benjamin, Mayor Bloomberg, President Bush, Chairperson Grasso, Endowed Teaching Chair Hilton
Capitalize titles of high-ranking government officials used with or without their names. Use lower case if the reference is general.	The President will visit the Middle East. The second president was John Adams.

Family relationships NOTE: When using a word such as <u>mother</u> or <u>father</u>, do not capitalize it unless you are using the word in place of the person's name.	Uncle Tai, Aunt Bessie I called Father today to ask him for money for textbooks. I called my father today to ask him for money for textbooks.
Groups and languages	African-Americans, Asians, Native Americans, Aleuts, French, Hebrew, Latin, Arabic, English, Spanish

Places

Geographical locations NOTE: when using the words <u>north</u>, <u>south</u>, <u>east</u>, or <u>west</u> for directions, do not capitalize them.	Arizona, Palm Beach County, the Rocky Mountains, Honduras, Gulf of Mexico, Pacific Ocean, Australia, Haiti, College Avenue Jose plans to move west after he graduates. Jose's family lives in the West.
Buildings, monuments (structures made by humans)	The Pentagon, Taj Mahal, Ritz Carlton Hotel, Philadelphia Museum of Art, Hoover Dam, Empire State Building, Golden Gate Bridge
Academic institutions, courses NOTE: Capitalize the title of a course but not the subject of the course	Michigan State University, University of Colorado, Valencia Community College History 101, Biology 2, English 2210 My favorite subject is <u>psychology</u>. I plan to take <u>Psychology 203</u> next semester.
Organizations, government agencies, institutions	Angel Flight, Internal Revenue Service, National Endowment for the Humanities, MADD, NFL

Things

Religious terms: religions and followers, holidays, holy books, words for deities	Islam, Christianity, Judaism, Buddhism, Easter, Ramadan, Yom Kippur, Kwanza, Allah, Bible, Torah, Koran, Book of Mormon, God, Vishnu
Historical periods, events, documents	Civil War, Dark Ages, Great Depression Bill of Rights, the Constitution
Time periods (days of week, months, holidays)	Sunday, July, Labor Day, Columbus Day, Thanksgiving

Company and product trademark ™ names	Bandaids, Microsoft, Apple, Verizon, Coke, Toyota, Nike, Big Mac, Levis
Awards	Oscars, Davis Cup, Grammy Awards, Nobel Prize, Pulitzer Prize
Planets, stars NOTE: Capitalize the word <u>earth</u> only when referring to it as a planet. Do not capitalize <u>earth</u> when used with <u>the</u> as in **the earth's climate**. Capitalize the words <u>earth, moon,</u> or <u>stars</u> in a sentence where they are used to refer to other astronomical bodies.	Little Dipper, Uranus, Earth, the Milky Way; Mars, Saturn, and Earth are planets in our solar system. The earth's atmosphere can support human life.
Major words in the titles of books, songs, plays, movies, articles. Always capitalize the first word and the last word, but do not capitalize articles (a, an, the), short prepositions, or conjunctions in a title.	*Lord of the Rings, Terminator,* "I Can't Get No Satisfaction," *The Godfather, Revenge of the Sith*

The Test Question
You will be presented with a sentence with three underlined parts. If a sentence contains an error, you must choose the answer that corrects an underlined part. If the sentence is correct, choose "No change is necessary."

SECTION 12 ◆ DIAGNOSTIC: STANDARD CAPITALIZATION

For each of the following questions, choose the option that corrects an error in the underlined portion(s). If no error exists, choose "No change is necessary." When you are done, check your work with the answers immediately following the diagnostic. Even if you get a perfect score here, go ahead and complete the exercises in this section; they are designed to help build confidence and to give you practice for future test success.

1. My <u>uncle</u> came to the United States to teach <u>mathematics</u> at the <u>University</u>.
        A   B   C
   A. Uncle
   B. Mathematics
   C. university
   D. No change is necessary.

2. Kien Nguyen, the son of an anonymous soldier and a wealthy <u>south</u> Vietnamese <u>mother,</u>
                                                      A   B

   gives an account of his difficult childhood in his book *The Unwanted*.
                                                      C
   A. South
   B. Mother
   C. unwanted
   D. No change is necessary.

3. In Sweden, the <u>Summer</u> solstice is a <u>national</u> holiday; the Swedish traditionally eat
                     A   B

    <u>strawberries</u> for dessert on that day.
           C

    A. summer
    B. National
    C. Strawberries
    D. No change is necessary.

4. The <u>red bush</u> is an exotic plant with needle-like leaves that was used to make tea
          A

    by the indigenous people of South Africa; in the late 1800s, <u>settlers</u> in <u>Cape Town</u>
                                                  B   C

    discovered how this tea was made.
    A. Red Bush
    B. Settlers
    C. cape town
    D. No change is necessary.

5. A popular artificial sweetener on the market suitable for people with <u>Diabetes</u>
                                                                    A

    is <u>Splenda</u>; it tastes just like sugar and contains maltodextrin and <u>sucralose</u>.
        B   C

    A. diabetes
    B. splenda
    C. Sucralose
    D. No change is necessary.

6. To get to the <u>airport</u>, go <u>North</u> on the <u>expressway</u> about twenty miles.
                  A   B   C

    A. Airport
    B. north
    C. Expressway
    D. No change is necessary.

7. In 1978, Florida was designated a <u>sanctuary</u> for <u>manatees</u> by the Florida
                                        A   B

    Manatee Sanctuary Act; these animals are considered an <u>endangered species</u>.
                                                      C

    A. Sanctuary
    B. Manatees
    C. Endangered Species
    D. No change is necessary.

Answers and Explanations to Diagnostic: Standard Capitalization

1. Answer   C

The word "university" is not capitalized unless it is part of its name.

False choices

    A The word "uncle" is not capitalized unless it comes before a person's name, such as Uncle
    Phil.

B   The word "mathematics" is not capitalized unless it is a name of a course, such as Intermediate Algebra I.

2. Answer   A

"South" should be capitalized because it is part of the name of a region.

False choices
   B   The word "mother" is not capitalized unless it is used in place of her name.
   C   This word "Unwanted" is part of the title of a book. The last word of a title is always capitalized. It's a good idea to memorize the specific capitalization rules for titles.

3. Answer   A

Names of seasons are not capitalized.

False choices
   B   The common noun "national" does not have to be capitalized.
   C   The common noun "strawberries" does not have to be capitalized.

4. Answer   D

All words are capitalized correctly in this sentence. "Red bush" and "settlers" are both common nouns and do not need to be capitalized.

5. Answer   A

Names of diseases are not usually capitalized.

False choices
   B   "Splenda" is a brand name and should be capitalized.
   C   The name of the artificial sweetener "sucralose" is a common noun and does not have to be capitalized.

6. Answer   B

Words indicating directions do not need to be capitalized.

False choices
   A   "Airport" is a common noun in this sentence and does not need to be capitalized.
   C   The common noun "expressway" does not require capitalization.

7. Answer   D

All capitalized words are correct. All of the word choices are common nouns.

SECTION 12 ◆ EXERCISES: STANDARD CAPITALIZATION

DIRECTIONS: *For each of the following questions, choose the option that corrects an error in the underlined portion(s). If no error exists, choose "No change is necessary."*

1. Dan spent the first eight years of his life in the <u>north</u>; then, he and
                                                          A
    his mother moved to the <u>South</u> during the <u>Summer</u>.
                                  B   C

    A. North
    B. south
    C. summer
    D. No change is necessary.

2. This semester, Javier is taking <u>History</u>, <u>Psychology 101</u>, and <u>English</u>.
                                            A   B   C

    A. history
    B. psychology 101
    C. english
    D. No change is necessary.

3. When I went to <u>high school</u>, anyone who did not follow the <u>Dress Code</u> was sent to
                        A   B

the <u>principal's</u> office.
          C
    A. High school
    B. dress code
    C. Principal's
    D. No change is necessary.

4. To get to the <u>Chinese</u> restaurant, go <u>west</u> on Glades Road to <u>northwest</u> 20th Street.
                           A   B   C
    A. chinese
    B. West
    C. Northwest
    D. No change is necessary.

5. All three of the *Lord Of The Rings* books, written by <u>J. R. R. Tolkien</u>, have been
                          A   B

adapted into successful movies that have won many <u>Oscars</u>.
                                              C

    A. *Lord of the Rings*
    B. J.r.r. Tolkien
    C. oscars
    D. No change is necessary.

6. I look forward to Sunday dinner after <u>church</u>; we all get together at my <u>Aunt's</u>
                                        A   B

house, and she always serves my favorite, <u>Kraft brand macaroni and cheese</u>.
                                                  C

    A. Church
    B. aunt's
    C. Kraft Brand Macaroni and Cheese
    D. No change is necessary.

7. The Declaration of Independence, written to justify America's <u>independence</u> from England,
                                                        A

was approved by <u>Representatives</u> of the <u>American Colonies</u> in 1776 and became one
                          B   C

of the most respected documents in America.
    A. Independence
    B. representatives
    C. american colonies
    D. No change is necessary.

8. Each year, <u>companies</u> such as Budweiser, Charmin, and Staples pay over two
             A

   million dollars to air a thirty-second <u>television</u> commercial to the 100 million viewers
                                      B

   watching the <u>Super Bowl</u>.
               C

   A. Companies
   B. Television
   C. Super bowl
   D. No change is necessary.

9. In a speech delivered to his supporters in January 2004, Howard Dean, <u>Governor</u> of
                                                         A

   Vermont, was publicly criticized for uncontrolled screaming. Some people felt that

   this speech, which was called <u>"I Have a Scream"</u> by Dean's critics, contributed to his
                                  B

   losing the <u>Presidential</u> nomination.
              C

   A. governor
   B. "I have a scream"
   C. presidential
   D. No change is necessary.

10. Sheila and Dave spent a romantic <u>New Year's Eve</u> together on <u>Sanibel Island</u>, where
                                A   B

   they watched a colorful fireworks display over the <u>Gulf of Mexico</u>.
                                         C

   A. New year's eve
   B. Sanibel island
   C. gulf of Mexico
   D. No change is necessary.

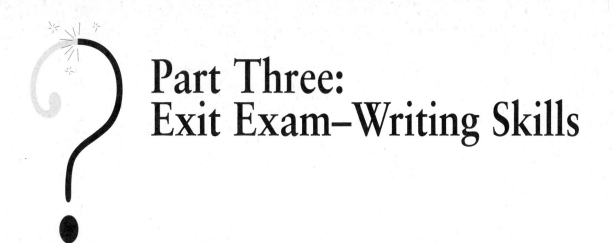

Part Three:
Exit Exam–Writing Skills

Read the entire passage carefully, then answer the questions. (Note: Intentional errors may have been included in the passage.)

(1) _____.

(2) At Columbine, 18-year-old Eric Harris and 17-year-old Dylan Klebold were generally seen as geeks or nerds from the point of view of any of the large student cliques—the jocks, the punks, etc. (3) Though excluded from mainstream student culture, they banded together and bonded together with several of their fellow outcasts in what they came to call the "Trench Coat Mafia." (4) As a result, trench coats became very popular attire among many students across the U. S. (5) The image they attempted to create was clearly one of power and dominance with their preoccupation with Hitler, the celebration of evil and villainy. (6) Harris and Klebold desperately wanted to feel important. (7) They amassed an arsenal of weapons, strategized about logistics, and made final preparations. (8) For more than a year, they plotted, planned, and conspired to put one over on their schoolmates, teachers, and parents. (9) In the preparations they made to murder their classmates, the two shooters got their wish. (10) Not a single adult got wind of what Harris and Klebold intended to do. (11) In their relationship, the two boys got from one another what was otherwise missing from their lives. (12) _____ they felt special, they gained a sense of belonging, and they were united against the world. (13) Family background can also be a factor in the actions of schoolyard snipers. (Adapted from James Alan Fox and Jack Levin, *The Will to Kill*, Boston: Allyn and Bacon, 2001.)

1. Which of the following sentences, if inserted into the blank labeled number 1, would provide the best thesis statement for the entire passage?
   A. On April 20, 1999, a school shooting occurred in Littleton, Colorado.
   B. In understanding the horrific actions of schoolyard snipers, it is important to examine friendships.
   C. The school shooting that occurred in Littleton, Colorado, altered the way people felt about school safety in many ways.
   D. Eric Harris and Dylan Klebold killed twelve students and one teacher on April 20, 1999.

2. Which of the numbered sentences is NOT supported by sufficient details?
   A. 6
   B. 8
   C. 11
   D. 13

3. Select the order of sentences 7, 8, and 9 that presents the details in the most logical sequence of ideas. If no change is necessary, select option A.
   A. They amassed an arsenal of weapons, strategized about logistics, and made final preparations. For more than a year, they plotted, planned, and conspired to put one over on their schoolmates, teachers, and parents. In the preparations they made to murder their classmates, the two shooters got their wish.
   B. For more than a year, they plotted, planned, and conspired to put one over on their schoolmates, teachers, and parents. In the preparations they made to murder their classmates, the two shooters got their wish. They amassed an arsenal of weapons, strategized about logistics, and made final preparations.
   C. In the preparations they made to murder their classmates, the two shooters got their wish. For more than a year, they plotted, planned, and conspired to put one over on their schoolmates, teachers, and parents. They amassed an arsenal of weapons, strategized about logistics, and made final preparations.
   D. They amassed an arsenal of weapons, strategized about logistics, and made final preparations. In the preparations they made to murder their classmates, the two shooters got their wish. For more than a year, they plotted, planned, and conspired to put one over on their schoolmates, teachers, and parents.

4. Which numbered sentence is the LEAST relevant to the passage?
   A. 2
   B. 4
   C. 5
   D. 12

5. Which word or phrase, if inserted into the blank in the sentence labeled number 12, would make the relationship between sentences 11 and 12 clear?
   A. As a result,
   B. However,
   C. Next,
   D. In summary,

Read the entire passage carefully, then answer the questions. (Note: Intentional errors may have been included in the passage.)

---

(1) _____.

(2) First of all, it may be difficult to meet the emotional needs of the child. (3) The demands of working and maintaining a home may be so overwhelming that a child's emotional needs may not be met adequately. (4) Telling a child that he or she is loved and demonstrating that love with quality time are ways to express love. (5) It also may be hard for the single parent to provide proper supervision for the child. (6) Making arrangements for the child's care and supervision is difficult and costly and may take a large share of the budget. (7) _____ because women tend to make less money than men, households headed by women can experience financial difficulties. (8) Finally, the single parent may experience unfulfilled emotional and sexual needs. (9) Unmet emotional needs can develop because of the lack of time to seek a relationship. (10) Because most single parents wish to hide their sexual involvement from their child, finding a time and place can present problems. (11) Divorce is not shameful as it used to be years ago. (12) It is important that single parents have sufficient financial, material, and emotional support to meet their own and their child's demands. (Adapted from David J. Anspaugh and Gene Ezell, *Teaching Today's Health*, 7th ed., San Francisco: Pearson, 2004.)

6. Which sentence, if inserted into the blank labeled number 1, would serve as the best thesis statement for the entire passage?
   A. There are over 11 million single parents in the United States.
   B. Divorce has many effects on a family.
   C. A single parent may experience a variety of problems.
   D. More than 15 million children are unsupervised from 3 to 8 p.m., which causes juvenile crime.

7. Which of the following sentences provides detailed support for sentence 6?
   A. Seventy-eight percent of mothers with 6–13 year olds work full time.
   B. Full-time daycare often costs as much as college tuition at a public university, yet 1 out of 3 families with young children earn less than $25,000 per year.
   C. Parents who receive child support have higher incomes.
   D. Many custodial parents have no provisions for health insurance and health care costs.

8. Which is the best placement for the sentence below to make the sequence of ideas clearer?

   A child needs some quality time with the parent every day; interacting with the child, actively listening and talking with him or her, and keeping it pleasant is quality time.

   A. Before sentence 4.
   B. After sentence 10.
   C. After sentence 4.
   D. Before sentence 8.

9. Which numbered sentence is the LEAST relevant to the passage?
   A. 3
   B. 6
   C. 8
   D. 11

10. Which word or phrase, if inserted into the blank in sentence 7, would make clear the relationship of ideas between sentences 6 and 8?
    A. In addition,
    B. Nevertheless,
    C. Then,
    D. Incidentally,

11. DIRECTIONS: Choose the most effective word or phrase within the context suggested by the sentence.

    At the age of three, Mariah's _____ for singing was apparent; she first performed in public when she was six and began writing songs when she was in elementary school.

    A. affection
    B. stubbornness
    C. aptitude

12. DIRECTIONS: Choose the most effective word or phrase within the context suggested by the sentence.

    The attorney tried to _____ the truth about the crime by examining all the evidence and thoroughly questioning the witnesses.

    A. ascertain
    B. presume
    C. disregard

13. DIRECTIONS: Choose the option that corrects an error in the underlined portion(s). If no error exists, choose "No change is necessary."

    Some people cannot <u>accept</u> a <u>complement</u> because <u>they're</u> not used to being praised.
                     A   B   C

    A. except
    B. compliment
    C. their
    D. No change is necessary.

14. DIRECTIONS: Choose the option that corrects an error in the underlined portion(s). If no error exists, choose "No change is necessary."

    Bryan <u>would of</u> shared an apartment with his girl friend, but his mom did not feel
            A

    <u>good</u> about the idea and <u>advised</u> against it.
       B   C

A. would have
B. well
C. adviced
D. No change is necessary.

15. DIRECTIONS: Choose the sentence in which the modifiers are correctly placed.
A. Uncle Fred finally found the restaurant driving around in his car.
B. The restaurant was found driving around in his car.
C. Driving around in his car, Uncle Fred finally found the restaurant.

16. DIRECTIONS: Choose the sentence in which the modifiers are correctly placed.
A. While watching a movie on television, the power went out.
B. While I was watching a movie on television, the power went out.
C. The power went out while watching a movie on television.

17. DIRECTIONS: Choose the sentence that expresses the thought most clearly and effectively and has no error in structure.
A. After the movie was over, we went to get pizza.
B. Although the movie was over, we went to get pizza.
C. While the movie was over, we went to get pizza.

18. DIRECTIONS: Choose the most effective word or phrase within the context suggested by the sentence.

When they play tennis doubles, Sean prefers to play the net position; _____, Rob likes the baseline position better.

A. finally
B. in addition
C. similarly
D. on the other hand

19. DIRECTIONS: Choose the most effective word or phrase within the context suggested by the sentence.

When I moved out, all of my bills became my responsibility, I could not control my freedom, and _____.

A. losing my volleyball scholarship.
B. I lost my volleyball scholarship.
C. lost my volleyball scholarship.

20. DIRECTIONS: Choose the sentence that has no error in structure.
A. Living in my home in Venezuela was very different from living in my home in the United States with respect to size, maintaining the yard, and security.
B. Living in my home in Venezuela was very different from living in my home in the United States with respect to the size of the rooms, the maintenance of the property, and security.
C. Living in my home in Venezuela was very different from living in my home in the United States with respect to size, maintenance, and security.

21. DIRECTIONS: Choose the option that corrects an error in the underlined portion(s). If no error exists, choose "No change is necessary."

Fashion design comes easy to <u>me I</u> can take something from the thrift store and make it look like it came from Saks Fifth Avenue.

A. me for I
B. me for, I
C. me, for I
D. No change is necessary.

22. DIRECTIONS: Choose the option that corrects an error in the underlined portion(s). If no error exists, choose "No change is necessary."

Even though I am too old to play on a softball <u>team I</u> enjoy sitting in the <u>stands and</u>
                                          A   B

watching my daughter play, cheering her <u>on, and</u> I remember how it used to be.
                                           C

A. team, I
B. stands, and
C. on and
D. No change is necessary.

23. DIRECTIONS: Choose the option that corrects an error in the underlined portion(s). If no error exists, choose "No change is necessary."

After three years of employment at <u>Kabooms. I</u> have found that the game of whirlyball can be fun or stressful to run, depending on how the people behave.

A. Kabooms; I
B. Kabooms I
C. Kabooms, I
D. No change is necessary.

24. DIRECTIONS: Choose the option that corrects an error in the underlined portion(s). If no error exists, choose "No change is necessary."

When I am ordering at <u>Checkers, I</u> feel like I am competing with the sounds of the
                                       A

traffic whizzing by about fifty feet from <u>me even</u> when I am <u>eating, I</u> still have to listen
                                              B   C

to people honk their horns or yell at each other in their cars.

A. Checkers. I
B. me. Even
C. eating; I
D. No change is necessary.

25. DIRECTIONS: Choose the option that corrects an error in the underlined portion(s). If no error exists, choose "No change is necessary."

After two months of taking orders at the drive thru, Linda had became frustrated with the rudeness of the customers.

A. become
B. has became
C. had become
D. No change is necessary.

26. DIRECTIONS: Choose the option that corrects an error in the underlined portion(s). If no error exists, choose "No change is necessary."

First, Bobby cooks Melinda a gourmet meal, then he asked her to marry him;
            A   B

she accepted his proposal.
        C

A. cooked
B. had asked
C. accepting
D. No change is necessary.

27. DIRECTIONS: Choose the option that corrects an error in the underlined portion(s). If no error exists, choose "No change is necessary."

My favorite ride at Disney World, Big Thunder Canyon, takes me on a wild trip through an abandoned canyon mine at sixty miles per hour; my body shook in every direction.

A. shakes
B. had shaken
C. had shook
D. No change is necessary.

28. DIRECTIONS: Choose the option that corrects an error in the underlined portion(s). If no error exists, choose "No change is necessary."

After completing two years at the community college, each of the students in my class plans
                                                                                        A

to get a four-year degree; a few of them intends to go out of state while most of them
                                            B

choose to transfer to a school in Florida.
    C

A. plan
B. intend
C. chooses
D. No change is necessary.

29. DIRECTIONS: Choose the option that corrects an error in the underlined portion(s). If no error exists, choose "No change is necessary."

Linda's new jeans, which she says <u>is</u> the latest fashion trend, <u>look</u> like someone <u>has</u> cut
                     A   B   C

holes in the knees.

A. are
B. looks
C. have
D. No change is necessary.

30. DIRECTIONS: Choose the option that corrects an error in the underlined portion(s). If no error exists, choose "No change is necessary."

Every student should pay <u>his or her</u> fees before the semester begins; otherwise, <u>he or she</u>
                              A   B

may be dropped from <u>their</u> classes.
                                C

A. their
B. they
C. his or her
D. No change is necessary.

31. DIRECTIONS: Choose the option that corrects an error in the underlined portion(s). If no error exists, choose "No change is necessary."

<u>I</u> have always liked meeting my friends at Don Carter's every Friday night, but now the
A

bowling alley is so crowded that <u>you</u> cannot get a lane as easily as <u>I</u> used to.
                                         B   C

A. We
B. I
C. you
D. No change is necessary.

32. Choose the option that corrects an error in the underlined portion(s). If no error exists, choose "No change is necessary."

At our restaurant, most of the customers <u>we</u> serve are senior citizens who are often rude
                                               A

and short tempered toward <u>us</u>; although their behavior makes us angry, <u>I</u> have to provide
                                  B   C

good customer service by being patient with them.

A. I
B. me
C. we
D. No change is necessary.

33. Choose the option that corrects an error in the underlined portion(s). If no error exists, choose "No change is necessary."

The delivery room keeps Wildcard Systems running efficiently because <u>they distribute</u> the pre-paid credit cards to our customers.

A. the employees distribute
B. it distributes
C. the department distributes
D. No change is necessary.

34. DIRECTIONS: Choose the option that corrects an error in the underlined portion(s). If no error exists, choose "No change is necessary."

In honor of Tony and Mandi's college graduation, Pat, Kim, and <u>I</u> are planning a surprise
                A

party; the decision about the location is up to <u>me</u>, but <u>us</u> three will work together on
                B   C

everything else.

A. me
B. I
C. we
D. No change is necessary.

35. DIRECTIONS: Choose the option that corrects an error in the underlined portion(s). If no error exists, choose "No change is necessary."

The toad jumped <u>quickly</u> into the pool of standing water and waited <u>patient</u> for a <u>tasty</u>
             A   B   C

insect to gobble.

A. quick
B. patiently
C. tastily
D. No change is necessary.

36. DIRECTIONS: Choose the word or phrase that best completes the sentence.

Elijah's voice is the _____ in the choir.

A. loudliest
B. louder
C. loudlier
D. loudest

37. DIRECTIONS: Choose the option that corrects an error in the underlined portion(s). If no error exists, choose "No change is necessary."

Waiting at the dealership for my car to be repaired is an <u>inconvienence</u> to me.

A. inconveniance
B. inconvenyence

C. inconvenience
D. No change is necessary.

38. DIRECTIONS: Choose the option that corrects an error in the underlined portion(s). If no error exists, choose "No change is necessary."

She was the only <u>female, that</u> I have ever <u>known to</u> choose a male-dominated
               A   B

<u>career, automotive</u> engineering.
      C

A. female that
B. known, to
C. career; automotive engineering
D. No change is necessary.

39. DIRECTIONS: Choose the sentence that is correctly punctuated.
A. Lila asked when the research papers were due.
B. Lila asked when are the research papers due.
C. Lila asked when the research papers were due?

40. DIRECTIONS: Choose the option that corrects an error in the underlined portion(s). If no error exists, choose "No change is necessary."

My <u>doctor's</u> magazine subscriptions must have run out because the most recent
     A

<u>Reader's Digest</u>, *Time*, and *Sports Illustrated* are from the <u>Fall</u> of 2004.
     B   C

A. Doctor's
B. *Readers digest*
C. fall
D. No change is necessary.

Part Four: Correspondence Charts for Test Questions

Skill Tested	Question Number
Identifies a thesis statement or topic sentence	1, 6
Recognizes adequate support provided by generalized and specific evidence	2, 7
Arranges ideas and supporting details in logical patterns	3, 8
Identifies supporting material that is relevant or irrelevant to the thesis statement or topic sentence	4, 9
Recognizes effective transitional devices within the context of a passage	5, 10
Chooses the appropriate word or expression in context	11, 12
Recognizes commonly confused or misused words or phrases	13, 14
Uses modifiers correctly	15, 16
Uses coordination and subordination effectively	17, 18
Recognizes parallel structure	19, 20
Avoids fragments, comma splices, and fused sentences	21, 22, 23, 24
Uses standard verb forms	25
Avoids inappropriate shifts in verb tense	26, 27
Maintains agreement between subject and verb	28, 29
Maintains agreement between pronoun and antecedent	30
Avoids inappropriate pronoun shifts in person	31, 32
Maintains clear pronoun references	33
Uses proper case forms	34
Uses adjectives and adverbs correctly	35
Uses appropriate degree forms of adjectives and adverbs	36
Uses standard spelling	37
Uses standard punctuation	38, 39
Uses standard capitalization	40

Ques. No.	Skill Tested	Ques. No.	Skill Tested
1.	Identifies a thesis statement or topic sentence	18.	Uses coordination and subordination effectively
2.	Recognizes adequate support provided by generalized and specific evidence	19.	Recognizes parallel structure
3.	Arranges ideas and supporting details in logical patterns	20.	Recognizes parallel structure
4.	Identifies supporting material that is relevant or irrelevant to the thesis statement or topic sentence	21.	Avoids fragments, comma splices, and fused sentences
5.	Recognizes effective transitional devices within the context of a passage	22.	Avoids fragments, comma splices, and fused sentences
6.	Identifies a thesis statement or topic sentence	23.	Avoids fragments, comma splices, and fused sentences
7.	Recognizes adequate support provided by generalized and specific evidence	24.	Avoids fragments, comma splices, and fused sentences
8.	Arranges ideas and supporting details in logical patterns	25.	Uses standard verb forms
9.	Identifies supporting material that is relevant or irrelevant to the thesis statement or topic sentence	26.	Avoids inappropriate shifts in verb tense
		27.	Avoids inappropriate shifts in verb tense
		28.	Maintains agreement between subject and verb
10.	Recognizes effective transitional devices within the context of a passage	29.	Maintains agreement between subject and verb
11.	Chooses the appropriate word or expression in context	30.	Maintains agreement between pronoun and antecedent
12.	Chooses the appropriate word or expression in context	31.	Avoids inappropriate pronoun shifts in person
13.	Recognizes commonly confused or misused words or phrases	32.	Avoids inappropriate pronoun shifts in person
14.	Recognizes commonly confused or misused words or phrases	33.	Maintains clear pronoun reference
15.	Uses modifiers correctly	34.	Uses proper case forms
16.	Uses modifiers correctly	35.	Uses adjectives and adverbs correctly
17.	Uses coordination and subordination effectively	36.	Uses appropriate degree forms of adjectives and adverbs
		37.	Uses standard spelling
		38.	Uses standard punctuation
		39.	Uses standard punctuation
		40.	Uses standard capitalization

Skill Tested	Question Number
Identifies a thesis statement or topic sentence	1, 6
Recognizes adequate support provided by generalized and specific evidence	2
Arranges ideas and supporting details in logical patterns	3, 8
Identifies supporting material that is relevant or irrelevant to the thesis statement or topic sentence	4, 9
Recognizes effective transitional devices within the context of a passage	5, 10
Recognizes adequate support provided by generalized and specific evidence	7
Chooses the appropriate word or expression in context	11, 12
Recognizes commonly confused or misused words or phrases	13, 14
Uses modifiers correctly	15, 16
Uses coordination and subordination effectively	17, 18
Recognizes parallel structure	19, 20
Avoids fragments, comma splices, and fused sentences	21, 22, 23, 24
Uses standard verb forms	25
Avoids inappropriate shifts in verb tense	26, 27
Maintains agreement between subject and verb	28, 29
Maintains agreement between pronoun and antecedent	30
Avoids inappropriate pronoun shifts in person	31, 32
Maintains clear pronoun reference	33
Uses proper case forms	34
Uses adjectives and adverbs correctly	35
Uses appropriate degree forms of adjectives and adverbs	36
Uses standard spelling	37
Uses standard punctuation	38, 39
Uses standard capitalization	40

Part Five:
Student Answer Sheets

ANSWER SHEET FOR PRETEST ◆ EXIT EXAM

Student Name: _____   Date: _____

Pretest/Exit Exam: _____

1. _____   2. _____   3. _____   4. _____   5. _____   6. _____

7. _____   8. _____   9. _____   10. _____   11. _____   12. _____

13. _____   14. _____   15. _____   16. _____   17. _____   18. _____

19. _____   20. _____   21. _____   22. _____   23. _____   24. _____

25. _____   26. _____   27. _____   28. _____   29. _____   30. _____

31. _____   32. _____   33. _____   34. _____   35. _____   36. _____

37. _____   38. _____   39. _____   40. _____

Thinking Through the Test: My thoughts about my answers and my performance . . .

_____

_____

_____

_____

_____

_____

_____

_____

_____

ANSWER SHEET FOR WORKBOOK DIAGNOSTICS AND EXERCISES

Student Name: _____ Date: _____

Workbook: _____

Chapter & Skill: _____

Diagnostic

1. _____ 2. _____ 3. _____ 4. _____ 5. _____ 6. _____ 7. _____

Exercises

1. _____   2. _____   3. _____   4. _____   5. _____   6. _____

7. _____   8. _____   9. _____   10. _____   11. _____   12. _____

13. _____   14. _____   15. _____   16. _____   17. _____   18. _____

19. _____   20. _____

Thinking Through the Test: My thoughts about my answers and my performance . . .

_____

_____

_____

_____

_____

_____

_____

_____

Part Six: Answer Keys

ANSWERS TO THE PRETEST

1.	C	2.	A	3.	B	4.	A	5.	D	6.	C
7.	C	8.	D	9.	D	10.	A	11.	B	12.	A
13.	B	14.	B	15.	C	16.	B	17.	A	18.	D
19.	C	20.	C	21.	A	22.	C	23.	B	24.	A
25.	A	26.	B	27.	B	28.	C	29.	B	30.	A
31.	C	32.	B	33.	C	34.	C	35.	A	36.	B
37.	D	38.	C	39.	B	40.	B				

ANSWERS TO THE WORKBOOK EXERCISES

CHAPTER 1: *CONCEPT SKILLS*

1. The Topic Sentence

1.	C	2.	D	3.	B	4.	D	5.	B
6.	B	7.	A	8.	C	9.	B	10.	D

2. Supporting Details

1.	A	2.	B	3.	D	4.	C	5.	C
6.	C	7.	B	8.	A	9.	D	10.	B

3. Logical Patterns

1.	B	2.	C	3.	B	4.	C	5.	A
6.	D	7.	B	8.	A	9.	D	10.	C

4. Relevance of Details

1.	D	2.	B	3.	A	4.	A	5.	C
6.	C	7.	D	8.	B	9.	A	10.	D

5. Transitional Devices

1.	C	2.	D	3.	A	4.	B	5.	D
6.	C	7.	B	8.	A	9.	D	10.	C

CHAPTER 2: *LANGUAGE SKILLS*

1. Choosing Proper Expressions (Context Clues)

1.	B	2.	A	3.	C	4.	B	5.	C
6.	A	7.	B	8.	C	9.	B	10.	A

2. Confused or Misused Words/Phrases

1.	C	2.	C	3.	A	4.	A	5.	C
6.	A	7.	B	8.	C	9.	B	10.	B

CHAPTER 3: *SENTENCE SKILLS*

1. Modifiers

1.	C	2.	A	3.	B	4.	B	5.	A
6.	C	7.	A	8.	B	9.	C	10.	A

2. Coordination and Subordination

1.	A	2.	D	3.	C	4.	B	5.	B
6.	A	7.	C	8.	A	9.	B	10.	C

3. Parallel Structure

1.	A	2.	C	3.	B	4.	B	5.	C
6.	B	7.	C	8.	D	9.	C	10.	B

4. Fragments, Comma Splices, and Fused Sentences (Run-ons)

1.	B	2.	C	3.	B	4.	A	5.	D
6.	A	7.	B	8.	D	9.	C	10.	A
11.	B	12.	A	13.	D	14.	B	15.	A
16.	C	17.	C	18.	A	19.	B	20.	C

CHAPTER 4: *GRAMMAR SKILLS*

1. Standard Verb Forms

1.	B	2.	D	3.	C	4.	A	5.	C
6.	C	7.	A	8.	B	9.	C	10.	C

2. Shifts in Verb Tense

1.	B	2.	C	3.	A	4.	C	5.	B
6.	A	7.	D	8.	B	9.	C	10.	B

3. Subject and Verb Agreement

1.	A	2.	C	3.	C	4.	B	5.	C
6.	A	7.	B	8.	C	9.	D	10.	A
11.	B	12.	A	13.	C	14.	A	15.	A
16.	B	17.	B	18.	A	19.	C	20.	D

4. Pronoun and Antecedent Agreement

1.	A	2.	D	3.	B	4.	C	5.	B
6.	C	7.	A	8.	C	9.	B	10.	D

5. Pronoun Shifts

1.	B	2.	C	3.	C	4.	A	5.	B
6.	C	7.	C	8.	A	9.	D	10.	B

6. Clear Pronoun Reference

1.	B	2.	C	3.	A	4.	B	5.	C
6.	A	7.	A	8.	B	9.	C	10.	D

7. Pronoun Case Form

1.	A	2.	B	3.	C	4.	C	5.	C
6.	D	7.	A	8.	B	9.	D	10.	B

8. Adjectives and Adverbs

1.	A	2.	C	3.	B	4.	B	5.	D
6.	C	7.	B	8.	A	9.	C	10.	A

9. Degree Forms of Adjectives and Adverbs

1.	C	2.	B	3.	A	4.	B	5.	C
6.	D	7.	A	8.	D	9.	C	10.	B

10. Standard Spelling

1. B	2. A	3. A	4. C	5. C
6. D	7. B	8. B	9. A	10. B

11. Standard Punctuation

1. C	2. B	3. A	4. B	5. D
6. D	7. A	8. C	9. B	10. A

12. Standard Capitalization

1. C	2. A	3. B	4. C	5. A
6. B	7. B	8. D	9. C	10. D

ANSWERS TO THE EXIT EXAM

1. B	2. D	3. C	4. B	5. A	6. C
7. B	8. C	9. D	10. A	11. C	12. A
13. B	14. A	15. C	16. B	17. A	18. D
19. B	20. C	21. C	22. A	23. C	24. B
25. C	26. A	27. A	28. B	29. A	30. C
31. B	32. C	33. A	34. C	35. B	36. D
37. C	38. A	39. A	40. C		

ANSWERS TO THE PRETEST ◆ WITH EXPLANATIONS

1. **Skill tested:** Identifies a thesis statement or topic sentence. **Answer:** C. **Explanation:** Choice C is the best topic sentence for the passage. The authors use the Ice Man as an example to illustrate how DNA was used to find out information about him.

2. **Skill tested:** Recognizes adequate support provided by generalized and specific evidence. **Answer:** A. **Explanation:** No examples or other support is provided for the sentence.

3. **Skill tested:** Arranges ideas and supporting details in a logical pattern. **Answer:** B. **Explanation:** The pattern follows chronological order, describing the Ice Man and the items found along with him.

4. **Skill tested:** Identifies supporting material that is relevant or irrelevant to the thesis statement or topic sentence. **Answer:** A. **Explanation:** Sentence 12 adds information about a dinosaur fossil; however, it is neither supported by nor connected to the main idea of the passage.

5. **Skill tested:** Recognizes effective transitional devices within the context of the passage. **Answer:** D. **Explanation:** The word "currently" takes the reader from the story of the Ice Man discovery to his location at this time.

6. **Skill tested:** Identifies a thesis statement or topic sentence. **Answer:** C. **Explanation:** The paragraph explains the ways in which ethical standards are violated, which is best expressed in answer C.

7. **Skill tested:** Recognizes adequate support provided by generalized and specific evidence. **Answer:** C. **Explanation:** The passage does not discuss the systems for citing others' ideas.

8. **Skill tested:** Arranges ideas and supporting details in a logical pattern. **Answer:** D. **Explanation:** The sentences describe the ways in which plagiarism violates ethical standards. Transition words indicate the logical pattern. The second sentence of the group uses the transition word "also." "Finally" is used in the third sentence of the group to indicate that the idea is the last way.

9. **Skill tested:** Identifies supporting material that is relevant or irrelevant to the thesis statement or topic sentence. **Answer:** D. **Explanation:** Sentence 13 gives a specific effect on a student if he or she plagiarizes, but the passage does not discuss specific effects of plagiarism on an individual.

10. **Skill tested:** Recognizes effective transitional devices within the context of the passage. **Answer:** A. **Explanation:** The phrase "for example" is appropriate because the sentence introduces an example to illustrate the main idea.

11. **Skill tested:** Chooses the appropriate word or expression in context. **Answer:** B. **Explanation:** The word "deficient" means lacking or inadequate.

12. **Skill tested:** Chooses the appropriate word or expression in context. **Answer:** A. **Explanation:** The word

"oblivious" means lacking a conscious awareness of. The sentence implies that the subject is no longer bothered by the noise of the planes flying overhead.

13. **Skill tested:** Recognizes commonly confused and misused words or phrases. **Answer: B. Explanation:** The possessive form "whose" is the correct word while the word in the sentence, "who's," is the contracted form of who + is.

14. **Skill tested:** Recognizes commonly confused and misused words or phrases. **Answer: B. Explanation:** The words "number" and "amount" are often confused. "Number" is used for things that can be counted while "amount" is used for things that are not countable. Therefore, "number" is correct because calories can be counted.

15. **Skill tested:** Uses modifiers correctly. **Answer: C. Explanation:** A modifier must have a word to modify. If not, it "dangles." Choice C places the modifier before the subject, "they," which clearly shows who was "sitting on the beach."

16. **Skill tested:** Uses modifiers correctly. **Answer: B. Explanation:** For clarity and meaning, a modifier must be placed next to the word or phrase that is being modified; otherwise, it is misplaced. Choice B places the modifier "that was moldy" next to "cheese spread," which is the word group it modifies.

17. **Skill tested:** Uses coordination and subordinating effectively. **Answer: A. Explanation:** This type of question requires that you carefully consider the relationship between ideas within the sentence. The sentence shows a cause and effect relationship best expressed by Choice A. The dependent clause that begins the sentence tells why.

18. **Skill tested:** Uses coordination and subordination effectively. **Answer: D. Explanation:** This sentence consists of two independent clauses connected with a semicolon. The word that fills in the blank, a conjunctive adverb or transition word, must show a relationship between the two sentences. Choice D shows effect; as a result of the dog's aggression, it must be kept in a cage.

19. **Skill tested:** Recognizes parallel structure. **Answer: C. Explanation:** This sentence contains a list. When listing items in a sentence, you must be sure that each of the items is written in the same grammatical structure. The list could contain all words, all phrases, all clauses, or all sentences. In the sentence, the first two phrases in the list begin with *-ing* words, so the third

item in the group should also. C is the only choice that has the same grammatical structure.

20. **Skill tested:** Recognizes parallel structure. **Answer: C. Explanation:** As in question 19, this sentence also contains a list, so once again you must choose the list that has structurally parallel items. Each of the items in the list in Choice C begins with the base form of a verb: ride, take, and borrow.

21. **Skill tested:** Avoids fragments, comma splices, and fused sentences. **Answer: A. Explanation:** You must determine whether the sentence has any of these problems: is incomplete (a fragment), has a comma separating two independent clauses (a comma splice), or lacks appropriate punctuation between two independent clauses (fused). The underlined portion of the sentence is the last word of the first sentence and the first word of a new sentence. Since it is not punctuated appropriately, it is considered a fused sentence. Choice A corrects the sentence by placing a period after the word "school" and capitalizing "Sometimes." This separates the two independent clauses correctly.

22. **Skill tested:** Avoids fragments, comma splices, and fused sentences. **Answer: C. Explanation:** You must determine whether the sentence has any of these problems: is incomplete (a fragment), has a comma separating two independent clauses (a comma splice), or lacks appropriate punctuation between two independent clauses (fused). This sentence offers three options. Choice C is correct. The comma between "pressure" and "if" creates a comma splice. The semi-colon corrects this error.

23. **Skill tested:** Avoids fragments, comma splices, and fused sentences. **Answer: B. Explanation:** You must determine whether the sentence has any of these problems: is incomplete (a fragment), has a comma separating two independent clauses (a comma splice), or lacks appropriate punctuation between two independent clauses (fused). The underlined portion of the sentence is the last word of the first sentence and the first word of a new sentence. The second word group in the sentence is a fragment. Choice B corrects this fragment by replacing the period with a comma.

24. **Skill tested:** Avoids fragments, comma splices, and fused sentences. **Answer: A. Explanation:** You must determine whether the sentence has any of these problems: is incomplete (a fragment), has a comma separating two independent clauses (a comma splice), or lacks appropriate punctuation

between two independent clauses (fused). This sentence offers three options. Choice A corrects the error, which is a fragment: "When my mother first came to the United States." This dependent clause begins the sentence, so it should be followed by a comma.

25. **Skill tested:** Uses standard verb forms. **Answer:** A. **Explanation:** The past participle of "spoke" is "spoken." This verb form, "had spoken," is necessary to show that the first action in the past was completed before the second action in the past.

26. **Skill tested:** Shift in verb tense. **Answer:** B. **Explanation:** This sentence contains a shift in verb tense. The three verbs in the sentence should all be in the simple past tense; however, B is not. Choice B, "looked," corrects "is looking."

27. **Skill tested:** Shift in verb tense. **Answer:** B. **Explanation:** The verb in the underlined portion of the sentence, "dive," is in the present tense, but the rest of the sentence is in the simple past tense. "Dove" is the past tense form of the verb "dive."

28. **Skill tested:** Subject and verb agreement. **Answer:** C. **Explanation:** This question tests your ability to determine whether the subject of an independent or dependent clause agrees with its verb. In this sentence, the problem is in the dependent clause "if there is any drug sales." The subject of that clause is "sales," which is plural, so the verb must be in the plural form, "are."

29. **Skill tested:** Subject and verb agreement. **Answer:** B. **Explanation:** This question tests your ability to determine whether the subject of an independent or dependent clause agrees with its verb. This error tests your knowledge of the rule for subject-verb agreement when *neither* and *nor* are used as subjects. In this situation, the word after "nor" determines the form of the verb. In this sentence, "flowers" follows nor. Because "flowers" is plural, the verb must be plural in form, "need."

30. **Skill tested:** Pronoun and antecedent agreement. **Answer:** A. **Explanation:** In the sentence the pronoun "their" is incorrect. "Their" is a plural pronoun, but the word it refers to, "each" (the subject of the sentence), is singular. The correction is "his or her." "His or her" is used because the reader does not know the gender of the children, so both the masculine and feminine forms of the pronoun are used separated by "or" to indicate it could be either gender.

31. **Skill tested:** Avoids inappropriate pronoun shifts in person. **Answer:** C. **Explanation:** Choice C corrects the shifted pronoun "you."

32. **Skill tested:** Avoids inappropriate pronoun shifts in person. **Answer:** B. **Explanation:** The pronoun "we" marks a shift from the other two pronouns, "they." To correct the shift in person, "they" should replace "we."

33. **Skill tested:** Maintains clear pronoun references. **Answer:** C. **Explanation:** In this sentence, the reader does not know what the pronoun "it" refers to. Choice C, "an antique car," replaces the pronoun with a specific noun.

34. **Skill tested:** Uses proper case forms. **Answer:** C. **Explanation:** Choice C corrects the incorrect pronoun "I." When a pronoun is an object of a preposition, it must be in the objective form. "Between" is a preposition, so the correct object pronoun must be "me."

35. **Skill tested:** Uses adjectives and adverbs correctly. **Answer:** A. **Explanation:** "Safely," the adverb, must be used to modify the verb "live." "Safe" is the adjective form.

36. **Skill tested:** Uses appropriate degree forms of adjectives and adverbs. **Answer:** B. **Explanation:** A comparison is implied in this sentence. The weather is not as good as it was; it is getting "worse." "Worse" is the correct comparative form.

37. **Skill tested:** Uses standard spelling. **Answer:** D. **Explanation:** "Broccoli" as it appears in the sentence is the correct spelling.

38. **Skill tested:** Uses standard punctuation. **Answer:** C. **Explanation:** The sentence begins with a dependent clause and ends with an independent clause. The independent clause contains compound verbs, "organizing" and "helping." No comma is needed to separate these compound verb phrases.

39. **Skill tested:** Uses standard punctuation. **Answer:** B. **Explanation:** This question tests your knowledge of the question mark and the apostrophe. The sentence is an indirect question, so no question mark is necessary. The apostrophe is needed to show possession; the jerseys belong to the team members. The apostrophe follows "members," indicating that "members" is a plural possessive.

40. **Skill tested:** Uses standard capitalization. **Answer:** B. **Explanation:** The South is a region of the country and is capitalized.

1. **Skill tested:** Identifies a thesis statement or topic sentence. **Answer: B. Explanation:** The passage focuses on the friendship of Harris and Klebold as an example of "horrific actions of schoolyard snipers."

2. **Skill tested:** Recognizes adequate support provided by generalized and specific evidence. **Answer: D. Explanation:** No support is provided for the sentence about family background.

3. **Skill tested:** Arranges ideas and supporting details in a logical pattern. **Answer: C. Explanation:** The first sentence in the group makes a statement that the two boys wanted to feel important. This sentence supports the previous sentence (6). The next two sentences build on the first of the group.

4. **Skill tested:** Identifies supporting material that is relevant or irrelevant to the thesis statement or topic sentence. **Answer: B. Explanation:** The passage does not focus on how popular trench coats became because Harris and Klebold wore them.

5. **Skill tested:** Recognizes effective transitional devices within the context of the passage. **Answer: A. Explanation:** "As a result" indicates that the sentence is expressing the effect of the previous sentence.

6. **Skill tested:** Identifies a thesis statement or topic sentence. **Answer: C. Explanation:** The passage explains the various problems a single parent may experience.

7. **Skill tested:** Recognizes adequate support provided by generalized and specific evidence. **Answer: B. Explanation:** Sentence 6 points out that child care can be costly. Choice B provides information about the cost of full-time day care compared to family income.

8. **Skill tested:** Arranges ideas and supporting details in a logical pattern. **Answer: C. Explanation:** This detail supports the sentence before it, sentence 4, which says that spending quality time with a child is a demonstration of love. This sentence gives an example of quality time as "interacting with the child, actively listening and talking with him or her."

9. **Skill tested:** Identifies supporting material that is relevant or irrelevant to the thesis statement or topic sentence. **Answer: D. Explanation:** The passage does not discuss how society views divorce, so the sentence is not relevant to the topic.

10. **Skill tested:** Recognizes effective transitional devices within the context of the passage. **Answer: A. Explanation:** Sentence 7 adds to the point

made in sentence 6, so "in addition" is appropriate and effective.

11. **Skill tested:** Chooses the appropriate word or expression in context. **Answer: C. Explanation:** "Aptitude" means talent, a natural ability.

12. **Skill tested:** Chooses the appropriate word or expression in context. **Answer: A. Explanation:** "Ascertain" means to find out or learn with certainty, which is what the subject of the sentence tried to do.

13. **Skill tested:** Recognizes commonly confused or misused words or phrases **Answer: B. Explanation:** "Compliment" and "complement" are often confused. A "compliment" is an expression of praise; a "complement" is something added that completes, such as adding some flowers to a beautifully set table.

14. **Skill tested:** Recognizes commonly confused or misused words or phrases **Answer: A. Explanation:** "Would have" is the grammatically correct form.

15. **Skill tested:** Uses modifiers correctly. **Answer: C. Explanation:** For clarity of meaning, modifiers must be placed next to the word or phrase that is being modified; otherwise it is misplaced. Choice C places the modifier, "Driving around in his car," before the word(s) it modifies, "Uncle Fred."

16. **Skill tested:** Uses modifiers correctly. **Answer: B. Explanation:** A modifier must have a word or phrase to modify. If not, it "dangles." Choice B tells the reader who was watching the movie on television.

17. **Skill tested:** Uses coordination and subordination effectively. **Answer: A. Explanation:** This type of question requires that you carefully consider the relationship between ideas within the sentence. The sentence shows a time relationship best expressed by Choice A. "After" is used in the dependent clause to explain the sequence of actions in the sentence.

18. **Skill tested:** Uses coordination and subordination effectively. **Answer: D. Explanation:** The sentence contrasts the two positions that each person prefers in doubles tennis, so "on the other hand" is the appropriate choice to coordinate these two sentences.

19. **Skill tested:** Recognizes parallel structure. **Answer: B. Explanation:** The sentence contains a list. When listing items in a sentence, you must be sure that each of the items is written in the same grammatical structure. In other words, the list could contain all words, all phrases, all clauses, or all sentences. In

this sentence, the list is a series of sentences, and Choice B is the only option that is a sentence.

20. **Skill tested:** Recognizes parallel structure. **Answer:** C. **Explanation:** This sentence contains a list. Each item in the list must be written in the same grammatical structure. In Choice C, all of the words in the list are nouns.

21. **Skill tested:** Avoids fragments, comma splices, and fused sentences **Answer:** C. **Explanation:** This sentence fuses two independent clauses. One way to correct this problem is to add a comma and a coordinating conjunction between the two independent clauses. Choice C is the only answer that has the comma before the coordinating conjunction.

22. **Skill tested:** Avoids fragments, comma splices, and fused sentences **Answer:** A. **Explanation:** The beginning of the sentence is a dependent clause. A comma must follow an introductory dependent clause. Therefore, Choice A is the option that corrects the error in the sentence.

23. **Skill tested:** Avoids fragments, comma splices, and fused sentences **Answer:** C. **Explanation:** Choice C corrects the error in the sentence. "After three years of employment at Kabooms" is a dependent clause. Placing a period at the end of it creates a fragment. Always put a comma at the end of an introductory dependent clause.

24. **Skill tested:** Avoids fragments, comma splices, and fused sentences **Answer:** B. **Explanation:** Two sentences are fused because there is no punctuation after the word "me," which ends the first sentence of the two. Choice B corrects the error with a period after "me" and a capital "E" to begin the next sentence.

25. **Skill tested:** Uses standard verb forms. **Answer:** C. **Explanation:** The past perfect verb tense is formed by combining "had" and the past participle verb form of "become": had + become.

26. **Skill tested:** Avoids inappropriate shifts in verb tense. **Answer:** A. **Explanation:** The sentence begins with the verb in the present tense but the verb shifts to the past in the second independent clause. The verb in the independent clause after the semicolon is also in the past tense. To keep the verb tense consistent in the sentence, the first verb must be changed to the past tense, "cooked."

27. **Skill tested:** Avoids inappropriate shifts in verb tense. **Answer:** A. **Explanation:** This sentence begins in the present tense with "takes" and finishes in the past with "took." Choice A corrects the verb shift, so both verbs are in the present tense.

28. **Skill tested:** Maintains agreement between subject and verb. **Answer:** B. **Explanation:** The subject of the independent clause beginning with "a few of them" is "few," which is plural. Therefore, the verb must be in the plural form, "intend." "Intends" is the third person singular form.

29. **Skill tested:** Maintains agreement between subject and verb. **Answer:** A. **Explanation:** The verb "are" agrees with the subject, "jeans." The dependent clause modifies "jeans," and the word "which" refers to "jeans," so the verb must be in the plural form.

30. **Skill tested:** Maintains agreement between pronoun and antecedent. **Answer:** C. **Explanation:** Pronouns must agree with their antecedents. In this sentence, the subject of the sentence is student, which is singular. All of the pronouns refer to that subject (the antecedent), so they must all be singular. "His or her" is the correction for "their."

31. **Skill tested:** Avoids inappropriate pronoun shifts in person. **Answer:** B. **Explanation:** The pronoun shifts from "I" to "you" and then back to "I." "You" should be replaced with "I" for consistency.

32. **Skill tested:** Avoids inappropriate pronoun shifts in person. **Answer:** C. **Explanation:** The pronoun shift in the sentence is "I." The other pronouns used are "we" and "us," both forms of the first person plural. To correct the error, "I" must be replaced with "we."

33. **Skill tested:** Maintains clear pronoun references. **Answer:** A. **Explanation:** In the sentence, the reader is not told what "they" refers to. The employees are the ones who distribute the credit cards.

34. **Skill tested:** Uses proper case forms. **Answer:** C. **Explanation:** An object pronoun cannot be used as a subject. The second independent clause in the sentence is compound; that is, it consists of two independent clauses joined by a comma and a coordinating conjunction. The subject follows the coordinating conjunction "but." The subject is "three," but a pronoun is used as part of the subject "three."

35. **Skill tested:** Uses adjectives and adverbs correctly. **Answer:** B. **Explanation:** "Patient" is an adjective, but in this sentence "patient" does not modify any noun in the sentence. The adverb "patiently" corrects the error.

36. **Skill tested:** Uses appropriate degree forms of adjectives and adverbs. **Answer:** D. **Explanation:** The sentence compares more than two things, so the superlative form must be used.

37. **Skill tested:** Uses standard spelling. **Answer:** C. **Explanation:** "Inconvenience" is spelled correctly.

38. **Skill tested:** Uses standard punctuation. **Answer:** A. **Explanation:** No comma should appear before a relative pronoun, in this case "that," which begins an essential dependent clause. The dependent clause "that I have ever known" is essential to the meaning of the sentence.

39. **Skill tested:** Uses standard punctuation. **Answer:** A. **Explanation:** The sentence contains an indirect question correctly punctuated with a period at the end of the sentence.

40. **Skill tested:** Uses standard capitalization. **Answer:** C. **Explanation:** Seasons are not capitalized.

ANSWERS TO WORKBOOK EXERCISES ◆ WITH EXPLANATIONS

CHAPTER 1: CONCEPT SKILLS

1. The Topic Sentence

1. Answer   C

This sentence is the best choice for the main idea because it summarizes all the supporting ideas in the passage. The passage gives six disadvantages of e-mail in a business environment.

2. Answer   D

This topic sentence is the best choice because it provides a summary of the supporting details in the passage that discuss gender equality in the military.

3. Answer   B

Jaime Escalante's success as a teacher was a result of the methods he used with his students to help them achieve. The passage gives examples of those methods.

4. Answer   D

The purpose of this paragraph is to describe the physical and psychological symptoms of anorexia nervosa. This topic sentence achieves that purpose.

5. Answer   B

The paragraph covers the history of the standardization of bare-knuckle boxing between the late 1800s and the early 1900s. Choice B clearly indicates this.

6. Answer   B

This topic sentence is an effective unifying summary of the supporting details in the paragraph. Examples of the different messages communicated by eye movements are provided.

7. Answer   A

The passage describes how the albatross is equipped to live at sea, and this topic sentence is the best summary of the topic. The paragraph explains the features of the albatross that help it survive: its salt tolerance and its wingspan.

8. Answer   C

This sentence works well as a topic sentence because it covers the reasons athletes use anabolic steroids and the effects they could experience.

9. Answer   B

The topic sentence reflects the content of the paragraph, which shows how parents and children can learn about computers from each other and increase their self-confidence, strengthening their relationship.

10. Answer   D

This topic sentence is effective for the content of the paragraph. The passage explains the benefits of highlighting.

2. Supporting Details

1. Answer   A

This sentence cites another disadvantage of e-mail, but the passage offers no discussion of the privacy issues and is, therefore, not supported.

2. Answer   B

This sentence brings up a new point, whether being able to serve in combat is a privilege or a burden, but the author does not discuss it.

3. Answer   D

Sentence 11 provides specific support for sentence 10 in the passage. It gives an example of a way Escalante changed his method of instruction.

4. Answer   C

Sentence 9 is a transitional sentence in the paragraph. It shifts the discussion of anorexia to more than an eating disorder. Sentence 10 adds the idea that it is a psychological disorder, too, with a wide range of disturbances. Thus, sentence 10 supports 9.

5. Answer   C

Periodic efforts to outlaw boxing are not discussed in the passage.

6. Answer   C

No support is provided for sentence 8, which says that eye movements can signal a positive or negative relationship.

7. Answer   B

The sentence that provides specific support for sentence 4 in the passage is sentence 5. It explains how the salt-excreting glands in the albatross dispose of excess salts.

8. Answer   A

Sentence 13 supports sentence 9 because it gives an example of a physical problem that can occur from using anabolic steroids. Sentence 9 introduces the idea that these substances can cause physical and mental problems.

9. Answer   D

Sentence 9 is not supported by specific details. No examples of how children interact with the computer as if it were alive are provided.

10. Answer   B

Sentence 4 provides specific support for sentence 3 in the passage. It explains what sifting and sorting is. Sentence 3 explains that highlighting is a process of sifting and sorting.

3. Logical Patterns

For this section, only the correct answer is explained. The question asks you to select the arrangement of sentences that provides the most logical sequence of ideas and supporting details in the paragraph. Therefore, it is unnecessary to explain why the other answers are false.

1. Answer   B

This is the best arrangement for the series of sentences. The passage gives the disadvantages of e-mail communication in the workplace. The first sentence of the group introduces the second disadvantage of the passage, which talks about the fact that e-mail provides no paper trail. The point made in sentence 6 should follow because it directly supports sentence 4; it explains the ease of reading and deleting e-mail instead of printing a copy for your files or moving it to an electronic folder. Sentence 5 begins with the transition "As a result." This phrase logically follows sentence 6 because it gives the effect of what happens when messages aren't printed or saved; they are forgotten or lost.

2. Answer   C

This group of sentences follows sentence 10, which introduces the idea that there is a debate over whether women should serve in combat. Sentence 13 presents the first point of debate, that women are less suited for combat because they have less body strength than men do. The sentence begins with the word "Some." It makes sense logically that sentence 11 should follow. The sentence begins with the word "Others," showing that another point of view is being expressed. Sentence 12 addresses the two previous opinions given in sentences 13 and 11 by stating that there are critics of both of those points.

3. Answer   B

Sentences 11, 12, and 13 are supporting details for sentence 10. Sentence 10 introduces the idea that Escalante changed the system of instruction that the students had experienced at their high school. Sentence 13 is logically the first point that supports this. His first step was to get the students to think of themselves as a team and of him as their coach because they were preparing for the national math exams. Next, he fostered team identity; sentence 12 gives examples of how this was accomplished. They wore hats and clothing items that identified them as a team. Moving from establishing their identity as a team and fostering that identity, Escalante had his students do warm-ups before each class, getting them ready to work together and learn.

4. Answer   C

The paragraph begins with a definition of anorexia nervosa as a loss of appetite in sentence 2 but explains that the meaning does not fit the disease. Sentence 4 supports this statement: a person with anorexia is hungry but denies it in fear of becoming fat. The use of the transition word "Therefore" beginning sentence 5 leads the reader to the effect of the fear as well as introduces the reader to the first characteristic of the illness: severe weight loss. Sentence 3 adds information about the anorexic's approach to weight loss.

5. Answer   A

The sequence of sentences in the passage is the most logical sequence. These sentences describe the stages of a bare-knuckle boxing fight. The other arrangements of sentences do not make sense as a sequential description.

6. Answer   D

The best placement for the sentence is immediately after sentence 14. Sentence 12 presents the detail that eye contact can change psychological distance between you and someone else. Sentence 13 gives the example of catching someone's eye at a party, which brings the two people psychologically close. Then sentence 14 explains how avoiding eye contact increases the psychological distance. The new sentence gives another example of increasing distance.

7. Answer   B

Sentence 7 in the passage begins the transition to a discussion of the albatross's flight abilities. Sentence 8 talks about the wingspan, and sentence 9 describes how the albatross's long wings give it sufficient lift to stay up in the air for hours. The new sentence explains how the feathers insulate it from the chill of the sea wind and how they keep the bird dry because they are coated with oil. This is an appropriate placement because it further explains how the albatross can handle the environmental conditions it is exposed to while gliding on wind currents over the ocean.

8. Answer   A

The sentence suggested for placement in the passage gives another effect of anabolic steroids on the mind. It supports the sentence immediately before it, sentence 11, which begins the discussion of the mental effects. Both sentences support sentence 9; this sentence refers to the serious physical and mental effects of anabolic steroids. Sentence 12 moves the discussion forward to the internal effects.

9. Answer   D

The best placement for the sentence is after sentence 7. It gives another example of how children can teach their parents how to use computer programs and Internet communication. Sentence 3 gives the main supporting detail, and sentences 4, 5, 6, and 7 provide the minor details. The suggested sentence would serve as the last example in the series. Sentence 8 summarizes the examples that were discussed.

10. Answer   C

The suggested sentence is best placed after sentence 8. Sentence 7 begins the discussion of another benefit of highlighting, a new supporting detail; it helps you discover how facts and ideas are organized and are connected. Sentence 8 adds another detail: highlighting shows you whether or not you have understood what you have read. The suggested sentence further supports this idea. The author says that if your highlighting was difficult or not helpful, then you did not understand the passage you read.

4. Relevance of Details

For each of the following explanatory answers, the topic sentence for each passage is provided as the first piece of information. A detail's relevance is best judged against the main idea, for good writing ties every detail either directly as a major point or indirectly as a minor point (that supports a major point) to the main idea.

1. Topic Sentence: Although electronic mail has become a medium of choice for business communication, e-mail has disadvantages for users.

Answer: D. The 1986 Electronic Communications Privacy Act considers e-mail to be the property of the company paying for the mail system.

The Electronic Communications Privacy Act is least relevant to the main idea as stated in the topic sentence. The paragraph does not discuss who "owns" the company's e-mail system.

2. Topic Sentence: Military service is still a controversial issue of gender equality.

Answer: B. In 1981, the Supreme Court ruled that male-only registration for the military did not violate the Fifth Amendment.

The beginning of the paragraph establishes that men and women are treated differently in the military. The first support is that only men must register for the draft when they turn 18. However, the history of the male-only registration for the military ruling moves the discussion off the main topic into another direction that is merely stated and not developed or related to the point of the paragraph.

3. Topic Sentence: Jaime Escalante's dramatic success in teaching calculus to students in an East Los Angeles inner-city school plagued with poverty, crime, drugs, and gangs was a result of changes he made to classroom instruction.

Answer: A. When Escalante first came to the United States, he worked as a busboy and attended Pasadena Community College.

This sentence does not support the topic sentence. It has nothing to do with the changes Escalante made to his instruction in the classroom. Instead it tells the reader about Escalante's past when he first came to this country.

4. Topic Sentence: The central features of anorexia nervosa are a complex mixture of symptoms.

Answer: A. There is a strong argument that eating disorders are a form of addiction.

This sentence is not relevant for two reasons. First, the passage does not discuss all eating disorders, just one, anorexia nervosa. Next, although the passage mentions the psychological aspects of the disorder, it neither lists addiction as one of the aspects nor attempts to provide any further discussion of that idea.

5. Topic Sentence: Boxing began as a largely unstructured sport, but by 1900, new rules standardized the sport.

Answer: C. Currently there are eight major professional divisions.

This sentence has no relationship to the discussion of the changes to boxing by 1900.

6. Topic Sentence: Eye movements communicate a variety of messages.

Answer: C. Your pupils enlarge when you are interested or emotionally involved.

The change in the size of a person's pupils is not supported in the passage. The passage focuses on eye movements, not the pupils.

7. Topic Sentence: Only a few birds can live at sea, but the albatross is a model of fitness for its environment.

Answer: D. Their scientific name, *Diomedea exulans*, means exiled warrior in Greek.

This is the least relevant sentence in the paragraph. While it is interesting to know the scientific name of the albatross, the information does not add to the details explaining how the albatross is well-suited for its environment.

8. Topic Sentence: While using anabolic steroids is a fast way to increase general body size, their health hazards support the argument for banning their use in athletics.

Answer: B. Black market sales bring in up to $400 million a year.

This sentence has no relevance to the passage. The illegal sale of anabolic steroids does not support the idea that steroids can be hazardous to a person's health.

9. Topic Sentence: Sharing information and teaching each other about their computer and the Internet can strengthen the parent-child relationship.

Answer: A. Children are more apt to interact with the computer as if it were alive.

This sentence is least relevant because the passage is about sharing information, not about how children interact with the computer. This does not help the reader understand how a child is able to master a program, whether through persistence or intuition.

10. Topic Sentence: Highlighting is an extremely effective way of making a textbook review manageable.

Answer: D. One mistake to avoid is highlighting almost every idea on the page.

The paragraph explains the many ways in which highlighting is effective. Its purpose is not to point out mistakes people make when highlighting.

5. Transitional Devices

1. Answer   C

"Finally" indicates that the last point is being made. In this passage, the final disadvantage of e-mail is that writing on a computer screen often encourages people to drop their inhibitions and write things in e-mail that they would not write in a letter or say on the phone.

2. Answer   D

"However" is the best choice, for it indicates contrast with the sentence that precedes it. Sentence 7 explains the services women performed during the Persian Gulf War and sentence 8 states that the policy does not allow them to serve as combat pilots in the navy and air force or on navy war ships.

3. Answer   A

"First" is the best choice because it indicates that the statement is the first in a series of details explaining the methods Escalante used with his students. His first task was to show his students that they could learn successfully.

4. Answer   B

"In fact" is the best choice because it clarifies the information presented in the sentence before it. Sentence 9 states that anorexia is more than a simple eating disorder. Sentence 10 begins with "In fact" to say that in actuality, anorexia is a distinct psychological disorder.

5. Answer   D

"In addition" indicates that new information of equal value is being added. In the passage, another change to bare-fisted boxing is added to the previous two already mentioned.

6. Answer   C

"Moreover" indicates an addition of information. In the passage, "Moreover" appropriately begins sentence 9, which adds a new detail expressing another way eye movements communicate.

7. Answer   B

"Along with" means in addition to. Sentence 7 in the passage uses "Along with" to show that the albatross not only has salt tolerance but also has extraordinary flight abilities.

8. Answer   A

"Moreover" indicates an addition of information. In the passage, sentence 13 adds another serious physical effect of overdosing anabolic steroids.

9. Answer   D

"For example" alerts the reader that a specific support is going to follow a more general statement. In the passage, sentence 4 provides the first example to support the point that a child may be able to teach a parent a computer or Internet skill.

10. Answer   C

"First" indicates that a specific idea is going to be introduced. In this passage, "First" is used in the sentence to express the first benefit of highlighting.

CHAPTER 2: *LANGUAGE SKILLS*

1. Choosing Proper Expressions (Context Clues)

1. Answer   B

"Detect" means to discover the presence of. Good vision helps animals discover the presence of their prey or predators from a distance.

2. Answer   A

"Integrated" means incorporated into a larger unit. The computer has become incorporated into our daily lives. In other words, using a computer has become part of our lives without our thinking about it. We use the computer informally for e-mail, Internet searches, and chats. Many of us use computer technology in some way in the workplace.

3. Answer   C

"Restore" means to repair, to renew. The context of the sentence makes this an ideal choice. Sleep enables the body to renew itself by repairing the body.

4. Answer   B

"Reveals" means to make known, to show. The purpose of research is to prove a theory, so "reveals" makes sense within the context of the sentence.

5. Answer   C

"Distinguishing" means seeing the difference between. This is the best word based on the context of the sentence. Critical thinking involves being able to distinguish the difference between fact and opinion.

6. Answer   A

"Expression" means representation in words, art, or music. The context of the sentence makes this the best word. The Harlem Renaissance was a literary and artistic movement that expressed African-American pride.

7. Answer   B

"Created" means produced or caused. This word works well within the context of the sentence. A contrast is set up by the structure of the sentence in which the dependent clause that begins the sentence describes a more positive effect of the September 11 attacks. The second part of the sentence gives the negative effect: the attacks caused people to feel more vulnerable.

8. Answer   C

"Significant" means large, meaningful, important, or having a major effect. Within the context of the sentence, this is the best word choice. In the past fifty years, major changes in marriage practices have occurred and have been noted by social scientists.

9. Answer   B

"Eradicate" means destroy, do away with, get rid of. The context of the sentence makes this word an ideal choice. A person would get rid of body odor if he or she thought it was a problem.

10. Answer   A

"Present" has several meanings, but in this sentence it is used as a verb to mean show or make evident by showing. This is the best choice based on the context of the sentence. Test stress can present itself in distinct physical symptoms.

2. Confused or Misused Words/Phrases

For each of these questions, the definition for each underlined word in the sentence and the definition for its corresponding option is provided. Notice that the correct answer/definition is given first, followed by its counterpart definition. To clarify your understanding, you should insert the definitions into the sentence.

1. Answer   C
   has passed   has moved forward to catch up and then continued beyond (verb)
   has past   a nonstandard (incorrect) form of "has passed."

2. Answer   C
   between   measuring one thing with another, used with two items
   among   with each other, used with more than two items

3. Answer   A
   set   to put or place (verb)
   sit   to bend one's knees and rest on one's buttocks

4. Answer   A
   number   expression of a quantity, used with countable nouns
   amount   expression of a quantity, used with noncountable nouns

5. Answer   C
   already   by this time
   all ready   fully prepared

6. Answer   A
   stationery   envelopes and paper used for writing letters

   stationary   not moving

7. Answer   B
   accept   to approve of
   except   but, excluding

8. Answer   C
   sight   in view; at or within a reasonable time
   site   place of something

9. Answer   B
   affect   have an influence on or cause a change in (verb)
   effect   a result (noun)

10. Answer   B
   lose   to be unsuccessful in retaining possession of
   loose   not tight

CHAPTER 3: *SENTENCE SKILLS*

1. Modifiers

For each of these questions, to avoid needless repetition of information, only the correct option is explained. The type of error is also identified: dangling modifier or misplaced modifier.

1. Answer   C   Dangling Modifier
The modifier "Having entered the gym" must be followed by a noun or pronoun identifying the individual who entered the gym.

2. Answer   A   Dangling Modifier
The modifier "To revise my paper" must be followed by a noun or pronoun identifying the individual who needs to revise it. Otherwise, the modifier "dangles" because it doesn't have a reference.

3. Answer   B   Dangling Modifier
The modifier "While I was watching a movie on television" correctly identifies who was watching a movie on television.

4. Answer   B   Misplaced Modifier
The correct sentence identifies which of the two, the father or the son, was five when he learned to ride his bicycle without the training wheels. The clause "when I was five" corrects the sentence.

5. Answer   A   Dangling Modifier
The modifier "Riding on the escalator" must be followed by the person riding on the escalator. The correct sentence follows that modifier with "I."

6. Answer   C   Dangling Modifier
The foreign student is the person who does not get to see her mother; therefore, the modifier "As a foreign student studying in the U.S." should be followed by the pronoun "I."

7. Answer   A   Dangling Modifier
The pronoun "we" must follow the modifier "After

writing a check and signing the documents" to indicate who wrote the check and signed the documents.

8. Answer   B   Dangling Modifier
The correct sentence supplies a subject "I" to identify who was fishing on the ocean with his friend.

9. Answer   C   Dangling Modifier
The reader needs to know who removed the label at the neckline of the T-shirt. Adding the word "I" to the modifier clarifies the sentence by identifying the actor in the sentence. Otherwise, the reader would think that the T-shirt removed its own label.

10. Answer   A   Dangling Modifier
The correct sentence supplies the pronoun "I" to indicate who ran the red light.

2. Coordination and Subordination

For each of the following questions, the correct definition for each transitional phrase is provided, and the correct relationship between ideas is explained.

1. Answer   A
Although: contrast. The dependent clause that begins the sentence suggests that having a baby can be joyous; the independent clause indicates the contrasting idea that it can strain a relationship.

2. Answer   D
Moreover: addition. The first independent clause explains the class' plan to study at the University of Seville in the summer. The second independent clause adds information: they also intend to see the famous historical sites.

3. Answer   C
So: cause and effect; indicates a result. The second independent clause gives the result of the first.

4. Answer   B
Who: relative pronoun used at the beginning of an adjective clause (dependent clause) to describe a person. The "who" clause modifies the word "person" at the end of the opening independent clause.

5. Answer   B
Therefore: cause and effect; indicates the effect. The independent clause that begins the sentence explains that Andrea's job is demanding. The effect, as stated in the second independent clause, is that she can only take two classes per semester.

6. Answer   A
Because: cause and effect. The dependent clause that begins the sentence gives the cause, "Because the bus was late." The independent clause that completes the sentence explains the effect: "I missed my first class."

7. Answer   C
After: time order; indicates that one thing occurs later than the other. In the sentence, the person plans to trans-

fer to a four-year university "after" he or she receives a two-year degree from the community college.

8. Answer   A
Who: relative pronoun used at the beginning of an adjective clause (dependent clause) to describe a person. The clause "who is flying this airplane" modifies the word "pilot."

9. Answer   B
So that: cause and effect. The dependent clause "so that I can improve my vocabulary" is the effect of the independent clause that begins the sentence, explaining that the person has to learn fifty new words in reading class every week.

10. Answer   C
Even though: contrast. The sentence contrasts the knowledge that fast foods are high in calories with the decision to eat it despite this knowledge.

3. Parallel Structure

For each of these questions, to avoid needless repetition of information, only the correct option is explained.

1. Answer   A
The three verbs in the sentence are correctly expressed in the same past tense: inserted, selected, and filled.

2. Answer   C
The three verbs in the sentence are correctly expressed in the same present tense: look, read, and buy.

3. Answer   B
In this sentence, independent clauses are listed in the same grammatical structure: her friends were calling her, her brother was blasting his stereo, and her dad was mowing the lawn.

4. Answer   B
This sentence has a series of independent clauses in a list; each one begins with "they" and is followed by a verb in the present tense: take, say, and hug.

5. Answer   C
The sentence is grammatically parallel, with verb phrases used in a series: brushes her teeth, takes a shower, and walks the dog.

6. Answer   B
In this sentence, the verbs "storing" and "writing" must be balanced with "taping."

7. Answer   C
The answer, "cried," is consistent with the other verbs in the series, all in the past tense.

8. Answer   D
The verb "use" matches the verb "pay."

9. Answer   C
In this sentence, there are three noun phrases in a list that must be consistent in grammatical form; the phrases begin with a noun and end with a prepositional

phrase. Therefore, "a scholarship for tuition" is the grammatically parallel answer.

10. Answer   B
Two noun phrases complete the sentence. To match grammatically, each of the items must begin with a noun and end in a prepositional phrase. "The shallowness of the water" is the correct match.

4. Fragments, Comma Splices, and Fused Sentences (Run-ons)

Due to the difficulty of this skill, twenty questions have been provided; however, only the first ten questions are explained. You will find two types of questions in this exercise. Some of the questions require that you decide whether the underlined portion needs to be corrected; if so, then you select from the options. The other type of question asks you to read each of the three underlined portions of a sentence for a possible error. The underlined portions are labeled in alphabetical order, "A" through "C." Each of the answer options is a possible replacement for the words in the question.

1. Answer   B
The semicolon in the original sentence is not correctly used; semicolons separate two independent clauses. The word group that comes after the semicolon is missing a subject, which makes it a fragment. This fragment "and hand it in to the instructor" is corrected by eliminating the punctuation at that point in the sentence.

2. Answer   C
A dependent clause begins this complex sentence. When a dependent clause comes at the beginning of a sentence, follow it with a comma.

3. Answer   B
This sentence contains three independent clauses. The last independent clause is not punctuated, created a run-on error (fused). Choice B is the correction. The semicolon indicates that a new, related sentence is beginning: "now searching online is quick and easy."

4. Answer   A
"Therefore" is the conjunctive adverb used to join the two sentences. In this case, place a semicolon before "therefore" and follow it with a comma.

5. Answer   D
The sentence is correct as written.

6. Answer   A
A comma corrects the semicolon error in the sentence. Placing a semicolon after a dependent clause creates a fragment.

7. Answer   B
The sentence is fused. Placing a period between the first independent clause that ends with "friends" corrects the error. The first word of the next independent clause must be capitalized, "Studying."

8. Answer   D
The sentence is correct as written.

9. Answer   C
The compound verbs in the sentence, "put" and "likes," should not be separated by a comma.

10. Answer   A
The use of the semicolon is correct in this sentence because it separates two independent clauses. "For example" is the transitional expression that begins the second sentence. A comma is correctly placed after "For example."

11. Answer   B
The semicolon corrects the comma splice in the sentence.

12. Answer   A
A semicolon, not a comma, is required to separate two independent, related sentences.

13. Answer   D
The sentence is punctuated correctly as written.

14. Answer   B
The sentence beginning with "Whenever" and ending with "party" consists of two dependent clauses. It is a fragment. To correct the fragment, a comma should be added following "party."

15. Answer   A
A comma before the words "such as" indicates that the examples given are nonessential.

16. Answer   B
The semicolon after "classroom" separates the two independent clauses.

17. Answer   C
A period placed after "home" corrects the comma splice.

18. Answer   B
The semicolon corrects the comma splice error.

19. Answer   B
No punctuation is needed to separate a verb from its objects.

20. Answer   C
A comma should be used after an introductory phrase.

CHAPTER 4: *GRAMMAR SKILLS*
1. Standard Verb Forms

1. Answer   B
The verb "come" must be changed to the past tense "came" because the rest of the sentence is in the past tense.

2. Answer   D
The verbs in the sentence are correct. They are all in the past tense and use the correct past tense forms.

3. Answer   C
In this sentence, the incorrect past tense form of fall, "falled" is incorrect. "Fell" is the correct form.

4. Answer   A

The correct verb form to use with "had" is the past participle. "Approached" is the correct past participal form, so the answer is "had approached."

5. Answer   C

"Stealed" is not the correct past tense verb form of "steal." "Stole" is the correct form.

6. Answer   C

"Burst" is the correct past participle for the verb "burst."

7. Answer   A

The past tense of the verb "fly" is "flew."

8. Answer   B

The first part of the sentence uses the past perfect tense of the verb "had forgotten" to indicate that the action expressed occurred before the next action. "Had become" is incorrectly used in the next part of the sentence because her sunburn occurred later. The simple past "became" corrects the error.

9. Answer   C

"Lays" is an incorrect form of the verb "lie" meaning to recline. The phrase "Last Sunday," which begins the sentence, indicates that the action of the sentence is in the past. "Lay" is the past tense of "lie."

10. Answer   C

In this sentence, the past participle of the verb "eat" is incorrect. "Eaten" is the past participle, so the answer is "had been eaten."

2. Shifts in Verb Tense

1. Answer   B

The sentence is written in the present tense; therefore "forgot" must be changed to the present tense, "forget."

2. Answer   C

The actions in the sentence occurred in the past, so all of the verbs must be in the past tense. "Suspends" should be changed to "suspended."

3. Answer   A

In this sentence, the verbs should all be in the past tense. "Is trying" is in the present progressive tense and needs to be changed to "tried."

4. Answer   C

This sentence uses the simple present tense to express habitual action. In the sentence, the person performs the same activities, feeds the dog and takes him for a walk. The present progressive "am taking" should be replaced by the simple present "take."

5. Answer   B

The past tense of the verb "work" is incorrect in this sentence. The future is indicated; the second action of the sentence cannot happen until the first is completed. "Worked" should be changed to "will work."

6. Answer   A

All the verbs in this sentence should be in the past tense because the details of the sentence describe something that happened in the past. "Has flown" should be changed to "flew."

7. Answer   D

The sentence is correct. The use of the past and past perfect tenses show that one action in the past was completed before another action in the past.

8. Answer   B

This sentence explains that one action in the past occurred while another was still going on in the past. "Sleeps" is in the present tense; the verb should be in the past progressive tense.

9. Answer   C

This sentence sets up an if . . . then condition. The present tense of the verb is the correct choice for the "if" clause that begins the sentence.

10. Answer   B

In this sentence, both the present and past tenses are used. In the first part of the sentence, the reader learns that Suzanne does not work at her previous job. She "found" a new job; this happened and was completed at some point in the past. Right now she likes it better than the job in the bakery.

3. Subject and Verb Agreement

1. Answer   A

"Was" is the correction for "were" in the sentence. When two subjects are joined by "neither . . . nor," the verb agrees with the closer subject (the word after "nor").

2. Answer   C

The subject of the dependent clause is "each," which is a singular indefinite pronoun. Therefore, the singular form of the verb, "needs," is required. When a singular indefinite pronoun is the subject of a sentence, the verb will always be singular. Don't be fooled by the prepositional phrase that may come between the subject and the verb. Even if the object of the prepositional phrase is a plural word, such as "speakers" in the question, you should disregard it.

3. Answer   C

"Each" is the subject of the dependent clause that begins with "because." "Each" is a singular subject, so the verb must be singular, "has." Don't be fooled by the prepositional phrase that may come between the subject and the verb. Even if the object of the prepositional phrase is a plural word, such as "birds" in the question, you should disregard it.

4. Answer   B

The dependent clause beginning with "that" modifies "lecture series," which is singular; although the word "series" may be plural, the compound noun "lecture series" is considered a unit. Therefore, the verb must be singular. The helping verb "have" should be changed to the singular "has."

5. Answer   C

The dependent clause in this sentence begins with "which"; "which" takes the place of the subject of the clause. Therefore, you need to find the word that "which" refers to: "peanut butter and jelly." Although "peanut butter and jelly" appears to be two items, it is viewed as one, so the verb should be in the singular form, "is."

6. Answer   A

The subject of the sentence, *Stand and Deliver*, is the name of a movie. Titles are considered singular, so the present tense verb form must be singular to agree with the subject. The third person singular present tense form of a regular verb ends with an –s, in this case "tells."

7. Answer   B

The verb is part of a dependent clause that begins with "who." You need to find the word that the clause modifies to determine whether the verb of the dependent clause is singular or plural. In this sentence, "who" refers to "scientists," so the plural form of the verb, "perform," is correct.

8. Answer   C

"Few" is the subject of the last independent clause in the sentence. "Few" is a plural indefinite pronoun, so the verb must also be in the plural form, "pass."

9. Answer   D

The sentence is correct.

10. Answer   A

The subject "shelters" requires a plural verb, "offer." Remember, plural verbs do not end in –s.

11. Answer   B

The second independent clause of the sentence has a compound subject: "a beverage and a small package of salted peanuts." The verb must be plural to agree: "do."

12. Answer   A

The subject of the sentence, "Briana," takes a singular verb, "has." The intervening prepositional phrase should be ignored.

13. Answer   C

The subject of the second independent clause in this compound sentence is "one," which is singular. The verb must be singular, "looks." The third person singular present tense form of a regular verb ends with –s.

14. Answer   A

"Accommodations" is the subject of the sentence and is plural, so the plural verb form must be used, "have."

15. Answer   A

The subject of the sentence, "statistics," is singular. The singular verb form "is" agrees.

16. Answer   B

"Is" is the correct verb which agrees with the subject "variety." This second independent clause in the sen-

tence begins with the transition words "in addition." The word "there" is not a subject. In sentences that begin with "there is" or "there are," the subject usually follows the verb.

17. Answer   B

The dependent clause begins with "who." To determine whether this "who" subject is singular or plural, you must find the word the dependent clause modifies. It is "the French." "The French" is considered plural, so the verb form is plural, "are."

18. Answer   A

The subject of the sentence is "news," which is considered singular. The verb must also be singular, "makes." Remember, the third person singular present tense form of a regular verb ends with –s.

19. Answer   C

"Few" is the subject, which is a plural indefinite pronoun. Therefore, the subject should be plural, "get." The third person plural form in the present tense does not end in –s.

20. Answer   D

The sentence is correct.

4. Pronoun and Antecedent Agreement

1. Answer   A

"Each" is the singular subject of the sentence. The pronoun that refers to it must also be singular. Therefore, "their" is incorrect because it is a plural pronoun. Of the choices, "her" is the only possible correction. "Its" is not used to refer to people, and "our" is plural.

2. Answer   D

The sentence is correct. When two subjects are joined by "either . . . or," the pronoun must agree with the antecedent closest to the verb (after "or"). A band or choir is a thing, so "its" is the appropriate choice.

3. Answer   B

"Company" is the singular subject of the sentence to which the pronoun refers. For the pronoun to agree, it must be singular. In addition, "company" is a thing, so "its" is the correct choice, not "him" or "her."

4. Answer   C

The two subjects of the second part of the sentence are joined by "neither . . . nor." In this situation, the pronoun must agree with the word closest to the verb (after "nor"), which is "boater." Therefore, "his" is the correct choice, for it is the only one of the three choices that is singular.

5. Answer   B

The pronoun in this sentence refers to the subject, Pete. It must be the singular "his." This is the only possible answer because the other two choices are plural.

6. Answer   C

The pronoun "them" is the correction, replacing "him." The pronoun refers to the subject "They" (Andrea and

Sebastian), so it must take the objective plural pronoun "them."

7. Answer   A
The pronoun "its" agrees with the subject "committee." "Committee" is considered singular in this sentence because the members are acting as a unit.

8. Answer   C
The pronoun must agree with the singular "parent." "His or her" is the correct choice. Without knowing the sex of the parent, the choice of "his or her" is appropriate.

9. Answer   B
The pronoun refers to the subject, "neither the students nor the professor." In this situation, the pronoun must agree with the word closest to the verb (after "nor"), which is the "professor." "Professor" is singular, so the pronoun that refers to it must also be singular. "His" is the correct choice.

10. Answer   D
The sentence is correct.

5. Pronoun Shifts

1. Answer   B
The second person viewpoint "you" is established in the sentence with "you," so the word "one" must be replaced with "you" to avoid a shift in perspective.

2. Answer   C
The sentence is written in the second person plural with the pronouns "us" and "we" and must be continued with the possessive form, "our."

3. Answer   C
The sentence is written in the third person plural viewpoint with the pronouns "their" and "they" and must be continued with by replacing "one" with "they."

4. Answer   A
The third person singular is established with the pronouns "he" and "his." Therefore, "you" must be replaced by "he" to avoid a shift in perspective.

5. Answer   B
The third person singular is established with the pronoun "his," which is used twice in the sentence. This perspective must be continued by replacing "you" with "he."

6. Answer   C
In this sentence, the second person plural is established with "we" and "our." To avoid a shift in perspective, "we" must replace the "he."

7. Answer   C
The third person plural is established with "their" and "they." To avoid a shift in person, "they" must replace "you."

8. Answer   A
Third person plural is established in this sentence with "them" and "their." Replacing "we" with "they" corrects a shift in person.

9. Answer   D
Third person plural is used consistently and properly throughout this sentence.

10. Answer   B
In this sentence, first person singular is established by "my" and "I." To avoid a shift in person, "you" must be replaced with "I."

6. Clear Pronoun Reference

1. Answer   B
The word "they" in the original sentence does not refer to any word in the sentence; its antecedent is missing. "The manager" provides the missing information. The manager is the one doing the interview.

2. Answer   C
In this sentence, there is no way to know what the pronoun "it" refers to. "The picture" is now crooked.

3. Answer   A
As the sentence is written, the pronoun "it" seems to refer to the phone, which cannot answer itself. "Tavar" should replace the pronoun to clarify that he did not answer the phone.

4. Answer   B
In this sentence, the pronoun "it" does not refer to any word in the sentence. The newspaper does not "say" anything; "the reporter" does.

5. Answer   C
As this sentence is written, it is difficult to know to what the pronoun "it" is referring. "It" should be replaced with "the table."

6. Answer   A
The pronoun "they" does not specify who helped edit the paper in the writing lab. Replacing "they" with "the lab assistants" clarifies this.

7. Answer   A
The use of the pronoun "it" is confusing because it does not appear to refer to anything in the sentence. The pronoun must refer to "college preparatory courses," so the pronoun "them" corrects any misunderstanding.

8. Answer   B
Two women are mentioned in this sentence, and although the reader may know that Doreen is the best worker, there is no clue to that fact in the sentence as it is written. Repeating the name of the person near the pronoun, "she, Doreen," clarifies any possible confusion.

9. Answer   C
Two men are mentioned in this sentence, and although the reader may know that the tour is for Mr. Linger's students, there is no clue to that fact in the sentence as it is written. Replacing the pronoun "his" with "Mr. Linger's" clarifies the meaning.

10. Answer   D
All of these pronouns clearly refer to their antecedents.

7. Pronoun Case Form

1. Answer A
"Me" is the object of the preposition "between."

2. Answer B
"Me" is the object of the preposition "to."

3. Answer C
"Me" is the object of the preposition "for."

4. Answer C
"They" is the subject of the verb "were exhausted."

5. Answer C
"Me" is the direct object of the verb "believe."

6. Answer D
All of the pronouns are used properly in the sentence. "Them" is the object of the preposition "to," "They" is the subject of the verb "use," and "us" is the object of the preposition "of."

7. Answer A
"I" is the subject of the verb "will be."

8. Answer B
"She" is the subject of the verb "was walking."

9. Answer D
All of the pronouns are used properly in the sentence. "Us" is the object of the verb "told," "us" is the object of the preposition "of," and "who" is the subject of the verb "does."

10. Answer B
"We" is the subject of the verb "have."

8. Adjectives and Adverbs

1. Answer A
"Peacefully" is the adverb that modifies the infinitive verb "evacuate." "Peaceful" is an adjective.

2. Answer C
"Artistically" is the adverb that modifies "was executed." "Artistic" is an adjective.

3. Answer B
"Well" is an adverb modifying "sang." "Good" is an adjective.

4. Answer B
"Tightly" is an adverb modifying "held." "Tight" is an adjective.

5. Answer D
The adjectives and adverb are used correctly in this sentence. "Challenging" is an adjective modifying "job," "frequent" is an adjective modifying "shopping trips," and "frivolously" is an adverb modifying "spent."

6. Answer C
"Really" is an adverb modifying the adjective "bad." "Real" is an adjective; it cannot modify another adjective.

7. Answer B
"Good" is a predicate adjective describing the subject, "actress." Predicate adjectives describe the subject of the sentence through a linking verb such as "looked."

8. Answer A
"Terrible" is a predicate adjective (also called a complement) describing the subject, "Renzo." Predicate adjectives describe the subject of the sentence through a linking verb such as "felt."

9. Answer C
"Well" is an adverb modifying "felt." Although "felt" is a linking verb, the adverb "well" is used when referring to health.

10. Answer A
"Surely" is an adverb modifying the verb "enjoyed." "Sure" is an adjective.

9. Degree Forms of Adjectives and Adverbs

1. Answer C
The comparative "better" is required because "of the two guitar players" indicates a choice between two players.

2. Answer B
The superlative "most beautiful" is required because the comparison is with more than two mountain ranges. The word "among" is used to describe more than two. Three syllable words form the superlative by adding "most" before the word.

3. Answer A
The superlative "worst" is required because the comparison includes more than two years. "Since 1992" indicates more than two years.

4. Answer B
The superlative "most handsome" is required because Brad Pitt is being compared to all actors, not just one other actor. Two-syllable words not ending in –y often require the addition of "most" before the word for the superlative form.

5. Answer C
The comparative "more effectively" is required because Josh is being compared to one other person, "I." Words of more than three syllables form the comparative by adding "more" before the word.

6. Answer D
The comparative "farther" is required because two distances are being compared.

7. Answer A
The comparative adverb form "more diligently" is required. Studying for the final is compared to studying for the midterm. Words of more than three syllables form the comparative by adding "more" before the word.

8. Answer D
The comparative form "more enthusiastically" is correctly used in the sentence. Hai's and Kim's routines are

compared. Words of more than three syllables form the comparative by adding "more" before the word.

9. Answer   C

The comparative form "harder" is required to compare the difficulty of the exercises with the person's perception about how hard they might be. One-syllable words form the comparative by adding –er to the end of the word.

10. Answer   B

"Easier" is the required comparative form to compare math with English. One-syllable words ending in –y form the comparative by dropping –y and adding –ier.

10. Standard Spelling

1. Answer   B

There are three spelling issues that can be confusing with the word "knowledgeable": the silent "d," the addition of the suffix, and the choice of the suffix, -able or -ible. The suffix –ible is less commonly used than –able; therefore, it is a matter of memorizing the correct ending. When adding –able to a word that ends in –e that is not pronounced, usually you drop the –e; however, "knowledgeable" is one exception to this rule.

2. Answer   A

3. Answer   A

The word "truly" is an exception to the spelling rule. Usually, when you add –ly to a word ending in a vowel, you retain the vowel; however, you do drop the –e to spell "truly."

4. Answer   C

The word "license" is frequently misspelled. Most often the c and the s are reversed; however, in the incorrect choice c is used in place of s.

5. Answer   C

Although the word sounds as if it begins with ex, the correct spelling is "ecstasy." The word ending is –asy, not –acy.

6. Answer   D

The correct spelling involves double consonants.

7. Answer   B

The correct spelling involves double consonants.

8. Answer   B

The correct spelling involves double consonants.

9. Answer   A

The word "argue" does not retain the final –e before the suffix –ment.

10. Answer   B

The correct spelling involves two sets of double consonants.

11. Standard Punctuation

1. Answer   C

The sentence does not ask a direct question, so it does not require a question mark as end punctuation.

2. Answer   B

The comma before "because," between the first independent clause and the dependent clause that follows it, is not necessary.

3. Answer   A

Commas are used to separate elements of a date.

4. Answer   B

No comma is necessary after "such as."

5. Answer   D

The sentence is punctuated correctly.

For questions 6–10, only the correct option is explained to avoid unnecessary repetition of information.

6. Answer   D

The first punctuation issue is the comma after the word "off." This comma is required because along with the coordinating conjunction "so," it marks the separation between two separate complete sentences. The apostrophe used in "two weeks' vacation" is required. "Weeks'" is the plural of "week's." It is also a possessive. To form the possessive of a plural word ending in –s, you add an apostrophe after the –s.

7. Answer   A

In this sentence, no comma is required before "but" because the word does not begin another independent clause. The apostrophe is correctly placed after the y in "somebody's" to show possession.

8. Answer   C

The word "month's" requires an apostrophe because the word is possessive. Since it is only one month, the apostrophe is correctly placed after the h. The comma after "mother" indicates that the dependent clause is non-essential. The sentence is declarative, not a question, so a question mark is not required.

9. Answer   B

The semicolon after "equipment" is not necessary because it does not separate one independent clause from another. The semicolon is not used to introduce a list. The other error is the comma after "pets." This comma is not necessary because a separate independent clause does not come after the "and," which would indicate a compound sentence.

10. Answer   A

The sentence requires one comma placed after "powers" to set off the examples given. No comma is necessary after "away" to separate the two examples. The semicolon would not be used to introduce a series of examples. Finally, the two commas, one before and one after "and" in sentence D is incorrect; the first comma is not used to separate two examples, and the second comma is unnecessary.

12. Standard Capitalization

1. Answer   C

Seasons are not capitalized.

2. Answer   A

The word "history" should not be capitalized because it is not a specific course title.

3. Answer   A

Neither the "h" nor the "s" of the word "high school" needs to be capitalized. They are capitalized only when used with the name of the school.

4. Answer   C

The word "Northwest" is part of the name of a street address, so it should be capitalized.

5. Answer   A

The title of the book is not capitalized appropriately. Short prepositions and articles are not capitalized in titles of books and other works.

6. Answer   B

The word "aunt" is capitalized only when used in place of the person's name.

7. Answer   B

Official titles do not need to be capitalized when they are not accompanied by a person's name.

8. Answer   D

All words in this sentence are capitalized correctly.

9. Answer   C

The word "presidential" does not need to be capitalized. It is not used as a title.

10. Answer   D

All words in this sentence are capitalized correctly.

Appendix

The second part of the Florida College Basic Skills Exit Test is a timed writing sample. You will be required to compose either an essay or a paragraph in 50 minutes. Writing under pressure can be stressful. However, if you apply the strategies in this section, you will be able to meet the challenge with confidence.

Understanding the Topics

You will be given a choice of two topics to write about. One of the topics is subjective; you can approach this subject by using personal experience. The other topic is objective; you can develop the topic by using information you know about it from something you have read or heard or something you have learned in a class. Although you will not know what the specific topics are before the test, you can understand how the topic is written and know the categories from which the topics are developed.

How the Topic Is Written

The topic consists of two parts: the subject and the qualifier, a word or phrase that limits the subject. You can narrow the subject down further, but you cannot change it. If you do not address the topic, your paper will be considered "off topic," and you run the risk of failing the exam. Here are some examples of subjective and objective topics.

Subjective Topics

1. A family tradition that you plan to continue

Subject	A family tradition
Qualifier	that you plan to continue

   Have any ideas popped into your mind when you heard the topic? What about a family reunion or a holiday celebration? A tradition from your ethnic or cultural background?

2. An experience that made you change something

Subject	An experience
Qualifier	that made you change something

3. A first impression that was either right or wrong

Subject	A first impression
Qualifier	that was either right or wrong

Objective Topics

1. A place that people should visit

Subject	A place
Qualifier	that people should visit

2. A job that is beneficial for a teenager

Subject	A job
Qualifier	that is beneficial for a teenager

3. A topic in the news that upsets people

Subject	A topic in the news
Qualifier	that upsets people

Subjects from Which Topics Are Developed

You can see that the subjective topics often focus on a place, person, object, or personal incident. Objective topics may address an event in the news, an issue people feel strongly about, a person who has contributed to society, or an activity people participate in.

Understanding How Your Essay Will Be Scored

The Graders

Your writing sample will be graded by one or more readers whom you may or may not know. The reader may be your instructor or another instructor at your college. You can be certain that all readers are qualified in the field of English instruction and have experience both in teaching and in grading college writing.

Keep in mind that the graders do not expect a perfect piece of writing. They think of the writing sample as a rough draft, not as one that you worked on over a period of time. The grader wants to see that you can write a passing paper. Therefore, don't worry if your paper is sloppy because you may have crossed words or sentences out. You're not being graded on neatness!

The Grading Method

The graders use a method called holistic scoring to assess your papers. With this method, the grader reads each paper all the way through without writing comments or marking errors. He or she scores the writing sample according to the criteria established by the State. This way, **each grader uses the same standards**, not the particular standards he or she may require in an English course. As a result, holistic scoring prevents a grader from focusing on finding errors. Instead a paper is graded as a "whole" piece of writing in a more objective way.

The Grading Criteria

A number system is used to grade the writing samples. The scores range from 1, the lowest, to 6, the highest. You will need to achieve a 3 or higher to pass the exam. The grader will decide how well you have demonstrated that you can

- state a main idea
- develop the main idea with specific and sufficient details and examples
- show connections between ideas by using transitional words and phrases
- use a clear pattern of organization
- express ideas logically

- show effective use of vocabulary
- vary sentence patterns
- use correct grammar, spelling, capitalization, and punctuation

These are the same skills that you have been learning and practicing in your college preparatory English class.

The graders use the official "Scoring Criteria for the Florida College Basic Skills Exit Writing Sample." The criteria gives readers an overview of the scores, so although a paper may not have all of the characteristics of a particular score, it will clearly fall into the high, middle, or low range of that score. The complete scoring criteria follows the sample essays you are about to read.

Sample Essays

To help you see how other students have handled the writing sample and how the paper has been scored, read the examples that follow. Although some students will be asked to write a paragraph, most are required to write an essay. Therefore, the examples you will read here are essays. The writer of each sample essay responded to the topic "An activity or hobby that you enjoy." Four student essays have been selected to illustrate a failing score, a minimum passing score ("3"), a mid-range passing score, and a high passing score.

Failing Score

Shopping is one of my activity I enjoy. I enjoy spending an afternoon at different malls. Shopping with my friend Shantell. Shantell is the only person I bring to the mall with me, because Shantell is a outspoken person. We also knows how to shop for good sales.

The first thing I do before I go to the mall is find out what can of sale the store is having. For example, I enjoy shopping at Old Navy and when I find out that Old Navy is having a sale. I call Shantell on the phone and we go right to the store. While we are in the store. I spend hours in the store. Looking around and trying on different items. There is sometimes when I go to the store and I do not have any money on me to buy the items, we will go right to the bank to talke money out.

Another reason I bring Shantell shopping with me, she is a outspoken person. For example, if I try on a out fix that do not look good on me. She will tell me right a way. She do not wait until some one tells me that the outfix do not look good. There are times we go to the mall and we just look around, for fun. Not only she is good friend to shop with. She is also a good friend you can talk with all the times.

Low Passing Score

Two outs, bottom of the 9th, bases loaded with the winning run up at the plate. I have been in many situations like that and I love the feeling of it. It is the game of baseball and it is my most favorite sport to play. I have been playing this sport for many years and it never gets boring to me.

I love to play baseball because it is a very exciting game that takes lots of skill and practice. Whenever I get a chance to go to the park and throw a ball with someone it makes my day because I feel like I'm getting ready for another big game I have to win.

Another reason why I love playing baseball is because it is a team sport. I love to cheer on my teammates when they make a good play or get a great hit. I always cheer them on because I feel like I make them feel real good about themselves and they will make another play or get another hit the next time.

A third reason why I love playing baseball is that it keeps me active. If it wasn't for baseball I would not be the person I am today. Baseball has made me an outgoing person with a great personality and it has given me a great sense of humor as well.

The last reason why I love baseball is that it can make me some money in the future. In a couple of years, if I'm good enough, a major league team could draft me and I could be very rich just for playing the sport I love best.

Baseball has been something I have wanted to play my whole life and it is something that I will play for the rest of my life. I love to play the game of baseball and I will never give it up for anything.

Mid-range Passing Score

My favorite activity to do with my best friend is shopping. Shopping is something we do everyday. Clothes, accessories, jewelry, purses, shoes are all a part of our day when we are in the mall. When it comes to our items, most of them are designer brands. Coach, Louis Vuitton, Chanel, and Gucci sit in our closets, throughout our wardrobes. When we are not looking for designer items, we are buying cute, tacky t-shirts to wear on a not-so-dress up day. Shopping makes Jessica and I very happy and content. Shoes, clothes, jewelry and purses are all the items we buy to make our day better.

Clothes are an extremely big deal to Lisa and I. Between Juicy Couture, Rile, Rampage and XOXO, Lisa and I must own their whole line of clothes. To make the outfits a lot more fun, we buy accessories to go along with the outfits. Belts, chains, and headbands jazz our clothes up to make us look better. Jessica and I receive complements all the time for our cheesy accessories worn around our heads and waists. Clothes and accessories are only a few things that Lisa and I shop for.

Purses and jewelry are a very important asset to Lisa and I. Between the two of us, we must have at least 15 designer bags and a 100 different jewelry pieces. Chanel earrings, Gucci glasses, Louis Vuitton watches all shimmer on our wrists and ears. We also own a Tiffany and Company necklace, bracelet, and earring set. It is very special to us, so we only wear it on special occasions. Jessica has about four different Louis Vuitton styles and I have six different Coach purses. Having these expensive things makes Lisa and I feel good about ourselves because we work hard for all of these nice things. We buy everything with our own money that we worked for at our jobs.

Jessica and I really love to shop. We love the same things and share everything. All of these items seem important to us and we enjoy presenting them. It might seem conceited and vain to other people but we think it is better to spend our money on clothes than something else that could bet us into trouble. Shopping plays a big part in our lives and it is fun to do. We like to look nice for ourselves and other people, that is why shopping is our favorite activity to do.

Upper Range Passing Score

When I was growing up I enjoyed many activities. For example, I used to play basketball and soccer with my friends, or just collecting baseball cards, but now that I am older I enjoy two activities that I do by myself: playing guitar and writing poems.

I started to play guitar when I was sixteen years old. It started as a hobby that I enjoyed during the summer when I was not in school and I would not be playing basketball. When I turned seventeen, I quit basketball and dedicated my spare time to improving my skills with the guitar. As time passed by I was more interested in playing guitar, I wanted to learn all of my favorite songs from Pink Floyd or Black Sabbath, but soon I learned that playing guitar was not easy; you have to dedicate time and be patient. Once I learned to play guitar decently, I found out that girls liked a guy who could play the songs they liked, so to meet more girls, I learned to play popular songs that they liked.

Playing guitar goes hand in hand with writing poems. I started to write poems when I was around twelve or thirteen years old. I wrote poems because I felt that I needed to express myself in some way. I was a very shy kid and did not have many friends. I started writing about school and its problems, about meeting girls and falling in love. As years passed by and I lived more, my topics started to change. I wrote about lies, betrayal and very depressing experiences. My mom thought that I was having problems, but I was not. I just enjoyed writing about those subjects. When I was around seventeen, I started to write about experiencing with drugs. I could see that I was influenced by many artists but especially Pink Floyd. Also, by that time I started to date a lot more, so I started to write poems to girls. I kept a notebook with all the poems I wrote. Nowadays my writing has improved a lot. My topics vary from hate to love, from loneliness to friendship.

I enjoy playing guitar and writing poems because it is a way that I can relax. It is very peaceful to sit on my bed and just play guitar for hours or to write a poem about an experience I had. I have been playing guitar for almost ten years and it has made me more extroverted and organized. I have been writing poems maybe half of my life. It makes me happy because when I read a poem from when I was fifteen, it brings back memories. Above all, I enjoy playing guitar and writing poems because later I can see truly the person I am.

Scoring Criteria for the Florida College Basic Skills Exit Test Writing Sample

SCORE OF 6	• The paper has a clearly established main idea that the writer fully develops with specific details and examples. • Organization is notably logical and coherent. • Vocabulary and sentence structure are varied and effective. • Errors in sentence structure, usage, and mechanics are few and insignificant.
SCORE OF 5	• The paper has a clearly established main idea that is adequately developed and recognizable through specific details and/or examples. • Organization follows a logical and coherent pattern. • Vocabulary and sentence structure are mostly varied and effective. • Occasional errors in sentence structure, usage, and mechanics do not interfere with the writer's ability to communicate.
SCORE OF 4	• The paper has an adequately stated main idea that is developed with some specific details and examples. • Supporting ideas are presented in a mostly logical and coherent manner. • Vocabulary and sentence structure are somewhat varied and effective. • Occasional errors in sentence structure, usage, and mechanics may interfere with the writer's ability to communicate.
SCORE OF 3	• The paper states a main idea that is developed with generalizations or lists. • The paper may contain occasional lapses in logic and coherence and is mechanical. • Vocabulary and sentence structure are repetitious and often ineffective. • A variety of errors in sentence structure, usage, and mechanics sometimes interferes with the writer's ability to communicate.
SCORE OF 2	• The paper presents an incomplete or ambiguous main idea. • Support is developed with generalizations and lists. • Organization is mechanical. • The paper contains occasional lapses in logic and coherence. • Word choice is simplistic, and sentence structure is disjointed. • Errors in sentence structure, usage, and mechanics frequently interfere with the writer's ability to communicate.

SCORE OF 1	• The paper has no evident main idea.
	• Development is inadequate and/or irrelevant.
	• Organization is illogical and/or incoherent.
	• Vocabulary and sentence structure are garbled and confusing.
	• Significant and numerous errors in sentence structure, usage, and mechanics interfere with the writer's ability to communicate.

How to Prepare for the Writing Sample

1. Review the elements of a successful essay.

   You can find information on the parts of an essay in an appropriate English textbook, in the writing lab, or online. Many websites provide helpful information on essay writing.

2. Go over papers you've written.

   Look at all of the writing assignments you have completed in your writing class(es). What were your strengths and weaknesses? Did you have any problems with organizing your writing? Were there any grammar problems that seem to occur in more than one paper you've written? Do you make repeated punctuation errors? If you haven't paid much attention to comments your instructor made, read those comments and learn from them.

   If you aren't sure how to correct any problems you may have, get some help. Set up an appointment for a conference with your instructor. If you have a writing lab on your campus, set aside time to work on materials available there.

3. Practice, practice, practice

   You wouldn't sign up to run a marathon without training for it. You know that to become better at any skill you need to practice. The best way to prepare for the 50-minute timed essay exam is to write as many 50-minute timed essays as you can.

   • Simulate the conditions of the exam: find a quiet place where you will not be disturbed and use your watch or a clock to keep track of the time. Make note of the time you begin and the time you will finish. You might want to ask someone to signal you at specific intervals, such as at the 30 and 40 minute marks. Some people find it helpful to divide the 50 minutes into stages: 10 minutes to brainstorm, 30 minutes to write the essay, and 10 minutes to proofread and correct. On the other hand, you may find that limiting your time this way gives you more stress. As you practice, you'll figure out how you can make the best use of the time you have.

   • Choose one of the topics mentioned in this section or make up one of your own and write an essay. Follow the steps in the writing process that work for you. Do you like to brainstorm, make a web, or do a scratch outline first? Work through the introduction, body paragraphs, and conclusion.

   • When you have finished, think about your performance. Did you have trouble figuring out what to say about the topic? Did you spend too much time on any one part of the essay? Were you able to finish in the allotted time? Were you stressed? Think about how you behaved while writing the essay. This will help you become aware of the things you need to work on, whether they are aspects of the writing process or feelings of stress.

4. Read the next section, which walks you through the exam step by step.

How to Survive the Writing Sample on Test Day

If you follow these 9 steps, you should be able to write a passing essay.

1. **Keep your eye on the time throughout the test.**

   In order to finish in the allotted time, you need to keep track of those 50 minutes. Write down the time the test begins and ends. If you have practiced 50-minute timed essays on your own, then you will know how to divide your time to complete the different parts of the essay-writing process. If you haven't practiced, you can try the 10-30-10 method: 10 minutes brainstorming, 30 minutes writing, 10 minutes proofreading/editing.

2. **Choose one topic and don't change it.**

   Read each of the topics carefully. Make sure you know what the topics mean. Once you've selected your topic, don't be tempted to switch topics after you have started to write even if you do not like the topic. You won't have enough time to start over.

   Remember, you don't have to feel strongly about the topic. If you have no connection to either of the topics, try choosing the subjective topic. Most people find these easier to write about. You can always draw from your experience or even invent one; the reader won't know whether it was true or not.

3. **Figure out what the topic is asking you to do.**

   Here is a hypothetical topic: Lessons that you have learned in college

   This topic tells you that "lessons" is to be the subject of your essay. The qualifier, "that you have learned in college," tells you that you are expected to write about lessons you learned in college, not general lessons that all students learn in college. The "you" in the topic is an indicator that you can write about yourself.

4. **Use a prewriting strategy to generate ideas for your paper.**

   Prewriting strategies help you avoid writer's block and help you organize your thoughts. You can create a list of ideas, do a map (also called mind map or cluster), or make a scratch outline. Using one of these strategies keeps you actively involved in the process, so you won't have time to stress out. When you feel that you have found something to say, narrow your ideas down to three main points that you can easily support.

   Applying one of the strategies to the sample topic, you may have arrived at three specific lessons you have learned, such as scheduling time to study, going to bed at a reasonable hour, and managing your money.

5. **Write your thesis and decide on a plan of development.**

   When you write your thesis, you will also be deciding your plan of development. Following a plan of development will make your essay logical and coherent.

   Which organizational plan could be used for our topic "Lessons that you have learned as a college student"? You might give examples of various lessons you've learned as a college student, such as study skills, time management, cooking, housekeeping, or financial responsibility. Another way of discussing the lessons you learned might be to contrast the way you used to be before you started college with the way you are now that you are in college. For example, you could talk about how you used to spend your money on entertainment and clothing, but now you spend your money on books and tuition.

   One type of thesis statement that helps organize your essay is the thesis map. The thesis map is like a mini-outline of your essay. Here's an example:

   > Since I have enrolled in college, I have learned to be responsible for my schoolwork, to manage my time better, and to improve my study habits.

This thesis lists three supporting points to be discussed in the essay. From this thesis, you can easily see that the first body paragraph will discuss how the writer learned to be responsible, the second body paragraph will discuss how the writer learned to manage his time, and the third body paragraph will discuss how the writer improved his study habits.

6. **Write your introductory paragraph.**

The introductory paragraph will contain your lead-in and thesis statement. The lead-in gets your reader interested in the paper. Don't spend too much time thinking about writing an extensive, detailed introduction as you might if you were writing an essay at home with lots of time. Instead, use a few sentences to work up to the thesis. Think of a brief story (anecdote), give some background, use a quote that comes to mind, or ask a question or two. Follow your lead-in with your thesis statement. Placing the thesis at the end of the introduction tells the reader exactly what to expect.

7. **Write your body paragraphs.**

The body paragraphs will follow the organizational plan you have selected, which will be evident in your thesis. Each body paragraph should have a topic sentence, details that support the topic sentence, and a concluding sentence.

Use numerous specific details. For example, in our sample topic, one of the points of the thesis is that you have learned time management. To support this, tell specifically what things you did to manage your time, such as waking up to an alarm, setting aside three hours in the evening to study, and cutting down on television viewing. By doing this, you will be showing the grader that you can fully develop your main idea with specific details and examples. Your organization will be logical and coherent.

8. **Write your concluding paragraph.**

The concluding paragraph draws your paper to a close. For a 50-minute essay, you need only two or three sentences to conclude. Restating the main idea of your essay (thesis statement) is useful as it reminds the reader of what he or she has read. To complete the concluding paragraph, you can point out the effects, the importance, or the benefits of your topic.

9. **Proofread and edit your essay.**

You want to be sure to set aside time for reading what you have written. When the graders read your paper, they will be looking for your ability to use correct grammar and punctuation and write effective sentences as well as main idea, logic, organization, and supporting details. If you know that you have trouble with punctuation or grammar, check your paper for those problems.

One proofreading technique people find helpful is to read the essay backwards. Begin with the last sentence and continue until you have read the first sentence. This method helps you see each sentence separately so that you can analyze it. When you read your paper through from beginning to end, you tend to focus on the content and miss possible errors.

By the way, if you double-space your essay, you'll find it easier to add, remove, or change information.

The following is a sample essay on the topic "Lessons you have learned in college."

Lessons I Learned My First Semester in College

Before starting college, I thought it would be easy, and I would not have much work; however, I was wrong. **My first semester of college changed the way I think of school by teaching me to be responsible for my schoolwork, to manage my time better, and to improve my study habits. (Thesis statement)**

The first thing I learned was to be responsible for my schoolwork. (Topic Sentence) In high school, I skipped class a lot, and I was able to make up the work I missed. On the other hand, when I skipped one day of math class in college, I fell far behind the rest of the class. Unlike high school, in college I can't make up a test that I missed. I didn't come to class for my first test in my reading class. I went to class the next day hoping to make the test up, but my teacher would not let me. Also, I learned to pay attention in class because if I didn't, I would miss something; the teachers in college don't repeat themselves. For example, one day in my English class, I was sitting in the back of the classroom drawing and not paying attention to what the teacher was saying. Then, when it came time to do the homework, I had no clue what to do, and I also got a bad grade on the test. Another responsibility I learned was to bring my book to class. In high school, the teacher let me borrow a book if I needed it, but in college, if I don't have my book, the teachers tell me to leave the class. I forgot to bring my book to my reading class, and the teacher told me she would see me at the next class. Responsibility for my schoolwork was one major lesson I learned this semester.

Another lesson I learned my first semester was to manage my time better. (Topic Sentence) I am a person who always puts off something until the last minute. For example, I put off finishing my English, reading, and math lab hours, and now I am running around trying to get them done, so I can pass my classes. I found that I am not the only one who did this because the labs are full. If I had known how to manage my time, I would have used the entire sixteen weeks to do my lab hours, not the last two weeks. Not only did I put my lab hours off, but I also put off my homework assignments until the last minute hoping that they would be easy, and I could get them done quickly. For example, in my English class, we had to write paragraphs and essays, and I would wait until the morning that they were due to start writing them. I learned my lesson when I did not do well on them. Another thing I learned about managing my time was to work my job around my classes. I go to school in the morning until 10 a.m. and then go to work just to come back to school at 1 p.m. to finish my classes. Since I work as a lifeguard, and the pools are not crowded during the winter, I found that I could work my hours around my classes. This first semester really taught me to manage my time wisely.

The last lesson I learned in my first semester of college was to improve my study habits. (Topic Sentence) Since the tests and work in college are more difficult than the work I was used to in high school, my study habits have to be totally different. In high school, I talked to my girl friend while I studied. I also watched television and chatted on the computer all while trying to study. When I started my first semester, I did all of those distracting things while studying, but I soon realized that in college I can't do that. For college work, I really need to concentrate and understand what I am reading. Another study habit I learned was to study for at least a few hours each night. In high school, I only studied for about a half hour and thought that was enough. In college, I need to study at least two hours a day. With better study habits, I should do much better next semester.

When I first came to college, my advisor told me, "Look around you and see who is sitting beside you because 50% of the students you see will not survive the first semester." I believe this is true. I am thankful that in my first semester of college I learned to be responsible for my schoolwork, to manage my time better, and to improve my study habits. (Concluding Statement) If I use these throughout my college experience, I should get through with no problem.

Last Minute Tips

1. Be sure you know the day and location of the exam.
2. Wear a watch to monitor the time.
3. If you have to bring your own supplies, like a bluebook or lined paper and a pen or pencil, get them ahead of time and put them aside until the day of the essay. Treat yourself to a new pen to avoid running out of ink. As a matter of fact, if you are told to use ink, buy an erasable pen or a correction pen.